An OPUS book

EUROPEAN COMMUNITY

T264

European Community

THE BUILDING OF A UNION

Updated following the Maastricht Treaty

JOHN PINDER

Oxford New York

OXFORD UNIVERSITY PRESS

Oxford University Press, Walton Street, Oxford OX2 6DP

Oxford New York Toronto
Delhi Bombay Calcutta Madras Karachi
Petaling Jaya Singapore Hong Kong Tokyo
Nairobi Dar es Salaam Cape Town
Melbourne Auckland

and associated companies in
Berlin Ibadan

Oxford is a trade mark of Oxford University Press

First published 1991 as an Oxford University Press
paperback and simultaneously in a hardback edition
Reprinted 1992

British Library Cataloguing in Publication Data
Pinder, John 1924–
European Community: the building of a union. — (OPUS)
1. European Community
I. Title II. Series
341.2422
ISBN 0–19–219231–0
ISBN 0–19–289225–8 pbk

Library of Congress Cataloging in Publication Data
Data available

Printed in Great Britain by
Biddles Ltd, Guildford and King's Lynn

Contents

Acknowledgements

This book is the product of four decades of reflection about the European Community: why and how it has developed since its foundation. My view has been influenced during this period by the critique of sovereignty, leading to the idea of federal union, which was evolved in Britain in the decade up to World War II and of which Altiero Spinelli was the foremost post-war exponent, and by the example of Jean Monnet, who showed how union could be approached through a series of substantial steps.

I also owe much to countless other people from many countries who have helped me to acquire knowledge and generate ideas about the subject. Among the bodies that have provided a context for this I am particularly indebted to the Federal Trust in London and the College of Europe in Bruges. For comments on various chapters of the book I am grateful to Professor David Coombes, Richard Corbett, Professor Robert Hine, Edmund Neville-Rolfe, Michael Shackleton, Professor Dennis Swann, and John Young, and on the whole text to Pauline Pinder. The responsibility for any remaining errors and, for better or worse, for the ideas behind the book is entirely my own.

Foreword

The original text of this book was completed in December 1990. By the time that the third impression was about to go to press, the Treaty on European Union had been agreed at Maastricht in December 1991. As it was not possible to prepare a completely new edition, the text for this impression has been extensively revised to take account of the major changes that the new treaty will bring. This has been done by making revisions at each point in the book where these changes are likely to have a significant impact and by adding a postscript that summarises the background to the treaty, its contents and implications.

The use of the term 'Union' in the new treaty has required a further series of revisions. The original text defined a European Union as a Community with federal institutions and with the essential economic powers of a federation. While the new treaty provides the Community with most of these powers, however, it does not provide federal institutions. But as it is now appropriate to use the term Union in its new, official sense to denote what was agreed at Maastricht, I have qualified as a 'federal Union' what was simply termed European Union, or Union, in the original text. I hope that this change, necessitated by the new official usage, will not cause difficulty for those who compare the original text with the present one.

I have also taken the opportunity to update the text with respect to other salient events of 1991, such as the Swedish application for membership, the developments in the Community's relations with the European Free Trade Association and with the countries of Central and Eastern Europe and the former Soviet Union, and preparations for agricultural and budgetary reform.

The result may be less tidy than a completely new edition; but it does, I believe, give the reader a complete and clear picture of the Community's development up to and including the very important changes agreed at Maastricht.

January 1991   *John Pinder*

Abbreviations

ACP	African, Caribbean, Pacific countries
CFSP	Common foreign and security policy
Comecon	Council for Mutual Economic Assistance
Coreper	Committee of Permanent Representatives
CSCE	Conference on Security and Co-operation in Europe
EAGGF	European Agricultural Guidance and Guarantee Fund
EC	European Community
ECB	European Central Bank
ECSC	European Coal and Steel Community
ecu	European currency unit (equals £0.7, $1.3 at end 1991)
EEA	European Economic Area
EEC	European Economic Community
Efta	European Free Trade Association
EMI	European Monetary Institute
EMS	European Monetary System
Emu	economic and monetary union
EPC	European Political Co-operation
ERM	Exchange Rate Mechanism
ESCB	European System of Central Banks
Euratom	European Atomic Energy Community
Gatt	General Agreement on Tariffs and Trade
GDP	gross domestic product
GNP	gross national product
GSP	Generalized System of Preferences
IGC	Intergovernmental Conference
IMPs	Integrated Mediterranean Programmes
IT	information technology
Maastricht Treaty	Treaty on European Union
MCA	monetary compensatory amount

mfn	most-favoured nation
Nato	North Atlantic Treaty Organization
NCE	non-compulsory expenditure
OECD	Organization for Economic Co-operation and Development
OEEC	Organization for European Economic Co-operation
SEA	Single European Act
Union Treaty	*see* Maastricht Treaty
VAT	value-added tax
VERs	voluntary export restrictions

1 Creating the Community: Nation-State and Federal Idea

The European Community is a remarkable innovation in relations among states. Its institutions are more powerful than those of conventional international organizations, and offer more scope for development. Much of their specific character was determined in a few weeks in the summer of 1950, when representatives of the six founder members, France, the German Federal Republic, Italy, Belgium, the Netherlands, and Luxembourg, agreed on the outline of the Treaty to establish the European Coal and Steel Community. The initiative had been taken by Robert Schuman, the French foreign minister, who explained the gist of his proposal with these words:

... the French Government proposes to take action immediately on one limited but decisive point ... to place Franco-German production of coal and steel under a common High Authority, within the framework of an organisation open to the participation of the other countries of Europe.... The solidarity in production thus established will make it plain that any war between France and Germany becomes not merely unthinkable, but materially impossible.... this proposal will build the first concrete foundation of a European federation which is indispensable to the preservation of peace ...[1]

World War II, national sovereignty, the federal idea

World War II was a catastrophe that discredited the previous international order and, for many Europeans, the basic element in that order: the sovereign nation-state. In the Europe of such states, France and Germany had been at war three times in less than a century, twice at the centre of terrible world wars. Autarky and protection, fragmenting Europe's economy, had caused economic malaise and political antagonism. Fascist glorification of the nation-state had been revealed as a monstrosity; and many felt that insistence on its sovereignty, even without fascist excess, distorted and ossified the political perspective.

This critique pointed towards the limitation of national sovereignty. It was accepted by many people of the resistance, in Germany and Italy as well as the occupied countries. While the idea of limiting sovereignty in a united Europe was widespread, some influential figures were more precise. They envisaged a federal constitution for Europe, giving powers over trade, money, security, and related taxation, to a federal parliament, government, and court, leaving all other powers to be exercised by the institutions of the member states.[2]

Such ideas evoked a ready echo from those Europeans who asked themselves why the war had occurred and what could be done to ensure a better future; and they were encouraged by Winston Churchill who, in a speech in Zurich in September 1946, suggested that France should lead Germany into a United States of Europe. Not everybody noticed that he was reticent about the part that Britain should play in such a union; and many, impressed by the magnanimous vision of the wartime leader with his immense prestige, did not realize how hard it would be to accomplish. For despite the popularity of the federal idea in Continental countries, the structures of the states were gathering strength again and were to prove resistant to radical federal reform.

Some of this resistance stemmed from the principle of national sovereignty as a basic political value. General de Gaulle was to be the most powerful and eloquent exponent of this view. But most of the resisters were more pragmatic. Many bureaucrats, central bankers, and politicians would allow that sovereignty could in principle be shared on the right terms and at the right time: but the right terms were not on offer and the right time would be later. Such reactions have been widespread in Britain, although Mrs Thatcher was more Gaullist; and they were to pervade the governments of Continental countries to varying degrees at various times.

Two main strategies were devised to overcome the reluctance

of governments. One, promoted by the Italian federalist leader, Altiero Spinelli, was to mobilize popular support for a constituent assembly, in which the people's representatives would draw up a European constitution. But this idea bore little fruit until, with the direct elections to the European Parliament in 1979, Spinelli persuaded the people's newly elected representatives to design and approve a Draft Treaty to constitute a European Union. The other strategy, devised by Jean Monnet, was to identify a 'limited but decisive point', as Schuman's declaration put it, on which governments could be persuaded to agree and which, without going the whole way, would mark a significant step towards federation. With this idea, Monnet was to secure an early and spectacular success.

Founding the Community: the ECSC

Monnet's 'limited but decisive point' was the need for a new structure to contain the resurgent heavy industries of the Ruhr, the traditional economic basis for Germany's military might, which had been laid low as a result of the war. It was clear by 1950 that industry in West Germany must develop if Germans were to pay their way in the world and help the West in its rivalry with the Soviet Union, and that this required the revival of German steel production. Of the western Allies then responsible for West Germany, the United States and Britain were increasingly insistent on this. France, through history and geography more sensitive to the potential danger of German power, insisted that the Ruhr's heavy industries should be kept under control. But France lacked the means to restrain the Americans and British; and there were Frenchmen in key positions who realized that the perpetuation of an international Ruhr authority such as had been set up in 1948 to exert control over the Germans, apart from being unacceptable to the two Allies, would be an unstable arrangement, apt to be overturned by Germany at the first opportunity. Hence the idea of a common structure to govern the coal and steel industries, not only of the Ruhr but also of France and other European countries.

This idea was not the invention of Monnet alone. Officials in the French foreign ministry were also working on it.[3] But they would surely have created a conventional international organization, governed by committees of ministers, whereas Monnet was determined that the new institutions should have a political life independent of the existing governments: that they should be 'the first concrete foundation of a European federation'.

It is the theme of this book that the concept of European institutions which go beyond a conventional system of intergovernmental co-operation, however imperfectly realized so far, has given the Community its special character: its stability, capacity for achievement, and promise for the future. It is of course possible to argue that the Community is, on the contrary, essentially an intergovernmental organization to secure free trade and economic co-operation, and that the rest is frills and rhetoric. This book sets out a case for seeing it as more than that.

Monnet, from his vantage point as head of the French *Commissariat du Plan*, persuaded Schuman to adopt the more radical plan; and he did it at the moment when the French government was most apt to accept, because a solution to the problem of German steel could no longer be delayed. Monnet's solution had the merit of meeting not only the French national interest in the control of German steel but also a wider interest in the development of European political institutions. The proposal was immediately welcomed by the governments of West Germany, Italy, Belgium, the Netherlands, and Luxembourg; and it was enthusiastically received by the wide sectors of opinion in those countries and in France that could be called broadly federalist, in the sense of supporting steps towards a federal end, even if not all would be precise in defining this. The project also received strong and steady support from the United States.

Support for the federal idea had mushroomed in Britain too in 1939 and the first half of 1940, culminating with the government's proposal for union with France.[4] But after the fall of France in June 1940, with Nazi domination of the Continent, British interest in European union had ebbed. For more than a decade after the war, British governments wanted to confine their relationship with the Continent to no more than a loose association. They were not ready to accept the federal implications of Monnet's proposal. So the six founder members negotiated the Treaty establishing the European Coal and Steel Community (ECSC) without Britain or the other West European countries that took the same view.

As chairman of the intergovernmental conference that drew up the ECSC Treaty, Monnet was well placed to ensure that his basic idea was followed through. The High Authority was to be responsible for policy relating to the coal and steel industries in the member countries, and its decisions were to apply directly to the economic agents in each country, without requiring the approval of its government. The policies envisaged in the Treaty bore the mark of French planning ideas. Investment in the two industries was to be influenced by the High Authority, though not subject to much control. Prices and production could be regulated, but only if there were crises of shortage or over-production. Policies for training, housing, and redeployment were to cater for workers' needs. Competition was at the same time to be stimulated by rules on price transparency, as well as by anti-trust laws on American lines.

Monnet insisted on the principle of the High Authority's independence from the member states' governments because his experience as an international civil servant had convinced him that it would be hamstrung if they controlled it too directly. But that raised the question of the High Authority's accountability. Monnet, in his inaugural speech as the first President of the High Authority in August 1952, was to explain the Treaty's answer like this. The High Authority was responsible to an Assembly (now called the European Parliament), which would eventually be directly elected, and which had the power to dismiss it. There was recourse to the European Court of Justice in cases that concerned the High Authority's acts. In short, the powers defined by the Treaty would be exercised by institutions with federal characteristics, sovereign within the limits of their competences, and based on the principles of parliamentary democracy and the rule of law. The policy of the High Authority and those of the member states would be 'harmonized' by a Council of ministers, voting by majority 'save in exceptional cases'. Monnet ensured that the federal elements in the Community would be clearly explained by employing Spinelli's help in drafting the speech.[5]

Monnet's idea was that the European federation would be built over the years on this 'first concrete foundation' as new sectors of activity were brought within the scope of the pre-federal institutions; and the establishment of the European Economic Community and Euratom in 1958 lent remarkable support to this view. But he does not appear to have foreseen how much the Council would come to dominate the politics of the Community, as the political structures of member states came to assert themselves against the realization of the federal idea. This reaction of national sovereignty against the federal idea led to a long-drawn-out conflict within the Community, which began with a major assault by General de Gaulle as President of France and continued up to the 1990s, with Britain succeeding de Gaulle as champion of national sovereignty. But first, there was to be an early rehearsal in the political battle over the project for a European Defence Community.

The failure of the Defence Community

In June 1950, a few days after the conference to draw up the ECSC Treaty had begun, the Communist North Korean regime invaded South Korea. This, following the coup in Czechoslovakia and the Berlin blockade which had demonstrated Stalin's will to build up Soviet power in Central Europe, convinced the Americans that the defence of Western Europe required a military contribution from West Germany. As they began to press for this, France was again confronted by the question that had arisen when German steel production was to be expanded: how to square French security with a revival of German power.

Monnet was among those who found the same answer to the issue of defence as he had to that of steel: to pool the resources of France, West Germany, and other European democracies in a European Defence Community (EDC). The French proposal for a European army quickly secured the support of the governments of France's five ECSC partners and the six countries began to draw up an EDC Treaty. But this time the project 'touched on the core of national sovereignty', as Monnet was to put it, concluding that 'Now, the federation of Europe would have to become an immediate objective'.[6] The six governments did not at first appear to recognize the implications of this for their states, and negotiated about defence integration without paying much attention to the political structure to which the integrated forces were to be responsible. But this issue did not escape the notice of Spinelli, who had given much thought to the problem of integrating nation-states in a European federation. He persuaded the Italian government that federal institutions would be required to control a European army and the Italian government persuaded its five partners that such institutions must be envisaged.[7] They invited the newly established ECSC Assembly, slightly adapted for the purpose, to design a Treaty for a European Political Community. The result was a quasi-federal constitution to complement the EDC Treaty, which was itself ratified by West Germany and the Benelux countries (Belgium, the Netherlands, and Luxembourg), with the Italian parliament waiting on French ratification.

Here, however, the project ran up against the defence of national sovereignty, which was stronger in France than in the other five countries. Stalinist Communists and nationalist Gaullists were root-and-branch opponents; and they were joined by enough doubters from the centre parties to create, by 1954, a parliamentary majority against the EDC Treaty, which was accordingly abandoned by the Assemblée Nationale in August of that year. Many of these doubters had supported the proposal in principle, but feared that Germany would come to dominate the Community in the absence of British participation. But the British were, like the Gaullists, determined to preserve their national sovereignty. So the EDC project failed; and many doubted whether the federal idea could recover from this apparently decisive defeat.

The Treaties of Rome

Despite this setback, the federalist forces regained the initiative within a matter of months, returning to the economic field where national sovereignty seemed less directly threatened. The

Benelux countries put forward a proposal for a common market to cover the whole of trade, not just one sector like the ECSC. This appealed to economic liberals and the more dynamic businesspeople, particularly in Germany and the Netherlands; and to many it promised a European economy big enough to accommodate the scale and specialization required for contemporary technologies, and thus to compete with the United States, then still the world's unchallenged economic superpower. Monnet, continuing his sectoral approach, was meanwhile developing a scheme for an Atomic Energy Community, responding to one of the recurrent phases of European worry about energy supplies. This project was more popular in France, and the two together were taken up by the governments of the six ECSC countries at the Messina conference in June 1955, less than a year after the failure of the EDC. Again with strong American support, and against Britain's sceptical aloofness, the Six negotiated the two Treaties of Rome, signed in that city in March 1957, establishing the European Economic Community (EEC) and the European Atomic Energy Community (Euratom), which entered into force on 1 January 1958.

The EEC's institutions were modelled on those of the ECSC. It shared from the outset the same Parliamentary Assembly and Court of Justice. The significant difference lay, however, in the relationship between the EEC's executive and its ministerial Council. Instead of High Authority, the new executive was called the Commission; and this reflected a weakening of the federalist impulse and a strengthening of the ministers representing member governments over against the independent European executive. With de Gaulle as President of France from June 1958, this reaction was accentuated, and when the institutions of the three Communities were fully merged into one set of Community institutions in 1965, the merged executive was likewise called the Commission.

It was the scope of the powers which these institutions exercised that made the EEC a radical new departure. The creation of a common market for all goods and services was a project of great political and economic significance. The economies of the six member states had been separated by tariffs, quotas, and non-tariff barriers. The EEC Treaty set the aim of abolishing all these barriers on trade between them. The non-tariff barriers comprised a host of laws, regulations, and official practices that impeded trade, and their complexity made their removal difficult to ensure. The Treaty set the objective of removing them but left the methods to be settled later; and this remained largely undone until the 1980s, when the programme to 'complete the single market' was launched in order to attain the objective by the end of 1992. But the tariff was the great historic instrument of protection; and quantitative restrictions on imports, or quotas, had also been rife in the post-war period. The removal of all tariffs and quotas from the trade among member states was a truly radical project; and here the Treaty was decisive, setting out in detail a programme for eliminating them progressively over a transitional period of 12–15 years. On imports from outside the Community, the member countries' existing tariffs, above average for France and Italy, below for Germany and Benelux, were to be aligned on a common external tariff, itself generally at the average level, over the same transitional period.

While this customs union was the backbone of the EEC Treaty, the Treaty also provided for many of the other common economic policies to be expected in a federal system. Apart from the removal of non-tariff distortions to trade, there was provision for the free movement of workers, enterprises, and capital throughout the Community. There were chapters on agricultural, transport, and competition policy. Social policy was included, in the sense of policy relating to employment. A Social Fund and an Investment Bank were established. 'Overseas countries' (then colonies) and territories were to be associated. The policies were to be financed by a Community budget, whose income would eventually come from its 'own resources'—a euphemism for its own taxation which has persisted until now.

Euratom was given similar institutions to govern, like the ECSC, a particular sector of the economy: the 'nuclear industries' in their application to peaceful purposes. It was to promote research, investment, and infrastructure; create a common market for the sector; and ensure safety and the use of nuclear materials only for the intended purposes.

Euratom came too close to the heart of de Gaulle's concept of national sovereignty: his nuclear *force de frappe*. He marginalized it into an agency whose main function was to encourage research. Nor is it a coincidence that one economic power essential to a federal system with which the Economic Community was poorly endowed was the control of monetary policy, in particular the issuing of money by a federal bank. For this is seen as the citadel of economic sovereignty. The Treaties of Rome preceded de Gaulle's return to power as French President and champion of the cause of national sovereignty. But the forces defending the retention of this basic economic prerogative in the institutions of the member states were nevertheless too strong for the federalist-minded designers of the EEC Treaty to challenge.

Despite the eclipse of Euratom and the EEC's lack of monetary powers, the Community, as the three Communities collectively soon came to be called, forged ahead with the establishment of the customs union. With a booming economy and strong support from industry, the programme for tariff cuts was accelerated. At least part of the good performance of the Community economy in the EEC's early years was attributed to this wholesale removal of protection. The Community's external tariff, far from provoking protectionism in the international economy, was moreover the catalyst for multilateral tariff cuts on an unprecedented scale, particularly the Kennedy round of negotiations in the mid-1960s which led to cuts averaging one-third across the board by the industrialized countries. At the same time the common agricultural policy was put in place: a major political achievement even if it was later to become a sorcerer's apprentice, flooding the Community with wasteful expenditure and the world market with surpluses.

The successes of the ECSC and of the EEC in its early period were reflected in a theory which the American political scientists who developed it called neofunctionalism.[8] Their idea was that, once the political decision had been taken to establish supranational institutions in one sector, a new constellation of political forces would extend the area of integration to other sectors until it covered the main fields of political activity.

Political parties and interest groups would focus on the new institutions in the sectors of their initial competence. But the realization of their objectives would be frustrated by those institutions' lack of powers in related sectors, not yet integrated, where the effect of the supranational decisions could be negated. The new supranational political forces would help to resolve the contradiction by promoting the transfer of the related sectors to supranational competence.

The merit of this theory was to consider the novel circumstances of the Community, which has more federal elements than other international organizations but falls short of being a federation, whereas many federalists had concentrated on the idea of a federal constitution without giving much thought to the confederal system that was likely to precede it. The neofunctionalists also had the merit of going beyond a snapshot of the Community to treat it as a process of development over time. In the years of euphoria about the Community, up to the early 1960s, their ideas had much influence in Europe. But their fascination with the new institutions, and their addiction to the 'welfarist' tendency then prevalent to underrate the strength of other values and of existing institutions, led them to ignore the power of national sovereignty and the nation-state. They even went so far at times as to suppose that the process of transferring powers from member states to supranational institutions, or 'spillover' as they called it, would be automatic. This notion was rudely rebutted by de Gaulle, the leading contemporary embodiment of national sovereignty.

Stagnation

General de Gaulle made his concept of the Community quite explicit: '. . . there is and can be no Europe other than a Europe of the States—except, of course, for myths, fictions and pageants'.[9] Until 1962, de Gaulle was preoccupied with domestic French problems and with bringing the Algerian war to an end. This he succeeded in doing in that year, thus freeing himself to give his attention to his quarrels with the federalists in the Community and the 'anglo-saxons' outside it. His first offensive was his veto, in January 1963, on Britain's first attempt to join the Community, negotiations about which were by then far advanced. This was a blow not only to the British but also to the Community practice of taking decisions on EC matters collectively after thorough discussion, whereas de Gaulle's veto was announced at a press conference without discussion with his partners.

This episode was followed by a conflict over the financing of the Community budget, which was seen as a major French interest, since France had a strong agricultural production which the common agricultural policy was designed to help finance. But that interest would be secure only if other member governments lost the power to cut off the funds for the agricultural budget: that is, if the Community was to have its own budgetary resources, instead of depending on contributions from the member governments. The Commission and the Dutch, with support from other member governments, insisted that if tax money was to go direct to the Community, without the need for approval each year by member states' parliaments, its expenditure must be subject to the approval of the relevant elected representatives, that is of the European Parliament. This federalist logic convinced most of those who wanted further development of the Community. But it was anathema to de Gaulle. The Commission hoped that the French interest in securing the finance for agriculture would outweigh de Gaulle's concern for national sovereignty. But de Gaulle was not amenable to neofunctionalist spillover. He withdrew his ministers from the EC Council from 1 July 1965—the policy of the empty chair— and expressed his doubts about the future of the Community. Boycotted by its leading member government, the Community was in evident crisis. But in the first round of the French presidential elections in December, de Gaulle failed to get a majority. The French public was apparently not best pleased with what seemed like threats to withdraw from the Community. The second round was won by a de Gaulle who had started to speak less caustically about the Community; and in January 1966 he sent his ministers to Luxembourg to patch it up with his partners. The result was known as the Luxembourg compromise: a statement in which the French delegation asserted a right of veto in the Council 'when very important interests are at stake', while the other five maintained their stand in defence of the majority vote where the Treaties stipulated it. The issue of parliamentary control of the budget, which had ignited the quarrel, was shelved.

Some useful lessons can be drawn from this trial of strength between national sovereignty and federal reform. The first is that, even if some politicians may have grand notions of abandoning the Community for the principle of national sovereignty, the public is not keen to follow. This has been demonstrated in elections and referenda not only in France, but also in Britain and Denmark. A second is that, with France's participation essential to the Community, neither spillover nor federal reform stood a chance when faced with de Gaulle's stand on national sovereignty. A third, first shown by the grant of budgetary powers to the European Parliament after de Gaulle's departure in 1969, is that the logic of reform can outlast the nationalist leaders. Yet ministers and civil servants of member states continued to show themselves more than comfortable with the practice of continuing discussion in the Council until unanimity was reached, even if that should take a decade or more, which was one of the results of the Luxembourg 'compromise'. It was not until the Single European Act was signed in 1986 that majority voting began to become normal practice in the Council.

The unanimity procedure, or, more crudely put, the veto, was a major reason why even after de Gaulle's demise the Community faced a lengthy period of only slow development, apart from its enlargement from six member states to twelve. The enlargement was certainly a very substantial achievement. The accession of Denmark, the Irish Republic, and the United Kingdom in 1973, of Greece in 1981, and of Portugal and Spain in 1986 was a tribute both to the success of the Community, which made them want to join, and to its adaptability, which enabled them to do so. But the use of the Community's powers was dilatory and weak; and the development of its powers and institutions was limited, even though a number of steps were taken to strengthen them.

When Britain joined, with a grievance about the bias of the

Community's agricultural and budgetary system against it, the Regional Development Fund was set up, intended as a counterweight; and the Social Fund was expanded in the following years. The European Monetary System, which began to operate in 1979, was an important development. Institutional steps in a federal direction included powers of co-legislation for the European Parliament with the Council over part of the budget and the creation of the Court of Auditors to help budgetary control (1970 and 1975); direct elections to the Parliament (first held in 1979); and a steady growth in the role of the Court of Justice. The European Council of heads of state and government (from 1974) was a parallel innovation of an intergovernmental character, as was the 'European Political Co-operation' (from 1970) aiming to co-ordinate member states' foreign policies. With these and a number of other successes, some quite small but cumulatively significant, the Community arrived at the mid-1980s not only enlarged to include nine-tenths of the population of Western Europe, but also with its powers and institutions somewhat enhanced.

Apart from the Community's enlargement, however, the two decades from the mid-1960s to the mid-1980s can be seen as a long period of stagnation. Even if some steps were taken that strengthened the Community, its capacity to solve its principal problems was demonstrated to be dangerously weak. The agricultural budget in particular continued to consume between two-thirds and three-quarters of the Community's budgetary resources, aggravating the quarrel with Britain and the dissatisfaction of Germany, the other net contributor; provoking tension with the United States and others through the excessive subsidization of EC exports; pre-empting money that might have been used to finance new policies for the Community; and giving the impression of a Community that was incapable of action where it was really needed.

Enlargement brings with it objective problems: greater diversity and new interests to be accommodated. It also brought the British, less unyielding than de Gaulle but with a rooted objection to relinquishment of national sovereignty. The French, for their part, were only gradually to relax their attachment to de Gaulle's brand of nationalism; and as they did so, the Germans grew to feel more strongly that they were entitled to their share of autonomy too. Danes and Greeks proved awkward in various ways. Few were inclined to be amenable in a time of oil shocks and stagflation. All these things aggravated the fundamental problem of a polity confronted by growing pressures to take action on a wide front but depending heavily on securing agreement among a number of governments in order to do so.

It is not surprising that many observers concluded that the Community, after its initial flying start, had become stuck as a complicated intergovernmental organization, more powerful perhaps than most others but not essentially different. There was, according to this 'realist' school of thought, little prospect that it would become stronger in the future, let alone that there would be further steps in a federal direction. From the mid-1980s, however, this reductionist view, which had seemed to many plausible during the Community's years of stagnation, began to appear less realistic.

Regeneration

During the first half of 1984, when France occupied the Presidency of the Council, two long-standing problems were resolved: the terms of accession for Portugal and Spain, and the compensation for Britain to set against its net contribution to the Community budget. President Mitterrand also lent support to the European Parliament's federalist-oriented Draft Treaty to establish a European Union, which the Parliament, inspired by Spinelli, had approved by a large majority in February of that year. A year later, the European Council approved the Commission's ambitious programme, strongly supported by leading industrialists, to complete the single market by the end of 1992; and under the impulse of this and of the European Parliament's Draft Treaty, the member governments negotiated the first major revision of the Community Treaties, embodied in the Single European Act, which came into force in July 1987.

The Single European Act extended the scope of majority voting in the Council to include most of the decisions required for completion of the internal market, and gave the European

Parliament the right, under a new 'co-operation procedure', to a role in relation to those decisions that went some way beyond consultation, though still well short of co-legislation with the Council. The Act also defined a Community competence in the fields of environment, technology, and conditions at work; set monetary union as a Community objective and gave the European Monetary System a basis in the treaties; formalized the system of foreign policy co-operation, and extended it to the 'political and economic aspects of security'. Importantly for the new members from the Community's South, the Act recognized the need for 'cohesion', or financial support for the weaker economies in the Community, lest they should lose out in the freer trade resulting from the process of completing the single market.

Agreement on the Single European Act and progress with the decisions required to complete the single market gave the Community the momentum it needed to bind up the running sore of its agri-budgetary crisis. The Commission's President, Jacques Delors, put forward a comprehensive proposal to deal with it. This included 'stabilizers' to keep agricultural expenditure under control; a new tax resource to provide additional revenue, more fairly distributed among the member countries than hitherto; continued compensation to reduce Britain's net payment to the EC budget; and a doubling of the 'structural funds', as instruments for helping the weaker economies to meet the challenge of free trade. The European Council agreed a settlement along these lines in February 1988, resolving at least for a time a problem which had dogged the Community for a decade. Building on this success, the European Council charged a committee, chaired by Delors, to draw up proposals for an economic and monetary union (Emu). The project gathered support from businesspeople who saw it as a completion of the single market project; from public authorities that wished to reassert, collectively, the control over monetary policy that was being eroded by the opening of the economies and financial markets; and from those who saw it as a major element in political integration. So the Delors report led to an Intergovernmental Conference (IGC) to consider the treaty amendments needed to establish economic and monetary union.

The Community also responded to the radical reforms launched in Central and Eastern Europe in 1989, giving substantial help to these countries and facilitating the entry of East Germany into the EC in 1990 when it joined the Federal Republic. The desire to anchor the new, larger Germany in the Community, as well as to meet the political challenges of Emu and of the changes in Central and Eastern Europe, led to a second IGC, on political union; and the two IGCs culminated in the agreement at Maastricht on the Treaty on European Union, providing for Emu and for elements of political union.

There is no such thing as automatic spillover or inevitable progress towards federation. But the continued growth of interdependence in the real economies of the member countries, the strength of the political commitment to further unification, and the existence of solid Community structures on which further integration can be based, have provided the conditions for the dynamism that the Community has shown since 1985.

Federal institutions

In exploring this prospect in the chapters that follow, we face a semantic problem. The word integration, generally used to denote strengthening of the Community, is not precise enough for the analysis we have in mind. Nor is the description of the Community as *sui generis*, understandably popular among those who wish to avoid political discussion of sovereignty, much help in elucidating the directions in which it may develop. The choice in this book is to employ a word that has been much misused in discussion about the Community's future: that is, to use the word federal, precisely defined with reference to the Community.

Thus the EC institutions would be called federal if reformed to make majority voting in the Council the general rule for matters of Community competence, to make the Parliament a co-legislator with the Council so that Community laws have to be approved by both, and to give the Commission executive competence within the limits of Community law. These reforms would convert the Council and Parliament into a bicameral legislature and the Commission into a Community government.

Together with the Court of Justice, they would comprise the principal institutions of a federal system, which would be responsible for matters that are more effectively undertaken in common, while leaving competence in other matters with the member states.

With its institutions reformed, Emu added to its competences, and closer co-operation in foreign policy, the Community would embody the essentials of Union as it was envisaged by the European Parliament. The Maastricht Treaty is also called the Treaty on European Union. This being official nomenclature, the term European Union is used in this book to denote the arrangement agreed at Maastricht, while the Union envisaged by the Parliament, with its federal institutions, will be called a federal European Union or federal Union. Neither the new treaty nor the Parliament went so far as to give the Union control over the armed forces, which would make it a federation, or federal state.

The institutions of the Parliament's federal Union would nevertheless be substantially the same as those required for a European federal state. Steps towards such a Union will be called steps in a federal direction; and those who, like Monnet, wish to take them as steps on the way to such a Union will be called federalists. This may shock some British readers. But it is desirable to be clear about matters which are too often left unclear; and the word federal is the best to describe such a Union's institutions.

It is also desirable for the reader to know where the writer stands—but perhaps it is already plain enough that this one stands on the federalist side.

2 Institutions or Constitution

The specific character of the Community institutions derives mainly from the conviction that, in order to achieve more than conventional international organizations, they need to have more independence from the governments of member states.

This is most clearly demonstrated by the Court of Justice. It is the Court's duty to ensure that Community law is observed. In doing so, it affirms the primacy of Community law if there is a conflict with the law of a member state. The Court must judge whether member states, which like the Community institutions are bound by Community law, do in fact comply with it; and in order to ensure that member states' citizens benefit from their rights and discharge their obligations under Community law, the Court ensures that it applies directly to them, without the member governments standing in the way.

Part of Community law is embodied in the treaties. But a growing part is enacted by the Community institutions; and here, too, there is an element of independence, though less clear cut than in the case of the Court. Most of the laws are enacted by the Council, comprising representatives of the member governments. But the hold of a given government on the legislative process is weakened by the procedure of majority voting on many important matters. Independent bodies, moreover, have a part to play in the legislation. The Commission has the sole right to table most legislative proposals. The European Parliament and the Economic and Social Committee, both independent, have the right to be consulted; and the Parliament has significant powers in the legislative process. Once enacted, the Commission has major responsibilities for the implementation of Community laws.

The member governments, represented in the Council, are

still the predominant force in the Community institutions. But their behaviour is conditioned by the independent elements; and the question whether these elements are to be enhanced remains one of the most crucial facing the Community.

The Commission: a European executive

An independent executive was, for Jean Monnet, the keystone of the Community that he wanted to establish. The High Authority was the only institution about which the Schuman declaration was explicit. Monnet, in chairing the conference on the ECSC Treaty and then as the High Authority's first President, insisted on its multinational and independent character, which has been preserved in the Commission to this day.

The members of the Commission, although usually former ministers or high officials of member states, are bound by oath not to take instructions from governments or from any other outside body (article 157 EEC). To ensure that it is multinational, the Commission contains one member from each of the smaller member states, two from the larger ones. They are, according to the treaty (article 158 EEC), appointed by unanimous agreement among the ministers in the Council, although in practice the member states' nominations for their own nationals have always been accepted. However dissatisfied a government may subsequently be, it has no power to withdraw one of them during their term of office, which the Maastricht Treaty has increased from four to five years.

In the treaties, the Commission denotes this collegiate body of members, now numbering seventeen, though a reduction to one per member state has been proposed. They have recruited an equally multinational body of officials to carry out their tasks; and the name Commission is in practice given to the Commissioners and officials collectively.

In line with its designation as the Community's executive, one of the Commission's main functions is to execute the policies decided under Community law. For a policy such as that relating to agriculture, this is a big and complex task. Another is to represent the Community in international trade negotiations (article 113 EEC). Some of the Commission's tasks of implementation are given it directly by the treaties, rather than by decisions of the Council. An example is the competition policy (article 89 EEC); and the larger scope given to the ECSC's High Authority than to the EEC's Commission stemmed mainly from the policies enshrined in the ECSC treaty in this way. Despite the extent of its executive job, the Commission has remained a small body, with fewer officials than have many local authorities in the member countries. This it has done through delegation of much of the administration to the civil services of the member states, following an example that has been seen to work well in the relations between Bund and Länder in the Federal Republic of Germany.

The Commission's responsibilities go beyond plain implementation, in the duty that the treaties lay on it to ensure that their provisions and 'the measures taken by the institutions pursuant thereto' are applied (article 155 EEC). In this capacity the Commission is sometimes called the guardian, or 'watchdog', of the treaties. It brings infringements to the attention of those responsible, including member governments, and if necessary takes them to the Court.

The most innovative among the functions given to the Commission is, however, its role in legislation. Most governments, although called 'executives', in fact play a vital part in the legislative process, proposing draft laws which they expect the 'legislature' to approve, in more or less amended form. The Commission is weaker in relation to the Council than most governments are in relation to their legislatures. But on most subjects the Council cannot act without a proposal from the Commission; and the Commission has the right to make legislative proposals on its own initiative (article 155 EEC). These may take the form either of a Regulation, which is 'binding in its entirety and directly applicable in all member states'; or of a Directive, which is 'binding, as to the result to be achieved', but leaves it to the member states to choose 'the form and methods'; or of a Decision, which is 'binding in its entirety upon those to whom it is addressed' (article 189 EEC). Since there must be unanimous agreement in the Council in order to amend the Commission's proposal, member governments that want it changed may well have to persuade the Commission to withdraw and amend the draft itself. The Commission might stand a good chance of securing its passage instead, if this could be done by a simple majority. But where majority voting in the Council is stipulated, it is almost always by qualified majority, with over 71 per cent of the weighted votes; and for the most important matters the treaties specify unanimity, which the member governments in any case usually prefer to seek. Thus the Commission, if it wants a decision, is often obliged to withdraw and amend, even if it judges that this will unduly weaken or delay the measure.

The Commission is far from filling the shoes of a European government in the process of Community legislation. But it does play an essential part; and in the period of early EEC success, it was often called the motor of the Community, pulling the Council along behind it. Among the major actions that evoked this metaphor were the acceleration of the customs union programme, the realization of the common agricultural policy, and the conclusion of the Kennedy round of trade negotiations. Impressed by such achievements, the neofunctionalists invented the term engrenage (enmeshing), to express what they saw as the Commission's co-optation of member states' officials to help realize its European objectives.

The Commission was not as strong as the neofunctionalists had thought, when faced by a government that refused to be co-opted. The attack that de Gaulle launched in 1965 was against not only the European Parliament but also the Commission: 'this embryonic technocracy for the most part foreign'.[1] He did what he could to weaken it; and the practice of seeking unanimity in the Council, which lived on after him, did more. There was less talk of motors and engrenage.

The Commission never ceased to be indispensable. However much nationalists might resent it, the laws and policies required for an integrating economy and the European co-operation that was generally desired would not be feasible without an institution designed to articulate the common interest. The Commission has been the architect, and often the initiator, of many of the Community's achievements: less impressive, certainly, during the relatively stagnant period from the mid-1960s to the mid-1980s, but more recently gathering strong momentum again. There were significant successes, even before the regeneration of the Community following the Single European Act: already in the late 1970s the initiative by Roy Jenkins, as Commission President, to relaunch monetary integration, resulting in the European Monetary System; Viscomte Davignon's policies for steel and technology; the adoption of Lord Cockfield's internal market programme; the influence of the Delors Commission on the Intergovernmental Conference that drew up the Single European Act.

The Single European Act demonstrated the limits to the Commission's independence in relation to the Council. The Council had over the years encroached on the Commission's executive competence, in particular by setting up committees of member governments' officials to supervise its work. Seized of the consequent threat to the Community's efficiency, the Act required the Council to 'confer on the Commission . . . powers for the implementation of the rules which the Council lays down', but added the weasel words that the Council 'may impose certain requirements' (article 10 SEA). The Council had to act in this on a proposal from the Commission, which proposed committees in a form that would not be obstructive. The Council could amend this text only by unanimity, and included representatives of governments that had supported a more federalist version of the Single European Act. Faced with the prospect of fuller executive competence for the Commission, however, they unanimously agreed on a restrictive system of committees, objectionable to the Commission and causing the European Parliament to appeal to the Court of Justice to annul it on grounds of inconsistency with the Act. But the Court rejected the appeal on procedural grounds.

Despite this setback, the Commission continued to expand its influence. It designed the crucial agri-budgetary reform of 1988. President Delors was central to the project for economic and monetary union. With the agreement of the US and other OECD countries, the Commission was given the responsibility for co-ordinating the assistance of the advanced industrial countries to the emergent democracies of Central and Eastern Europe. But notwithstanding its creditable performance, the federalists' vision of the Commission as an incipient government for the Community has been frustrated, and for all its significant federal features, the member governments still dominate the Community. To judge the strength, durability, and consequences of the intergovernmental structures, we must examine the Council of ministers and the European Council of heads of state and government.

The intergovernmental bodies: Council, Coreper, European Council

The membership of the Council is that of a conventional international organization: a representative from each member government (article 146 EEC), usually a minister. Each minister is responsible to the government and parliament of his member state. Most ministers also realize that they have a responsibility to try to reach an agreement that will be of some benefit to the Community as a whole. Otherwise, nothing would get done. But the structure of the Council makes such agreements difficult.

Each minister is backed by a government department that will usually have a point of view on the matter at issue, sometimes deeply rooted and often lent a certain self-righteousness by being termed the national interest. Where unanimity is required or sought, which was generally the case following the Luxembourg 'compromise' of 1966 until the Single European Act of 1987, at least some are likely to resist the necessary compromises. Even a qualified majority may be hard to secure. It requires 54 of the votes, out of a total of 76, weighted so as to give more voting power to the representatives of larger member states: ten each for France, Germany, Italy, and the UK; eight for Spain; five each for Belgium, Greece, the Netherlands, and Portugal; three each for Denmark and Ireland; two for Luxembourg (article 148 EEC). A decision can be blocked by 23 of these weighted votes. Examples of such blocking minorities could be Italy, Spain, and Portugal or Greece, on matters of concern to the southern tier; Britain, Germany, and the Netherlands or Denmark, on matters of northern or of liberal trading concern; Britain, France, and Denmark, where there is a threat to the principle asserted by de

Gaulle in the Luxembourg 'compromise', that a government must not be outvoted on a matter that it, itself, defines as important.

To secure agreement that is more than an empty compromise is a thorny political problem. In organizations dominated by a hegemonial leader, the others can often be led. But it is a rewarding feature of the Community, and a basis on which democracy can be developed, that there is no hegemony: the larger states have been of similar size; and even the united Germany falls far short of being a hegemon. Leadership from the Commission might have been more consistently effective had the Council not checked its development. The member government whose turn it is to be President of the Council can exert influence, particularly if it represents a major member country and is working well with the Commission. But the procedure of rotation allows each government only six months in the presidency; and this is too short for a full development of the leading role, even in the foreign policy co-operation where the troika system provides for consultation with the preceding and succeeding presidencies.

Coherence is further undermined by the fragmentation of the Council on functional lines. So far from being a single group of ministers, the Council is a hydra-headed conglomerate of more than twenty functional Councils, each comprising the ministers with a given responsibility such as agriculture, finance, industry, trade, or transport. The foreign ministers, as well as meeting to deal with foreign affairs, sit as a General Affairs Council with the aim of co-ordinating the work of the other Councils. But ministers of agriculture, finance, etc. are not easily co-ordinated; and each Council when it meets has the equal right to act as the legislature for the Community. When the agriculture ministers have decided on a measure, the finance or foreign ministers have no power to rescind it; and it was only in 1988 that the agricultural budget began to be brought under control.

This unwieldy Council has enormous responsibilities. It has to enact the large volume of Community legislation. It has taken on itself the burden, much of which might have been left with the Commission, of taking a multitude of executive decisions. It also has to try to co-ordinate member states' policies in a wide area, such as macroeconomic policy and foreign policy, where the Community's method is still co-operation, not integration. So it combines legislative, executive, and diplomatic roles. An array of ministers, each flying into Brussels for a day or so at intervals, could not possibly come to grips with all this. In order to do so, and to reduce their dependence on the Commission, they have permanent delegations of their own government's officials stationed in Brussels, each one headed by a Permanent Representative, responsible for preparing the meetings for the whole set of that country's ministers. The Committee of Permanent Representatives, known by the French acronym as Coreper, meets weekly and goes as far as it can to reach agreement before the ministers come to meet in the Council. This it does to such effect that many measures are agreed without discussion in the Council.

Much of the work of day-to-day decisions which results from the Council's determination to keep the Commission on a tight rein is also delegated to member states' officials, sitting in the several hundred committees that the Council has set up for the purpose. Some of the committees are merely advisory, helping the Commission to take account of member states' views and circumstances. Others, such as many concerned with managing the common agricultural policy, can either persuade or force the Commission to think again, if they can muster a qualified majority against the Commission's decision. Yet others can block the Commission unless it gets a qualified majority on its side, so that the Commission's implementation can be prevented by a qualified minority of 23 votes, for example any two of the largest states plus one other; and in the field of trade policy, some decisions can be referred to the Council by a single member state. All this adds to the responsibilities and influence of the permanent delegations.

Already in the 1960s the neofunctionalists' idea of engrenage, or the co-optation of member states' officials to the Commission's sphere of influence, was challenged on the grounds that the member governments were the stronger, so the co-opting would be the other way about.[2] Although the Commission has maintained a creditable degree of independence, committees of the latter sort bear witness to the strength of the member governments' official machines. The Commission, appointed by the member governments, has lacked a political base that would enable it to be a match for them in any serious attempt to change the balance of political power. The European Parliament, with which the Commission has increasingly become allied, does not have the strength to offer such a base, at least as yet, though Maastricht gave it significant new powers. Coreper ranks high in the federalist demonology. But if the system is unsatisfactory, the over-burdened and dedicated Permanent Representatives are not to blame. It is they who have enabled it nevertheless to produce so many useful results.

With the intergovernmental method riding high, there were important developments in its institutions. One was the system of committees, with Coreper at the peak. Others were the European Council and the foreign policy co-operation—strengthened and with security added to it by the Maastricht Treaty.

Co-operation among member governments in their foreign policies should come readily in a Community with political aspirations and instruments of external economic policy. But it did not come in the 1960s, thanks to the quarrels between de Gaulle and his partners. It was in 1970 that the member governments' foreign ministers and the political directors of their ministries began to have regular meetings for the purpose; and the European Political Co-operation (EPC), as it was called following the division of labour between political and economic departments within the ministries of foreign affairs, evolved to the point where it was brought formally within the Community treaties, in the Single European Act (article 30).

The aim of the EPC was defined in the Act as 'to formulate and implement a European foreign policy', no less. But the means scarcely measured up to it: regular meetings of ministers and officials, and after the Act a small secretariat in Brussels. A relationship such as that between Commission and Council was not envisaged. There were useful results, such as many votes in common in the United Nations and joint declarations on a variety of topics. But they were modest compared with achievements of the EEC such as the trade negotiations and the Lome Convention. Although Maastricht strengthens the foreign policy co-operation, the system remains intergovernmental, and thus ill-adapted to producing a really effective common policy.

The other intergovernmental innovation that was initiated after de Gaulle and later incorporated in the treaties by the Single European Act (article 2) is the European Council, in which the heads of state and government and the President of the Commission meet at least twice a year, assisted by the foreign ministers and a Commissioner. When President Giscard d'Estaing launched the series of regular meetings during the French presidency in 1974, he seemed to have in mind intimate chats among the political heads of the member states (the President in France, Prime Ministers in the other countries). But the European Council was quickly sucked into the political vacuum at the centre of the Community: to take decisions that the Council of ministers was unable to take. These ranged from small details, such as demands for special treatment by Greece during its first years as a member, through the resolution of acute crises such as the British net contribution and the agri-budgetary imbroglio, to agreement on the treaty amendments in the Maastricht Treaty. The European Council has approved package deals that carried the Community into a new stage of development, such as that under French presidency in 1984 which combined the mechanism for Britain's budget rebate with the green light for Spanish and Portuguese accession, and under German presidency in 1988 which decided on the expansion of funds to assist the EC's weaker economies together with reform of the budget and of the agricultural policy. Initiatives are also taken that lead to important steps in developing the Community: to prepare direct elections to the European Parliament (French presidency, 1974); to launch the European Monetary System (Germany, 1978); to convene the Intergovernmental Conference (IGC) that drew up the Single European Act (Italy, 1985) and to agree on the Act (Luxembourg 1985); to respond vigorously to the reforms in Central and Eastern Europe (France, 1989); to prepare for the incorporation of East Germany into the Community on its accession to the Federal Republic (Ireland, 1990); to convene the IGCs on Emu (Spain, 1989), and on political union (Ireland, 1990), and to agree on the Maastricht Treaty (Netherlands, 1991). Thus the European Council has come to play a central part in taking many of the Community's principal decisions. So the quality of its performance can best be judged in the context of the performance of the institutions as a whole.

Results of the intergovernmental system

The Community has notable achievements to its credit, such as the customs union and trade policy, the successive enlargements, the survival through difficult times, and the resurgence that accompanied the launching of the 1992 programme. The common agricultural policy must also be counted among these, easing the reduction of agricultural employment by one-half in the original member countries and providing a cement that helped to keep France attached to its partners through the 1960s. So the existing institutions, with their intergovernmental predominance, have shown their ability to secure agreement on important matters, to continue working through the lean years, and to recover momentum when times are better.

This is incomparably better than Europe's performance in the decades before the Community was established. But the question remains: is it good enough? Can the Community in its present form work well enough in bad times, which will assuredly return one day? Can it deal with future needs, some of which, such as economic and monetary union or enlargement including Central European countries, can now be foreseen? Can it deal with current business in ways that satisfy the economic and political aspirations of its population?

The story of agriculture, if continued beyond the 1960s, invites scepticism. Already in 1968, Sicco Mansholt, the Commissioner for agriculture who had been the architect of the common agricultural policy, produced a memorandum for the Council stressing the need for a major programme of structural measures to avert the looming crisis of high cost and overproduction.[3] It was over four years before the Council approved some Directives, responding modestly to what Mansholt had proposed. Since Directives specify the result to be achieved but leave the member states to draft and enact their own legislation (article 189 EEC), another five years passed before they were actually applied in France; and in Italy there was still no action on some aspects of the Directives by 1980. Thus, over ten years after Mansholt's warning shot, the Community still had taken virtually no effective action to check the crisis, which as a consequence in the 1980s almost wrecked the Community. It was not until February 1988 that the European Council pulled back from disaster, with decisions that contained the problem for a time. The responsibility for the prolonged agony was that of the Council and the European Council, and theirs alone. The European Parliament had little power over the agricultural budget; and the Commission's proposals, had the Council accepted them, would have stopped the haemorrhage long before.

In agriculture, the Council's delays had spectacular effects. But a period of gestation of ten to fifteen years is by no means unknown for a Council decision on a tricky question in other fields. The decision on the structure of the value-added tax took that long, for example, even before enlargement had augmented the number of member governments' positions that had to be reconciled.[4] More recently, the programme of legislation to complete the single market has acquired a remarkable momentum, thanks to the Council's use of the provision in the Single European Act for majority voting on these matters (article 18 SEA). But overload in the Council, together with the search for unanimity on many important matters, continues to cause delay. Nor, with further monetary integration and other policies likely to flow from the fusion of the economies, is the pressure likely to abate. This can be seen as a consequence of the secular trend to economic interdependence; and when the interdependence links countries as diverse as the members of the Community now are, and with further enlargement increasingly may be, there cannot fail to be political consequences, which lend conviction to the argument that there will be a weaker Community, with loose co-operation and irregular application of its laws, unless there are stronger institutions.

Effectiveness is one arm of this argument. Democracy is the other. It is contended that laws made by ministers and not approved by an elected parliament transgress the norms of representative government. If such laws were not very important, they could be seen as examples of regulation delegated to the executive, which is widely practised in democracies. But with the volume and significance of the Community's present legislative programme, this justification wears thin. The criticism that laws are negotiated by interlocking technocracies, insufficiently accessible to the people's representatives, becomes more telling. The fact that the Council, as a legislature, conducts its proceedings in secret adds to the unease.

There are, then, grounds of both effectiveness and democracy that have led to demands for more federal elements in the Community's institutions.

Against the pull towards intergovernmental methods, there has been a current flowing towards stronger federal elements in each of the institutions. The Single European Act extended the scope for majority votes in the Council, stipulating qualified majority voting for most of the legislative harmonization required to complete the internal market (though unanimity remains for the harmonization of tax), and for the decisions on the regional fund, on health and safety at work, and on specific research programmes (articles 17, 18, 21, 23, 24 SEA). This not only made the Council more federal, but also strengthened the legislative role of the Commission, whose indispensability in resolving Community crises and problems has anyway been increasingly recognized. The powers of the European Parliament were enhanced by the Single European Act (articles 6, 7) as well as in other ways, particularly associated with the direct election of its members since 1979. The influence of the Court of Justice has been rising steadily. Maastricht further enhanced the institutions' federal elements. All this reflects awareness of a need for political integration, to set against the centrifugal tendencies of member states.

The Court of Justice and the rule of law

'The Court of Justice shall ensure that in the interpretation and application of this Treaty the law is observed.' Thus straightforwardly the EEC Treaty (article 164) sets down what the Court is for. Its full import can be grasped only if we remember that the member states had previously accepted no binding authority outside themselves. It was of course World War II, seen as the ultimate consequence of allowing relations among nation-states to be determined by power rather than law, that had induced the member countries to take this unprecedented step.

To provide a sound juridical basis for the Community and to gain the confidence of all the member states and their citizens, it was essential that the Court should be incontrovertibly impartial. It comprises one judge from each member state and, to make an odd number, one more nominated by each member state in rotation. The judges have to be chosen 'from persons whose independence is beyond doubt' (article 167 EEC) and the Statutes of the Court require them, before taking up their office, to take an oath to perform their duties 'impartially and conscientiously'. The Court is assisted by six Advocates-General, appointed in a similar way and likewise for six-year terms, to make 'reasoned submissions on cases brought before the Court' (article 166 EEC). Thus composed, the Court of Justice has been remarkably successful in securing respect for Community law.

It was in order to 'ensure . . . that the law is observed' that the Court established the principles of the primacy and direct effect of Community law. For if member states' law could override Community law, and if governments could stand between the law and the citizens, the law would soon be applied divergently in different countries and it would no longer be possible to say that the member states were bound by it. They would be sliding back to reliance on power relationships instead of law to settle their differences.

Having established the principles of primacy and direct effect for Community law, the Court applied them with as little European centralization as possible. The Court itself tries cases involving member states and Community institutions. But cases between individuals and between individuals and national authorities are tried in the courts of member states, with the Court of Justice intervening only to give a 'preliminary ruling' when asked to do so on a point regarding the interpretation of the treaties or the validity or interpretation of the acts of Community institutions (i.e. Community law). There have been few complaints that national courts are not impartial in applying Community law; and the member states have almost always complied with judgements of the Court which went against them, even if they have sometimes taken their time to do so.

Among the many hundred judgements made by the Court, some stand out as landmarks in the Community's development. In 1979, the judgement on Cassis de Dijon (case 120/78) initiated a new phase in the removal of barriers that fragment the EC market. The German authorities had forbidden imports of that French drink on the grounds that its contents did not comply with German regulations; but the Court found that the French regulations, which had been respected, were an adequate safeguard for health and must be recognized as such in other member countries. This judgement rested on article 30 EEC, which prohibited 'all measures having equivalent effect' to quantitative restrictions on intra-Community trade, and which the Court ruled should apply directly in member states in the absence of more specific legislation enacted by the Council. The sale of Cassis de Dijon on the German market went ahead, and set a precedent for the mutual recognition of member states' regulations, which became a major new strategy for completing the single market. A year later, in the isoglucose cases (138/79 and 139/79) the Court took a significant step towards establishing the European Parliament's legislative power. The Council had enacted a regulation for that substance without waiting for the Parliament's opinion; and the Court found the regulation invalid because the EEC Treaty required the Council to consult the Parliament. The Parliament could, thereafter, exert more influence on legislation, because it could delay the process until it was confident that its proposed amendments would be taken into account. In 1985, in a case (13/83) brought by the Parliament, the Court found that the Council was acting illegally in failing to decide on a common transport policy despite the duty clearly imposed on it by the EEC Treaty, over a quarter of a century before. This was the first sanction against the Council's habit of stunting Community development by indefinite delay.

Thus the Court has established itself as a significant actor in ensuring the development of the EC institutions as indicated by the treaties, as well as in promoting free movement within the Community and ensuring that Community law is applied in other ways. It has, like the Council, suffered from overload due to the expansion of Community activities; so the Single European Act (article 11) provided for a second Court, called a court of 'first instance' because all its cases are brought directly to it rather than going first to the courts of member states, to deal with a limited range of cases. The Maastricht Treaty broke new ground by giving the Court of Justice the power to fine member states that fail to comply with its judgements. In all, the Court continues to win growing respect and an expanding role, helping to ensure that 'as far as its legal system is concerned, the Community possesses most of the characteristics of a federation'.[5]

European Parliament and European democracy

The Schuman declaration contained no hint of a parliamentary assembly for the Coal and Steel Community. But on the suggestion of a French federalist member of parliament, the idea was introduced into the negotiations to establish the ECSC; and Monnet, in his inaugural speech for the High Authority, was able to say that 'the High Authority is responsible, not to the states, but to the European Assembly . . . the first European Assembly endowed with sovereign powers'.[6] Such a parliament was hardly necessary for the ECSC itself, but rather because it was seen as the first step towards a European federation; and in the same spirit the treaty provided that its members, initially designated by the member states' parliaments, would be directly elected by universal suffrage when the Council had decided how this was to be done.

The Council was to decide this by unanimous vote (article 21 ECSC, followed by article 138 EEC); and it was over a quarter of a century before the first direct elections were held. On becoming French President in 1974, Valéry Giscard d'Estaing consulted Jean Monnet on the steps he should take to put some new life into the Community, and decided to take the initiative on this, as well as on the creation of the European Council;[7] and the elections were duly held in June 1979. The authority of the European Parliament, as it was to be formally designated in the Single European Act, was greatly enhanced. It 'increased its influence dramatically', according to Britain's Permanent Representative during the period following the elections.[8]

One argument that had helped to strengthen the case for direct elections was the Parliament's acquisition of budgetary powers through the amending treaties of 1970 and 1975; and it had been given these powers because of the need perceived for democratic control of Community expenditure. It was the Dutch second chamber that bound its government to insist on control by the European Parliament if the Community was to be allocated its own tax resources. This federalist logic was, as we have seen, rejected by de Gaulle. But the Dutch Parliament and the federalist logic outlived him. The French government that followed his resignation in 1969 retained some of his attitudes, and managed to confine the Parliament to a mainly consultative role with respect to the agricultural budget and some other items of expenditure; but for the rest, the amending treaties made the Parliament and the Council a genuine two-chamber legislature, with the Parliament having the final say and hence the stronger power over that part of the budget (article 203 EEC). Because the Council eschewed the unanimity procedure in voting on the budget, and because the EEC Treaty stipulates that the Commission 'shall implement the budget . . . on its own responsibility' (article 205 EEC), thus giving it full executive power, this 'non-compulsory expenditure', as it is quaintly called, is subject to a fully federal relationship between the EC's legislature, executive, and judiciary: a bridgehead for federal institutions in a generally confederal or hybrid Community.

With agricultural expenditure predominant, the non-compulsory expenditure started small. But it grew steadily; and the expansion of structural funds agreed to meet the needs of the weaker economies in the single market was intended to bring it, after allocations for East Germany have been included, to some ecu 20 billion by 1992. For this part of the budget, the Parliament can add expenditure within limits prescribed by the treaties. This has enabled it to introduce new policies in matters such as research, education, and youth exchanges; give priority to food aid for the Third World; and increase the allocations for aid to Central Europe. The Parliament also has powers over the allocation of expenditure within the budget, which have enabled it, for example, to freeze aid to Turkey in reaction to violations of human rights.

The Parliament's powers over the budget as a whole are less impressive. It does have the right to adopt or reject the budget as a whole. But if it rejects the budget, the Community can continue to spend at the same monthly rate as in the previous year (article 204 EEC). Given inflation, this means a cut in real expenditure, which is not usually in line with the Parliament's wishes. The Parliament has not, indeed, been able to secure effective power over the agricultural expenditure, although in 1988 it did secure the right to ensure that the Council keeps that spending within agreed limits until 1992.[9] The Parliament is also responsible for granting Discharge for the whole budget (article 206b EEC), i.e. for affirming that a preceding year's expenditure has been properly implemented. Its capacity to scrutinize expenditure is strengthened by the Court of Auditors, which was created by the amending treaty of 1975 (article 206 EEC), following cases of fraud and other improprieties that the Parliament had unearthed in the early 1970s. A Commissioner for the budget went so far as to say he thought the Commission would have to resign if Discharge was refused.[10]

The Parliament also has the right to dismiss the Commission by a two-thirds majority (article 144 EEC). Such a power, already incorporated in the ECSC Treaty (article 24), led Monnet to say that its High Authority was responsible to the Parliament rather than to the member states. But if the Parliament were to dismiss the Commission, it would nevertheless stay in place, conducting current business, until the Council appointed a new one by unanimous vote. Unless the Council were to appoint a new Commission more acceptable to the Parliament, the result could be a public demonstration of the Parliament's lack of power. Since, moreover, the Parliament usually regards the Commission as its ally, it has never yet come near to exercising its power of dismissal. The British Permanent Representative cited earlier nevertheless observed that, as a result of the fear of dismissal, 'the Commission pays a great deal of attention to the views of the Parliament, in its preparation of draft legislation, in the line it takes in the Council . . . and in budgetary matters'.[11] The Commission has, however, other reasons to co-operate with the Parliament: it too needs political allies to strengthen it in its relations with the Council; the Parliament has the powers to upset the Commission's plans for the budget and to obstruct the Commission's proposals for legislation; and the Maastricht Treaty requires the Parliament's approval for the appointment of a new Commission. Life for the Commission would be harder in various ways if it did not accord substantial influence to the Parliament.

The EC treaties gave the Parliament the right to be consulted about Community legislation. Until 1979 this consultation on non-budgetary legislation brought little influence. The Commission was polite. The Council's attitude was cavalier. With the direct elections following on the grant of budgetary powers, the Parliament's legislative role became more important. The Court's ruling in the isoglucose case secured for the Parliament the right at least to delay; and some types of legislation could be influenced by its budgetary powers. But it was the Single European Act that brought the Parliament closer to the centre of the legislative process.

One of the impulses that gave rise to the Single European Act was the European Parliament's Draft Treaty for European Union (1984), which proposed a federal reform of the Community institutions, making the Parliament a co-legislator with the Council. The Draft Treaty and the Parliament's role were strongly backed by the Italian parliament and government; and most of the other member governments were open to the idea that the European Parliament's powers should be enhanced as the scope of Community legislation was increased. So the Act did something to strengthen the Parliament's powers. Under what is called the assent procedure, the Council cannot act on an application for membership of the Community without the assent of the Parliament, nor can association agreements with third countries be concluded without the Parliament's assent (articles 8, 9 SEA). Thus full co-legislation has been extended from the non-compulsory expenditure to apply also to these two essential elements in the

Community's external relations. The Parliament has used this power to secure, for example, some trade benefits for the Palestinians as a condition for accepting an extension of the association agreement with Israel; and applications for membership will give it an opportunity to insist that the Community's institutions are strengthened, not weakened, by enlargement.

For most of the legislation to complete the single market and for some other matters such as the Regional Development Fund and specific research programmes, the Single Act laid down a 'co-operation procedure', whereby the Council, voting by qualified majority, has to co-operate with the Parliament without giving it the full power of co-legislation (articles 6, 7 SEA). Under this procedure, if the Parliament rejects a measure that has been accepted by the Council, the Council can then enact it only by unanimous agreement. Thus if one member government agrees with the Parliament, the law cannot be enacted. A case in point was the measure to restrict exhaust emissions from small cars. Not only the Parliament, but also the environmentally conscious Dutch government, wanted a stricter limit than the majority of the Council had accepted. The combination of Parliament and Dutch would have been enough to bring the measure down.

The Parliament in fact secured the enactment of a stricter limit, by using its rights of amendment under the co-operation procedure. If amendments proposed by the Parliament are not supported by the Commission, they pass only if unanimously approved by the Council, not at all likely when the Council has already approved the existing text. But if the Commission accepts the Parliament's amendments, the Council can then change the revised text only by unanimous agreement, which is not likely to be forthcoming if, as in the case of the small car exhausts, there is a government that strongly agrees with the Parliament. So in such cases, the Parliament is well placed to persuade the Commission to support its amendments, as the alternative to the Parliament successfully rejecting the measure as a whole. Thus the Commission did support the Parliament's amendments and the Council enacted the stricter limit for exhausts. With the Commission's general desire to avoid conflict with the Parliament, combined with the sanction of rejection in the background, the Parliament has been able to secure the passage of between a third and a half of its amendments into Community law.

In order to deal with these complexities of the Single European Act, the Parliament adopted new rules of procedure; and its performance rapidly won it new respect in Brussels, and a considerable impact on the vast programme of legislation required to complete the single market by the end of 1992.

The Parliament has, then, over the years acquired a significant role with respect to the budget, the legislative process, and influence over the Commission. It has also become quite effective as a forum, airing citizens' problems, articulating European concerns, and being addressed by such luminaries as Mr Reagan and Mr Mandela. Its role is further strengthened by the Maastricht Treaty. But it still lacks the powers that would make it an equal partner of the Council in a two-chamber legislature. It was this subordination of the people's representatives to those of the governments that was a major motive behind Altiero Spinelli's resolve to persuade the Parliament to design and approve its Draft Treaty for European Union, following the first direct elections in 1979.

Intergovernmental institutions or constitutional government

Spinelli set out his critique of the Community's institutions in his Jean Monnet Lecture in 1983.[12] This focused on the dominance of the intergovernmental Council, which he attacked as both inefficient and undemocratic. Wherever possible the Council ignored the European Parliament and resisted institutional reform. To this it may be added that the Council enacts Community laws behind closed doors; the representatives of member states who do this are often not ministers but their substitutes; and much of the legislation is passed on the nod, having been already agreed by the Permanent Representatives. Ministers could in theory be controlled by the member states' parliaments. But if such control were to be really effective, the *de facto* legislature would be twelve separate parliaments, and the legislative process would be impossibly cumbersome. As it was, Spinelli found the Council unacceptably inefficient. With the rotation of presidency every six months, the Council could not effect a continuous development of policy, nor could a given member government achieve enough during its half-year in office; and the Council compounded its own defects by subjecting the Commission to detailed control by Coreper's web of committees. Yet the Council, Spinelli complained, insisted on arrogating to itself a load of political and executive responsibility which it was unable to carry. Spinelli's solution was the Draft Treaty for European Union, approved by the Parliament in 1984 for submission to member states, with its proposal for federal reform of the Community's institutions.

Spinelli made his critique at a low point in the Community's fortunes. The performance of the Council improved, and the European Council made some important decisions, after the relaunching of the Community by the Single European Act— itself partly a result of the Parliament's European Union initiative. But the Parliament continued to regard much of Spinelli's critique as valid, and reiterated in 1990 the principles on which the Draft Treaty of 1984 was based.[13]

The Draft Treaty provided for a general system of co-decision between the Parliament and the Council voting by majority, with respect to legislation, the budget, and the appointment of the Commission. The Commission would have full executive competences, which together with its right of legislative initiative would enable it to fulfil the function of a government for the Community. The jurisdiction of the Court of Justice would be filled out in certain respects, including its role in the guarantee of fundamental rights and freedoms established in the Union's constitution. Thus the Community's present institutions would be brought into a federal relationship with each other, as is at present the case with respect to the non-compulsory expenditure.

The Draft Treaty proposed to give these institutions competence not only to perform the Community's existing functions, but also to establish an economic and monetary union and to have power over Community tax as well as expenditure. External policy and security were also to come within the scope of the Union, but were to be dealt with by the method of intergovernmental co-operation, until a further decision should be taken to integrate them under the responsibility of the Union institutions.

In order to prevent the creation of the Union from being blocked by one or two member states, the Draft Treaty provided that it would come into force when ratified by a majority of the member states containing two-thirds of the population of the Community.

The Draft Treaty can be seen as an attempt to replace the predominance of intergovernmental relations in the Community institutions by a system of constitutional government, with the rule of law and with representative government.[14] The rule of law is already well developed within the sphere of Community competence. Law, including regular legal restraints on government, predominates over arbitrary power; and there is equality before the law, with access to impartial justice, for both citizens and public authorities. The Parliament's criticism was, rather, that the sphere of competence was too narrow, with inadequate powers over currency and monetary policy, and that the Community did not apply the principles of representative government. These require legislative and political authority to be vested in an assembly of representatives chosen in regular free elections: laws have to be enacted by an elected parliament, and the executive must be accountable either to the parliament or, as in the US, directly to the electorate. The Community scores badly in both these respects. The Council predominates in legislation, with a minor role for the elected Parliament; and although the Parliament has influence over the Commission, the Council has used its legislative and political power to secure the main control over it, with the help of Coreper's network of committees. Spinelli argued at the same time that the Community could not be as effectively managed by an intergovernmental system as it would be if power rested squarely with a normal democratic structure of institutions.

The member governments did not accept the Draft Treaty, substituting for it the less ambitious Single European Act; and it is often argued, particularly in Britain, that governments will not agree to federal reform of the Community institutions. But governments have accepted quite significant steps in that direction: establishment of the primacy of Community law; direct elections, budgetary powers, and substantial legislative influence for the Parliament; and majority voting for a wide range of decisions in the Council. The Parliament adopted a 'dual strategy', working for further specific steps towards federal institutions as well as promoting its project for a federal European Union as a whole. It also proposed that the member states mandate it to design a European constitution, on the lines of the Draft Treaty, for ratification by the member states; and this proposal was massively endorsed by the Italian electorate in a referendum in 1989. The federal Union project has also had substantial parliamentary support in Belgium, Germany, and Spain, as well as Italy; and the Draft Treaty was widely endorsed by Christian Democrat, Liberal, and Socialist parties in the Community, as well as by interest groups and substantial sectors of public opinion.[15] It was at the same time opposed by the Conservative and Labour parties as well as the government in Britain; Danish policy was against it but became more favourable in 1990; and official support was partial or lukewarm in several other member states, although there was a widespread swing in favour of federal reform by the time that the Maastricht Treaty was negotiated. We will return in Chapter 10 to the balance of forces for and against the development of the Community institutions into a federal structure and, in the Postscript, to the reforms of the Maastricht Treaty.

3 From Six to Twelve

Britain, Denmark, and the Irish Republic joined the Community on 1 January 1973, fifteen years after the EEC was established and over two decades after the ECSC. Why the delay? Was it just that the British, whose lead the other two followed, needed time to adjust their relationship with the Continent after their very different wartime experience? Or had 'a thousand years of history', as the Labour Party's leader Hugh Gaitskell put it in 1962 when he came out in opposition to the Conservative government's first application to join, built differences into the British economy and polity that would make it hard for the British to co-operate with the Continentals in the Community institutions? The question is still relevant. Britain has often been seen as an obstructive partner in the Community; and many of those who want the Community to become a federal Union believe that a core group of member states may have to move ahead on their own, leaving the British to catch up later if they wish. What does the story of the Community's enlargement tell us that can help to explain the effect of Britain, and of the other late arrivals, on the working of its institutions and its prospects for development?

In June 1940, ten years before the Community was launched by the Schuman declaration, it was the British government that had offered union to France; and this was the crest of a wave of British public support for the federal idea that had swept the country in 1939 and the first half of 1940, to the extent that an Archbishop said it had made a 'staggeringly effective appeal to the British mind', and Churchill was amazed by the enthusiasm with which the Cabinet approved the offer.[1] Even if the circumstances were exceptional, the British did show that they were capable of embracing the idea of federation. Then the fall of France turned Britain towards America. The British became disillusioned about the Continent, reliant on the United States, and, after the war was won, confident in the capacity of the British nation-state to do what was necessary for the British people.

The 1950s: Britain exclusive

After the war Jean Monnet, who was head of the French planning commission, began to seek an opportunity to create new institutions for European co-operation. He looked first to Britain, exploring the scope for economic integration between the two countries. But the British were not receptive. So Monnet turned to the Germans, who were ready to accept the sort of integration that Monnet had in mind. Having experienced, as its Deputy Secretary-General, the weakness of the pre-war League of Nations, he was determined that post-war Europe should have institutions that would not be emasculated by subordination to the governments of the member states. When Schuman on 9 May 1950 announced the proposal for a High Authority to control coal and steel production, the participants were to be France, Germany, and such other European countries as were prepared to be bound by the High Authority's decisions. Italy and the Benelux countries accepted. Britain did not.

The post-war Labour government's reaction was uncompromisingly negative. The project was seen, not as an opportunity to plan the coal and steel industries in common, but as a threat to give foreigners the right to shut down British mines and steelworks. Britain was perceived as a world power, a cut above its Continental neighbours, regarded as unreliable countries with which one would not care to have a particularly close association. So there was no serious interest in exploring exactly what the project might involve. It was seen as a 'rather fancy arrangement that the European constitutional theorists were indulging in', or as a 'federal Europe' in which British participation was out of the question.[2]

In 1950 France and Germany were bold to act without British participation or even approval, so soon after the war which had left Britain as the strongest West European power. But the success of the Coal and Steel Community demonstrated that the Continentals could go ahead without the British. The next Community venture showed that this ability still had its limits. In France, opposition to the Treaty for a European Defence Community (EDC) extended beyond the Gaullists and Communists to many politicians of the centre parties who were reluctant to accept such complete integration with Germany in the absence of any form of British association. But although the Conservatives had criticized the Labour government for their negative reaction to Schuman's proposal, they maintained, once in office after the election of 1951, a similar aloofness towards the nascent Community. Not only did the Conservative government regard membership of the EDC as out of the question, but no association or support was offered, such as might have encouraged the French National Assembly to ratify the Treaty; and in August 1954 the Assembly voted to let it drop.

This encouraged the British government to relapse into the comfortable assumption that the Continentals could not accomplish an important project without British help. The negotiations to establish the EEC and Euratom were, therefore, almost complete before the British government realized that it should act to protect British interests in relation to this new and potentially powerful entity. Membership was still regarded as out of the question, with the Community institutions similar to those that had been too strong medicine for the British when the Coal and Steel Community was created; and some of the economic provisions of the new treaties were inconvenient. The government therefore devised an ingenious scheme, known as the Free Trade Area, which would give British industry free access to the Community market without submitting to the Community's institutions or to the awkward economic stipulations.

The Free Trade Area, to which almost all of Western Europe, including the Community, would have belonged, would have been an intergovernmental organization without the federal elements of the Community's institutions. It would also have excluded some of the Community's functions, in particular the common external tariff and agricultural policy, which would cut across British trade with the Commonwealth, and the provision for 'social harmonization', i.e. harmonization of some elements of labour legislation. Compared to the Community, the idea was minimalist: free trade in industrial goods, with no alteration to tariffs on imports from outside the area.

France's five partners were, for the most part, eager for British involvement. But the more federalist among the Community's protagonists feared that the Free Trade Area might dissolve the Community 'like a lump of sugar in a British cup of tea'. France, which by the time the Free Trade Area negotiations came to a head in 1958 was led by General de Gaulle, had more traditional motives for opposing an arrangement that might give the British a leading role in Western Europe at the expense of the French. The British were exposed because their proposal was widely seen as solipsistic: tailored to British interests without regard to those of others, and in particular of France. The negotiations dragged on until they were broken off by de Gaulle in November 1958.[3]

The 1960s: Britain excluded

After their original Free Trade Area proposal had failed, the British went on to initiate the setting up of the European Free Trade Association (Efta), which applied the same minimalist free trade principles to Denmark, Norway, Sweden, Austria, Switzerland, Portugal, and the United Kingdom. But at the same time the British were rethinking their relationship with the Community. Much had changed since the initial rejection of Schuman's proposal. The British economy was becoming weaker than those of the neighbours on the Continent. The British Commonwealth was in the process of transformation into a loose association that might give Britain influence, but not the sort of power that had set it apart from its neighbours in the past. The Continent, on the other hand, was no longer weak and unreliable, but had made impressive economic and political progress, and was evidently capable of realizing such an important project as the Community had become. British industry wanted full access to this rich market nearby; and people in government did not want to see Britain 'relegated', internationally, 'to the second division'.[4] Prime Minister Macmillan decided to turn British policy around and seek membership of the Community.

Negotiations began in 1961 between the Community and Britain, together with two other Efta members, Denmark and Norway, and the Irish Republic. This time Britain accepted the Community's institutions and negotiated only to change some of its economic arrangements. Agriculture and Commonwealth trade were, as in the design of the Free Trade Area proposal, two of the main concerns, to which was added Britain's obligations to the other Efta members, which would be met by free trade with the Community for them as well. Macmillan justified the change of front regarding the institutions by aligning himself with de Gaulle's 'confederal' concept against those who were working for a federal system. Macmillan avoided any clear definition of these concepts, however, and the Permanent Under-Secretary of the Treasury was at the same time indicating that the idea of moving towards 'some kind of a federation' was acceptable.[5]

Most of the leaders in British government, business, and media soon swung round to support the idea of Community membership. But the public remained divided, and Macmillan had difficulty with the farmers' and Commonwealth lobbies, both influential with Conservative Members of Parliament. This made the British negotiators in Brussels cautious, looking over their shoulders towards London: from the point of view of the chief British official there, 'a sort of Whitehall exercise'.[6] The negotiations dragged; and, with Labour Party supporters increasingly doubtful, Gaitskell led Labour into opposing membership in October 1962. This did not pass unnoticed by de Gaulle, who could argue that the Party which was likely before long to form the next British government was against British accession. His relationship with Adenauer and his political position in France were at the same time strengthened, so that he was well placed to veto the continuation of the negotiations in January 1963.

Britain had moved far from its earlier post-war stance of aloofness from Europe; and the government had accepted the

Community institutions, even if with the proviso that de Gaulle was a guarantee against their becoming more federal, at least for some years ahead. But there was still much opposition, both to the European entanglement and to the federal elements in the Community. It appeared, for a time, that the rebuff of de Gaulle's veto might turn the British away from Europe again. But the Labour government, which had replaced the Conservatives in 1964, again applied for membership in 1967, only to encounter another veto from de Gaulle. The Labour government held to its new policy, however, and began to prepare a new application when de Gaulle resigned in 1969.

Georges Pompidou, who succeeded de Gaulle as President of France, did not share his rooted objection to British membership. German Ostpolitik was, moreover, raising French fears of a more independent and powerful Germany, to which Britain within the Community could act as a counterweight. At the same time the French saw the potential for getting the other Community member governments, which had been keen supporters of British entry, to accept conditions that were of interest to France. Above all, this meant agreement on securing the Community's 'own resources', i.e. its own tax revenue, with which to finance the common agricultural policy that France saw as a principal French interest in the Community. This was elegantly called 'completion', since it would complete outstanding Community business. At the same time, it was agreed that British entry would be accompanied by 'deepening' of the Community through the extension of its competences in monetary integration. Willy Brandt, by then Chancellor of the German Federal Republic, was a keen promoter of the project of monetary union; and European monetary integration to countervail the dollar and underpin the agricultural policy had for some time been a French concern. The French now had another motive. They had, from the beginning, feared that British participation would make the Community a looser and weaker organization. So the idea of deepening the Community at the same time as widening it seemed a suitable antidote— which would moreover lock Germany more securely into it. But the French government could not, so soon after de Gaulle, accept stronger Community institutions: functional integration, in the monetary field, appeared to be the perfect answer. The story of the ensuing attempt at monetary union is told in Chapter 7. Ironically, it failed in large part because France was not then ready to accept that monetary integration should have institutional consequences, on which Germany insisted. Equally ironically, the condition of 'completion', which was seen as a French interest in a more traditional sense, did lead to a strengthening of the Community institutions, because the payment of tax revenue direct to the Community, escaping the control of member states' parliaments, was accompanied by significant new budgetary powers for the European Parliament. Here, however, we need only note that enlargement of the Community does not have to result in its dilution through the greater diversity among the member states: it can be accompanied by the strengthening of the policies, powers, or institutions.

First enlargement: Britain, Denmark, Ireland

Although the Labour government had prepared Britain's ultimate, and successful, application to join, it was Edward Heath who carried it through after he became Prime Minister with the Conservative election victory in June 1970. He had long been convinced of the case for membership on both political and economic grounds. Politically, it was not just a matter of avoiding 'relegation to the second division', but of the positive merits that he saw in European unity. Economically, the argument was difficult. Since the common agricultural policy had been designed for the six founding members, it was ill adapted to the needs of Britain, with its particularly small agricultural sector and large imports of foodstuffs. It would impose high prices on the British consumer and, with the financial regulation that France was so eager to see completed, a heavy burden for the British taxpayer. A number of economic studies foresaw a direct, 'static' loss to Britain of ¾–2 per cent of gross domestic product, with a central estimate of 1¼ per cent.[7] There were some predictions of much heavier cost, in the belief that deflation would be required to stem losses to the balance of payments. But other studies suggested that the 'dynamic' effects of competition, innovation, and investment would, over the medium term, outweigh the static loss—which should build up gradually over a transitional period. Industrial leaders held fast to this view and continued to support entry. The White Paper with which Heath presented the case for membership to Parliament after the substance of the negotiations had been completed in July 1971 likewise emphasized 'improvements in efficiency and competitive power'.[8]

Heath had no doubts about the case and drove the negotiations forward as fast as possible. Solutions to many of the difficult problems relating to agriculture, the Commonwealth, and Efta had already been found during the first negotiations in 1961–3. Heath took care to establish a good relationship with Pompidou, insuring against a repetition of the veto of 1963. The European Movement ran a massive campaign to turn the public round from its initially hostile stance. Yet the negotiation was by no means all plain sailing.

The main issue for the British economy was the cost of the agricultural policy. A transition period of seven years was agreed, during which Britain would be eased incrementally into full participation in the Community budget. By then, it was argued from the Community's side, there would be new policies that would benefit Britain, offsetting the British loss on the hitherto predominant agricultural expenditure. But what if the burden on the British should still be excessive? Britain's negotiators did not succeed in getting any commitment to remedial action written into the Treaty of Accession. But the Community side assured the British, in the course of the negotiations, that if 'unacceptable' situations should arise 'the very survival of the Community would demand that the institutions find equitable solutions'; and this assurance was duly recorded in the White Paper.[9] The 'British budget question', though thus circumvented in the negotiations, was to remain an incubus for the Community until the mid-1980s.

The House of Commons remained sensitive about sovereignty, and the White Paper asserted that there was 'no question of any erosion of essential national sovereignty', adding that there was to be 'a sharing and an enlargement of individual national sovereignties in the general interest'.[10] This, like so many of the formulations about sovereignty, glossed over the hard questions. What national sovereignty was regarded as 'essential'? How much sovereignty was to be 'shared and enlarged' and how? The answers would depend on the future development of the Community and behaviour of the member states; and this would depend on the attitudes of their governments. Heath's attitude was favourable to integration; that of the British governments which succeeded his from 1974 onwards, less so.

The decade that followed the first enlargement lent support to those who had predicted that widening would be the enemy of deepening. Some significant steps were taken, such as the first direct elections to the European Parliament and the creation of the European Monetary System (EMS). But such steps were relatively few. The Community experienced a period of stagnation rather than development; and some aspects of the behaviour of new members were blamed for this.

Britain and Denmark, together, after 1981, with Greece, resisted proposals that they felt would erode national sovereignty; and the attitude of the British Labour government which replaced Heath's administration in 1974 was soured by the growing opposition in the Labour Party to the principle of membership itself. The government first tried to renegotiate the terms of membership, obtaining however only cosmetic adjustments. Then British membership of the Community was placed in question by a referendum on the issue in 1975. The electorate voted two-to-one for staying in. But ministers who had campaigned against remained in the government, continuing to represent Britain in the Community's Council. It is not surprising that they were often seen as obstructive, nor that Britain chose, when the EMS was created in 1979, to stay out of its central element, the Exchange Rate Mechanism. In 1980, the year after the Conservatives replaced Labour in government, the Labour Party Conference voted for unconditional withdrawal; and the Party campaigned for it in the 1983 election, which was, however, again won by the Conservatives. It was not until towards the end of the decade that Labour returned to a more positive policy.

Although Britain, as a new member, did little to help cure the

Community of its malaise in the 1970s, it was by no means the sole cause of the stagnation. French governments during that period were still in a post-Gaullist phase of vigilance against any federalist encroachment by Community institutions. Underlying many of the Community's difficulties, moreover, was the stagflation that pervaded the world economy, which had been initiated by the quadrupling of oil prices at the end of the year of the first enlargement. With rapidly rising inflation and unemployment, the mood of member states was protectionist rather than integrationist. Hopes of monetary integration were also set back by the divergence of economic performance among the member states. Britain and Italy, in particular, proved much more prone to inflation following the oil shock than most of the other members, while Germany became the model of stability. The idea of closer integration threatened inflation for the Germans, deflation and more unemployment for the Italians and the British. Divergence among the member states' economies became a key concept in the 1970s, causing concern about the future of the Community.[11]

When Mrs Thatcher won the 1979 election for the Conservatives, who had claimed to be 'the party of Europe', a more positive British attitude to the development of the Community was widely expected. After a further lapse of five years, this proved justified in one important respect: British support for the single market programme. But negotiation of the Single European Act in 1985 was hampered in many ways by British reluctance, as was again to be the case with the Maastricht Treaty in 1991; and the Community's development had, for five years, been blocked by the conflict over Britain's net contribution to the budget. There were good grounds to argue that, since new policies had not gone far to rectify the imbalance, the agricultural budget was causing an 'unacceptable situation' such as had been discussed during the entry negotiations; and Britain's partners were not quick to agree to a reduction in the net contribution that a British government could accept. But however the blame may be apportioned, the widening of the Community had hampered its deepening for a further five years. Apart from the commitment to the freeing of trade through the single market programme, moreover, Mrs

Thatcher's pronouncements as well as some of her actions in the later 1980s confirmed, for many among Britain's partner countries, the impression they had gained during the budget negotiations, that her view of the Community was reductionist, confined mainly to deregulation and freer trade.

It was President Mitterrand who, at the meeting of the European Council at Fontainebleau in June 1984, presided over the taking of decisions that led to the resolution of the British budget problem. At the same meeting he secured the breakthrough that brought Portugal and Spain into membership in 1986. This time, it was to be shown that enlargement need not impede the Community's development.

Southern enlargement: Greece, Portugal, Spain

Whereas the British had, initially, doubted the political stability of the Community countries, the southern members which brought its number from nine to twelve in the 1980s started from a diametrically opposite perspective. Greece, Portugal, and Spain had all become free of dictators in the 1970s. To them, the Community was a stronghold of democracy which could help to consolidate their own recently established democratic systems. Whereas Britain had, moreover, been richer than the member states when the Community was founded, for the new southern members it represented the prosperous, modern economy to which they aspired. Their perception of the Community was generally more favourable than that of the British had been.

There were problems, of course. The southern enlargement brought with it a new kind of economic divergence, after the economies of the existing member states, recovering from the shocks of the 1970s, had themselves begun to converge. The Greek, Portuguese, and Spanish economies were at a lower stage of development than that of the Community's mainstream. Among the existing members, only that of the Irish Republic was comparable. Average incomes were lower; a higher proportion of people worked in agriculture; industry was technologically less advanced. The integration of such economies with those of the existing members raised fears on both sides. The higher-paid existing members feared competition based on cheap labour—not only in manufacturing but also, for France and Italy, in Mediterranean agricultural products. The new member countries feared they would be unable to compete with the stronger industries of the North. Greece and Portugal had, admittedly, already been open to the competition of Community industries, in the Greek case under an association agreement and, for Portugal, through the free trading relationship that the Community had negotiated with each member of Efta. But membership of the Community would make this free trade more complete and rigorous, and less reversible. For Spain, which, because of the Community's objection to the Franco regime, had not qualified for a free trade arrangement, a wide range of industries which had been developing fast would have to face a new, chill north wind of competition.

For the existing members the southern enlargement presented no profound economic challenge. The acute fears were confined to a limited sector of agriculture in France and Italy. The worry was, rather, political. Would the Community, with this new diversity of interests and divergence of economic performance, be able to take the decisions necessary for the future? Or would its institutional machinery, at least partly unblocked by the resolution of the British budget problem, again become too difficult to operate? Solutions were sought in two directions. Federalists called for the institutions to be strengthened, so that there would be less chance for a small minority of governments to block decisions in the Council. Pragmatists considered various techniques, under names such as two speeds, two tiers, variable geometry, and Europe à la carte, to enable some member states to act while others opted out.[12] The new members from the South, with their weaker economies, were faced with more formidable economic problems, to which they reacted in different ways.

The Greek reaction was coloured by a political event, similar to that which the British had experienced after their accession. Entry had been negotiated by a Conservative government, which was soon after replaced by the Socialist opposition. As in

Britain, the new Greek government was not enthusiastic about the Community. It gained the reputation of tending to obstruct Community business whenever a problem arose for it. It made the negotiations for the accession of Portugal and Spain more difficult—and more difficult, it was contended, than the real problems of Iberian competition with Greece could justify. Greek demands did have a concrete result for the development of the Community, however. Its policy for the promotion of economic growth in the weaker regions was strengthened through what were called Integrated Mediterranean Programmes because they provided funds for regional development in a more co-ordinated way. With this and other experiences of working in the Community, the Greek government's attitude towards it evolved; and the Conservative government which gained power after the election in 1989 was yet more favourable.

Neither Spain nor Portugal suffered any such political inhibition after their accession in 1986. Their entry coincided with the regeneration of the Community following the solving of the British budget problem and the launching of the single market programme; and they provoked no accusations that they were obstructing the Community's development. The solution that they secured for their problem of divergence was similar in principle to the Integrated Mediterranean Programmes that had been devised for the Greeks, but on a grander scale. The first step was taken before they had actually joined. The juridical basis for the single market programme was formulated in the negotiations for the Single European Act (SEA), in the last few months of 1985. But working closely with the Commission, they managed to secure provision in the Act for a policy of 'cohesion', that is for 'reducing disparities between the various regions and the backwardness of the least-favoured regions' (article 23 SEA). Their argument was that, since the single market would expose them to more rigorous competition from stronger economies, they should be compensated with measures that would assist their economic development. The argument was accepted in principle by most member governments; and it was recognized that discontented members could make it hard to enact the complex legislation that the single market programme required. But it is one thing to secure agreement on a principle, quite another to ensure that the Community applies it adequately in practice. In this, too, the southern members and the Irish, who have a similar interest, succeeded, again with the Commission playing an essential part. By the first half of 1988, the Community could no longer delay a general reform of its budget. The chronic deficit caused by its agricultural spending had to be tackled and the arrangement to compensate Britain for its excessive contribution had to be renewed. The opportunity was seized to turn the principle of cohesion into a major financial commitment, with the doubling of the Community's 'structural funds' (regional development fund, social fund, and fund for 'agricultural guidance'), which it was agreed in 1989 should grow to a total of some ecu 15 billion by 1993.

Thus the southern enlargement has been accompanied by a significant enhancement of the Community's policy instruments and may well continue to be favourable to the Community's further development. But questions have been raised about the potential impact of other countries from which the Community has been attracting applications for membership.

And others?

Turkey lodged its application in 1987. Part of Turkey is geographically in Europe and the country is a member of the Council of Europe, although its membership has been troubled by failures to maintain the standards of fundamental rights, rule of law, and representative government to which its political élites generally aspire. Such principles of constitutional government are an essential condition for membership of the Community, in which the rule of law has to apply evenly throughout, elections to the European Parliament have to be freely and democratically conducted, and the ministers who enact laws and take other decisions in the Council must all come from properly representative governments. Doubts whether these principles are solidly based in the Turkish political system have clouded reactions to Turkey's application, and compounded worries about the Turkish economy which, though growing fast, is still at a lower level of development than that in the Community and prone to growing pains such as treble-digit inflation. While the Portuguese, Greek, and Irish economies are also much less developed than that of the Community in general, these are smaller countries; Turkey's population is as big as those of the Community's larger members and still expanding rapidly. The strain caused by economic divergence would be correspondingly greater.

Against doubts such as these, there are strong strategic arguments for consolidating Turkey's relationship with Western Europe, which, even if the end of the Cold War may have weakened them, can be reinforced by instability in the Middle East or Central Asia; and there are political grounds for giving what encouragement outsiders can to Turkey's still fragile democracy. These will certainly weigh with the existing member governments; and some will not object if further enlargement should place new obstacles in the path that would lead to a federal Europe. Other governments and parliaments would, on the contrary, object to this; and since treaties of accession must be ratified by all member states, their objections could prove decisive. Since the adoption of the Single European Act, moreover, applications to accede must also be approved by the European Parliament, which can be expected to be punctilious about the principles of fundamental rights, rule of law, and representative government. The Parliament's approval would almost certainly be withheld from any application which gave rise to doubts that these principles would be applied throughout the Community—or, to put it more positively, the Parliament would be likely to insist, before approving, that the requirement that all member states apply these principles be entrenched in Community law, with provision for the suspension of any state that should fall short of them.

The first step in the Community's procedure after receiving an application is for the Council to request an Opinion from the Commission. In 1990, three years after Turkey applied, the Commission produced its Opinion to the effect that no applications could be considered until after 1992 and that, despite significant progress, Turkey's economy and polity had some way to go before the Turks could meet the conditions for membership. The Council had no difficulty in accepting the Commission's view.

Austria's application for membership, presented in 1989, raises a quite different issue. There were no doubts about the compatibility of Austria's political system or of its economy with those of the Community. The problem has been Austria's neutral status resulting from the post-war settlement that ended the Allied occupation of the country. Sweden's application, which followed in 1991, came from another country with a compatible economy and polity and a policy of neutrality. But the Single European Act already provided for co-ordination among the member states with respect to 'the political and economic aspects of security'; and the Maastricht Treaty establishes a framework intended to produce a common foreign and security policy, including 'the eventual framing of a common defence policy, which might in time lead to a common defence'. Both the European Parliament and some member states will wish to ensure that enlargement will not impede these aims. The Maastricht Treaty allows for Irish neutrality with its provision that 'the specific character of the security and defence policy of certain member states' is not to be prejudiced; and applicants such as Austria and Sweden may hope that this would enable them to opt out of a common defence policy. But, while allowances may have to be made for existing member states, there will be fears that further exceptions would dilute the Community's political cohesion; and the European Parliament in particular may use its power in relation to the approval of new accessions as a means of requiring full commitment in all respects, including an eventual defence policy. Applicants such as Austria and Sweden may be able to accept such a requirement, particularly as Europe's new security constellation, following the changes in Eastern Europe, may be rendering the problem of their neutrality obsolete.

Austria and Sweden are not likely to be the last of the Efta countries to apply. Of those that may follow, Norway raises no problems relating to security. Norway was, indeed, one of the applicants at the time of the first enlargement, and failed to join only because the electorate voted by a narrow majority against when the issue of ratification was posed in a referendum. The

Norwegians are, perhaps more than the British and the Danes, sensitive about the idea of sharing sovereignty in the Community. If they overcome this reservation, there can hardly be an objection of principle to their membership—although the European Parliament could again seek to ensure that wider does not mean shallower, for example by using the occasion to secure some strengthening of its position in relation to the Council. Among other Efta members, security or neutrality has been an issue for Finland and Switzerland, as also for two other Community associates, Cyprus and Malta, which lodged their applications for membership in 1990. Since their reforms of 1989–90, Central European countries are also potential members. East Germany chose a fast track into the Community by uniting with the Federal Republic. The other Central Europeans will have to achieve stable pluralist democracies and competitive market economies before they can qualify for membership, and to ensure that their security policies do not create a problem for the Community. Other East European states have declared their interest in membership, although they have in general a longer way to go before they can satisfy the economic and political conditions.

Enlargement may, then, carry membership beyond twenty states, and eventually even to thirty or more. The implications of this prospect for Community institutions are profound. How could unanimous agreement on difficult questions be reached among so many and such diverse governments? How, indeed, could a basically intergovernmental system function effectively or democratically among them? In any or all of the cases of possible future enlargement, the European Parliament's right to refuse accession is likely to be used to secure that widening is accompanied by deepening, in the form of strengthening and democratizing the Community's institutions; and it will have some support from member states. By the time that the accession of new applicants would bring the number of members up to twenty or so, the Parliament and at least some member states are likely to withhold their consent unless the institutions are given a federal form.

4 From Customs Union to Single Market

Free trade versus protection is the classic issue of international economic policy. Britain's industrial supremacy in the nineteenth century was based on free trade. Germany and the United States sought to promote their industries by protecting them against British industrial power. Until the 1930s, both policies could show evidence of success. But in the 1930s, the rise of protectionism and autarky was associated with the world economic depression and the approach of war. When the war was over, there was a widespread determination not to let such things happen again.

The Americans led in establishing the liberal international economic order, in which the General Agreement on Tariffs and Trade (Gatt) was to ensure non-discriminatory tariffs and freer trade. But the founder members of the European Community wanted to go farther. Having suffered grievously during the war, they were ready to go to greater lengths to ensure that protectionism did not become a cause of future conflicts among them. Looking across the Atlantic at the wealth and power of the United States, they reasoned that Europe's divisions were a cause of their relative backwardness. In order to produce cars or planes as efficiently as the Americans, they wanted to have a unified continental market too.

The success of the customs union

Such were the motives that underlay the support for the idea of the customs union, which was the central economic feature of the EEC Treaty. The economic arguments went beyond the classical free trade case for cutting out production that was high-cost and concentrating it where there was a comparative advantage. Attention was drawn to the dynamic effects: the scope in the larger market for scale, specialization, and stronger competition; and the consequent opportunities for higher investment, more innovation, and faster economic growth.[1] The political arguments went beyond the reduction of friction between states. Merit was seen in a new relationship between the citizens of the states, in which for certain purposes they would all be equal before the law, without discrimination on grounds of nationality, thus planting deeper roots for the growth of peaceful relations among them. So the project itself went beyond a bare customs union, with tariff-free trade inside the union and a common tariff on imports from outside, to an area in which the 'four freedoms' prevail, that is free movement not only for goods but also for services, capital, and people going about their business; and the whole was to be the responsibility of institutions that could ensure the enactment of laws required for these purposes, the rule of law through the Community's juridical system, and any necessary executive action.

Despite the reaction against the autarky of the 1930s, there were still fears about the impact of free trade. The Germans and the Dutch were the most liberal among the six founders, the French and the Italians the most protectionist. When the common market project was first mooted, it seemed far from certain that the French would be ready to accept the removal of protection for their industry against German competition. So the designers of the EEC Treaty devised an ingenious method of allaying such fears while at the same time ensuring that the customs union would at the end of the day be completed. The removal of tariffs and quotas, or quantitative restrictions, from trade among member states would not be imposed at one swoop, but would be phased in incrementally over a transitional period of 12–15 years. Each member state would be able to adjust the rate of tariff reduction on individual products, freeing the imports of sensitive sectors more slowly, provided that the state's tariffs as a whole were reduced on average at the agreed rate. Similarly member states were to align on to the common external tariff by a series of three steps during the transitional period. In these ways protectionist pressures that could have impeded acceptance of the EEC Treaty were deflected; and France like the other five members entered a new phase in the development of a more open economy, with the first tariff cuts of 10 per cent at the end of 1958.

Had the expected economic gains not materialized, Monnet's idea of uniting Europe step by step might have progressed no farther. But evidence of economic success came surprisingly quickly. In the first couple of years after the EEC was established, the Patronat, which represented French industry, swung round from its earlier suspicion of the idea of opening the French market to support for accelerating the timetable of liberalization. The proposal for acceleration had political motives. The Commission wanted to maintain the momentum generated by its early success in sorting out the initial problems of launching the customs union. The Germans and the Dutch, together with the Commission, wanted the Community to start playing its part in a wider process of international liberalization; and they also wanted to make concessions to ease the impact on the British and other Efta countries of the Community's moves towards its common external tariff, which required them to raise their own relatively low tariffs on imports from those countries. The French, on the contrary, wished to ensure that the common external tariff remained intact, and to remove from the Dutch and the Germans any temptation to avoid imposing it on the trade partners in Efta. The resolution of this conflict of interests lay in acceleration of both the Community's internal tariff reductions and the first move towards the common external tariff, whose level was at the same time cut provisionally by one-fifth. This gave the Dutch and Germans faster progress towards internal free trade and towards international negotiations with a liberal orientation, while the French had secured the commitment they sought to the external tariff's implementation. The acceleration was strongly promoted by the Commission and the federalists. But the support of industry, including French industry, was also decisive.

Once they had been convinced that the customs union was going to be established, industrialists had begun to make their plans for doing business in the larger market. Having started to invest to produce for it, the delay that had been designed to meet protectionist fears became an irritant, standing in the way of early success for the new investments. Their support for acceleration indicated that the dynamic effects were materializing, and helped to give the customs union a clear run in the 1960s. Instead of a reduction of 30 per cent of the internal tariffs by 1962 or one of the two following years, as provided in the Treaty, the tariffs were in fact cut by half by the middle of 1962.[2]

The customs union continued to fulfil high expectations through the 1960s. Trade among the Community's member states grew twice as fast as trade in the wider international economy, quadrupling in the first decade after the Community was established in 1958. Gross domestic product expanded in the Community at 5 per cent a year, twice as fast as in Britain or the United States. There was no way of knowing how much of this growth had been due to the creation of the customs union, which was completed well ahead of time in mid-1968. But the Community had evidently provided a framework in which it had been possible. Although economists were unable to estimate dynamic effects, industrialists had been acting on the assumption that they existed. Their support for acceleration had soon been followed by the backing of British industry for the attempt to join the Community in 1961–3. The nature of the growth of trade within the Community in the 1960s consolidated industrial support. Protectionists had feared that whole sectors of industry would be competed out of existence in their own country. But trade in fact expanded on different lines. It was predominantly intra-sectoral trade, with each member state's exports and imports both growing in each sector. This was the consequence of the dynamic effect of greater specialization within each sector, and of larger scale in the production of these specialized products than would have been possible in the protected national markets. It was easier to adjust to this kind of change, because most people could continue to work in the same sector and place as before.

Politically, the Community suffered in the 1960s from de Gaulle's attack on its institutions. Expectations of steady progress towards political union on federal lines were dissipated. But the success of the customs union ensured that the Community would be valued for its existing achievements, not only for its potential as a step towards federal Union. This enabled the Community to weather the difficult period of stagnation in the 1970s and early 1980s, to expand from six to twelve, and to be ready to react to the problems of the 1980s with a further stage in the creation of a single market; and this in turn made further big strides towards Union appear politically feasible.

The need to complete the internal market

The dynamic phase of the late 1980s, with the single market programme as its focus, was the Community's response to the difficulties that had arisen in the 1970s. At the beginning of that decade, the hopes of Community development in the post-de Gaulle period had been placed on the combination of the first enlargement and the project of monetary union. But while the enlargement succeeded, the attempts to promote monetary integration, already weakened by disagreement between French and Germans over the relationship between monetary union and other elements of political and economic union, were blown off course by instability in the currency markets, which was an early warning of rough seas ahead.

After the exceptionally long boom of the 1950s and 1960s, inflation was starting to take hold of the international economy; and it hit very hard at the end of 1973, with the quadrupling of the price of oil. This injected a strong inflationary impulse into the European economies, and imposed heavy deficits in their external balances as they paid the new prices for their imported oil. Their main weapon to stem the inflation and correct the deficits was deflation, causing large-scale unemployment. For some time they suffered both inflation and unemployment; and, by the time inflation was generally under control, there was a second oil shock, when prices were doubled in 1979.

Quite apart from the political problems of accommodating the new entrants, and in particular the British, the Community was not well placed to promote further integration while its members were struggling against inflation and unemployment. On the contrary, they were tempted to lapse into measures of disintegration, as member governments sought to protect their hard-pressed industrial sectors: not with tariffs or quotas, to be sure, as these were not allowed by Community law which the member states did not wish to defy, but by subsidies to firms in trouble and, sometimes, by regulations which were overtly for purposes such as safety or consumer protection but which were in fact protectionist devices. Thus the fragmentation of the Community's tariff-free internal market by non-tariff barriers was intensified. Wherever they stood in the way, whether in the form of subsidies maintaining high-cost production or other government interventions, the more efficient firms were inhibited from producing for the wide Community market.

The pressure of unemployment which pushed the Community into this new and dangerous phase was intensified by new competitors from outside Europe. Japan, during the 1960s, had been establishing itself as an exporter far beyond its earlier image as a producer of cheap textiles with cheap labour. The Japanese had mastered the techniques required for the second industrial revolution, which had been pioneered by the Americans and applied in particular to the production of cars, consumer durables, and standard machinery. Their exports of such products began to make inroads into the European market. Hard on their heels came other, newly industrializing countries such as South Korea, Taiwan, Hong Kong, Singapore, Brazil, and India. While these still had cheap labour, they were climbing behind Japan up the ladder of technology, moving from textiles and shoes through consumer electronics to steel, shipbuilding, cars, and a range of capital goods. Protectionist pressures in Europe grew as Europeans began to doubt their ability to compete with these 'new Japans' in the products of the second industrial revolution.

Europeans sought a way out through more advanced technological development. But here they came up against the superiority of the Americans and Japanese in the new technologies, based on microelectronics and with information technology at the epicentre. By the early 1980s fears were widespread that Europe might become an industrial museum, the term Eurosclerosis was current coinage, and Europe's ability to compete in the world economy replaced unemployment as the focus of economic concern in the Community.

Various reports were produced on the declining competitiveness of the European economy.[3] They demonstrated how Europeans were losing ground to Americans and Japanese, both in the Community market and outside it, in many sectors where the newer or higher technologies were the key to success. They also drew attention to the fragmentation of the Community market caused by the non-tariff barriers and suggested that the Europeans, if they were to compete with the Americans and Japanese in the industries of the future, would have to follow the example of these most formidable competitors in establishing a single, barrier-free internal market.

This diagnosis and prescription were not just the brainchild of economists and officials. They were shared by leading industrialists in the most relevant sectors. Wisse Dekker, the head of Philips, one of Europe's foremost electronics manufacturers, went so far as to publish a report that recommended a programme for the Community to sweep away the non-tariff barriers by 1990. Not long after, in June 1985, the Commission published its White Paper, *Completing the Internal Market*, which set out a detailed timetable for enacting nearly three hundred measures to remove the barriers by the end of 1992.[4]

Like the idea of the customs union that was embodied in the EEC Treaty, the 1992 programme to complete the single market was supported by both economic liberals and federalists. But whereas in the 1950s the liberals had been concentrated mainly among the Germans and the Dutch, with French industry and government on the protectionist side, by the 1980s a liberal attitude towards trade, at least within Europe, was widespread throughout the Community. The leading industrialists, in France as elsewhere, strongly supported the 1992 programme; and a liberal view of economic policy was spreading among the member governments. Nowhere had it taken a stronger hold than in Britain, where Mrs Thatcher's government was distinctly unenthusiastic about most proposals for further development of the Community. However, she came to see the 1992 programme as a vast exercise in deregulation, led in the Commission by a former member of her government, Lord Cockfield, so she too championed the project. Thus it was supported by most member governments as well as by Europe's leading industrialists.

Federalists in the European Parliament had meanwhile taken an initiative that was to result in the Single European Act, which gave the 1992 programme its juridical form. This was the European Union Draft Treaty, which was the product of Spinelli's more general analysis of the Community's malaise, attributing it to the intergovernmental dominance in the institutions. The Draft Treaty proposed a thoroughgoing reform of the institutions to make them efficient and democratic, and thus capable of launching new projects such as monetary union as well as completing unfinished Community business, such as the removal of the non-tariff barriers within the internal market. The European Parliament approved the Draft Treaty in the first half of 1984, when France held the presidency. President Mitterrand went out of his way to emphasize his sympathy with the Parliament's aims; and he persuaded the European Council to set up an *ad hoc* committee to recommend what should be done about it. The committee's report commended many of the elements in the Draft Treaty, though with key reservations from the representatives of Britain, Denmark, and Greece in particular. But by the time the report came to be considered by the European Council, under Italian presidency in June 1985, Mitterrand was preoccupied by the political situation in France among other things, and failed to maintain his earlier support for the Parliament's project. The political momentum was however sufficient for the Italian presidency, itself the Parliament's strongest advocate among the member governments, to push through the decision to hold an Intergovernmental Conference to consider amendments to the Community treaties. At the same meeting the European Council approved the Commission's White Paper on the completion of the internal market. Since this was agreed by all the member governments, whereas other aspects of the Parliament's Draft

Treaty were not, the 1992 programme became the central element in the Single European Act that emerged from the Intergovernmental Conference. Spinelli and many other federalists felt this to be a grossly inadequate outcome, or even an undesirable distraction from the main task of creating the European Union. Yet it was the Act and the programme that lifted the Community from its stagnant to its dynamic phase in the late 1980s, opening out new opportunities for the proponents of Union; and it was the confluence of the political momentum generated by the Draft Treaty and the economic pressures for the 1992 programme that brought the Community to the point where the necessary decisions were taken.

The single market programme

The Commission's White Paper, with its nearly three hundred measures for completing the single market, proposed a vast programme of Community legislation. The Commission divided the barriers into three categories: physical, fiscal, and technical.[5]

The physical barriers were those that confronted people or goods as they cross the frontiers, that is, customs and immigration controls. The Commission argued that these barriers were, for the citizen, a manifestation of division within the Community, and that they imposed heavy costs on business. One of these costs was the time that lorries had to await clearance at the Community's internal frontiers, often for hours and sometimes for days. The lorry drivers were aggravated to the point of bringing such trade to a halt by a strike in the winter of 1983–4. The clerical work on providing documents for customs might be less uncomfortable, but was likewise costly. A study for the Commission on the costs of fragmentation of the market calculated that the cost of frontier checks on a consignment exported from Britain to France was ecu 131, while on one imported into Britain from Italy it was as much as ecu 280; and the total cost to the economy, including the public cost of the frontier controls, was estimated at ecu 8–9 billion.[6] The Commission proposed that these controls be removed altogether from within the Community.

The fiscal barriers that the Commission proposed to tackle were the indirect taxes: value-added tax, levied on most sales of goods and services; and excise duties, on alcoholic drinks, tobacco, and petrol. The Commission argued that wide differences in these taxes from one member state to another were a cause of frontier controls to prevent tax evasion through importing goods from a state with a lower tax rate to a state with a higher one, and that they also distorted trade in other ways. The Commission was to propose that member states harmonize their rates of value-added tax within two bands, one of 14–20 per cent for the normal rate and one of 4–9 per cent for lower-taxed goods such as food, while excise duties would be aligned on the average of the member states' existing rates. These proposals were controversial. It was argued that indirect taxes have both revenue-raising and social functions that are better left to the member states and that the problem of tax evasion can be approached in other ways, while the British government insisted on fiscal sovereignty. The Commission subsequently accepted many of the criticisms; and the Council agreed in June 1991 on a minimum general VAT rate of 15 per cent, with lower rates for some special items.

The third category, which the Commission called technical, is wide-ranging and by far the most important. The barriers that can more correctly be so called are the technical regulations and standards: these regulations (not to be confused with the term Regulation used for a general form of EC legislation) are statutory instruments which define the specifications of a product to assure the consumer of its quality and safety, while standards are defined by private standards institutes to similar ends. Where products have to fit each other in order to be usable, as a plug has to fit its socket, the specifications may also ensure what is called 'plug compatibility', which is also most important in the field of information technology. Guarantees of safety are wanted not only for products such as toys, electrical appliances, cars, and many articles of capital equipment, but also for services such as banking or life insurance, where the customer may be unable to judge whether savings or premiums are at risk because the financial institution is not maintaining proper standards of honesty or prudence.

Member states have developed their own standards and regulations for a vast range of goods and services. As these differ from country to country, and it is often not possible for a product that meets the specifications of one country to meet those of another without substantial adaptation, they constitute barriers that can be more costly than a tariff to overcome. Products can be adapted to meet the other country's specification, but that costs money and loses time while the product is tested and certified in the other country; and the need to spend this money and time makes the producer less competitive than an American or a Japanese firm that can establish its product rapidly and economically in a less fragmented home market. An estimate for the Commission put the cost of adapting a volume car to all the EC markets at ecu 286 million on top of the cost of development for a single market.[7] Such a sum takes more than the edge off a European manufacturer's competitiveness. The time and cost required to meet differing specifications bears most heavily on new technologies, where the development of new products can rapidly make the existing ones obsolescent. Getting such products on to the markets without delay and selling enough to pay for the costs of development before the next generation of products renders them unsaleable is a condition of survival.

New technologies are also hard hit in Europe by the other types of barrier that the Commission called technical, but which could more appropriately be called political. These result from the nationalistic bias imparted by public purchasing, state enterprises, and government subsidies to industry. It was estimated for the Commission that public purchases from other member countries were less than 2 per cent of the size of the market that should be open to them if there were no discrimination; and 'state aids' (or subsidies and other government assistance having equivalent effect) to industry amounted to between 5 per cent and 10 per cent of total industrial costs in France, Italy, and Britain, with 2–5 per cent in Germany and over 15 per cent in Belgium.[8] The problem was not just a deficiency in Community legislation, although laws to open up public procurement in energy, transport, water, and telecommunications remained to be enacted in the course of the 1992 programme. The difficulty is to ensure that the laws are enforced. Discrimination in public purchasing can be quite hard to establish; and member governments were not eager to co-operate in zealous implementation of the law. As for the state aids, the Commission is given powers by the EEC Treaty to find out whether they are being used as a form of protection against imports from other member countries and, if they are, to prevent their use in this way. But the Commission needs, in much of its work, the co-operation of member governments, so it has often been reluctant to antagonize them by demanding cuts in state aids that would cause them serious political problems. Nor did it wish to weaken its political position in the Community by being widely blamed for causing unemployment. Thus state aids were allowed to grow, during the difficult 1970s, to levels that substantially fragmented the Community market. Only since the 1980s, with governments themselves seeking to cut public expenditure, has the Commission felt able to pursue a more rigorous policy in this field.

With the regulations and standards, on the contrary, it was not so much the difficulty of enforcing the law as the difficulty of enacting it that was the cause of fragmentation in the Community market. The Commission initiated a systematic effort to remove these obstacles in 1969; but by 1984, when preparations for the White Paper were being made, it had been able to secure measures of harmonization at a rate of only about ten per annum.[9] Not only was this too slow to tackle the whole problem by the end of the century. In some sectors, where technological progress was fast, new regulations were being generated by member states faster than the Community was harmonizing the old ones, so that the market was becoming increasingly fragmented precisely in those sectors where the Europeans had most need to develop their industry as fast as the Americans and the Japanese.

The Commission's White Paper put forward two methods for breaking this legislative bottleneck. The first was a new approach to the harmonizing of member states' regulations. The Community's harmonized regulations had hitherto usually been bulky documents, defining every detail of the specifications required, which had been the subject of interminable negotiation among member states' officials and were then enacted by the Council of ministers who doubtless had only a remote idea of the significance of these lengthy texts. On one occasion, however, a Directive had been agreed which employed the much simpler method of 'general reference to standards'. This was the 'Low Voltage Directive' of 1973 and it laid down the general objective of safety, leaving it to the European Committee for Standardization, bringing together the authorized standards institutes of member states, to draw up the detailed harmonized specifications.[10] The Commission proposed that this method be generally used where harmonization was required.

The Commission also asked, however, whether harmonization was indeed generally required. This question had been stimulated by the Court of Justice, which had been frustrated by the Community's inability to give effect to article 30 EEC, prohibiting 'all measures having equivalent effect' to quantitative restrictions. Many of the technical regulations and standards clearly had an equivalent effect, reducing imports or preventing them altogether. But in the absence of harmonized regulations, the Community had for over two decades found no way to make this prohibition effective. In 1979, however, when the legality of the German regulation that prevented the import of Cassis de Dijon into the Federal Republic was challenged, the Court judged that the French regulations provided adequate assurance that it was safe for the consumer to imbibe, thus overriding the German regulation and opening up the German market to the French producers. Such 'mutual recognition of other member states' regulations' could, the Commission suggested, be much more widely applied, thus circumventing the laborious process of harmonization. With this 'new strategy', putting the emphasis on deregulation rather than re-regulation, the Commission hoped to ease the burden of legislating for the 1992 programme.

Most of the measures proposed in the White Paper did, nevertheless, involve the re-regulating process of harmonization, even if with the simplification of the new approach. Whatever the attractions of the ideology of deregulation, the member states with stronger protection for health and safety have not been willing to rely on the regulations of those where protection is weaker. Thus the legislative programme envisaged by the White Paper remained formidable; and it was far from certain that the Commission's new approach and strategy would suffice to ensure its success. A new political impulse and more efficient procedures for enacting Community laws might also be needed. It was a principal aim of the Single European Act to provide them.

The Single European Act: 1992 and beyond

Although the EEC Treaty established the principle that measures such as technical regulations or standards should not be allowed to restrict trade among the member states, the Treaty lacked two elements that would have helped to put this principle into practice. It contained no timetable for this, such as it had for the removal of tariffs and quotas; and there was no provision for majority votes for harmonizing such measures as laws, regulations or administrative action in member states that 'directly affect the establishment or functioning of the common market' (article 100 EEC). Failing these two elements, the search for unanimous agreement could be prolonged indefinitely.

The Single European Act (SEA) committed the member states to complete the internal market by the end of 1992, as 'an area without internal frontiers in which the free movement of goods, persons, services and capital is ensured in accordance with the provisions of this Treaty' (article 13 SEA). This, together with the Commission's White Paper, provided the necessary timetable. The SEA went on to introduce majority voting in the Council for a number of cases that had been left with the unanimity procedure in the EEC Treaty, including article 100 on harmonization, which was central to the single market programme. Majority voting did not reach to fiscal harmonization (article 99 EEC), which still depends on unanimous agreement among the member governments. Those countries with high standards in matters such as health, safety, or the environment are moreover protected against having their standards harmonized downwards because they can opt out of Community laws that would have such an effect, provided that the Court of Justice does not find that they are making 'improper use' of this right, i.e. using it for the purpose of trade protection (article 18 SEA). While this does not give the countries with high standards a veto over Community legislation, it does warn member governments not to override such a country when it has a convincing case. Nevertheless, the agreement to extend the scope of majority voting in the SEA has in fact been followed by a sharp increase in its use and in the rate at which Community legislation is enacted.

A major political impulse was needed to launch the single market programme successfully; and the new provision for majority voting contributed significantly to it. The SEA as a whole also helped by embodying agreement on a range of treaty amendments to develop the Community's powers in the economic and social fields and to formalize the co-operation in foreign policy as a Community activity; and the enhanced role for the European Parliament in internal market legislation gave it a higher political profile. All these things added to the sense of political momentum. But the Commission still feared that, after political agreement on the grand principle, protectionist interests and bureaucratic inertia might impede the programme in practice. So they decided to demonstrate the general economic benefits that could be set against the particular interests and resistances.

The result was known as the Cecchini report, after the name of the former Commission official who directed it.[11] It was a massive study, based on research undertaken by over a score of institutes and consultancy firms throughout the Community, including surveys of particular sectors and problems as well as macroeconomic surveying and modelling. In these ways it was possible to estimate some of the dynamic effects of creating the single market, which economists working on the basis of customs union theory had previously not been able to do. The result boiled down to an estimated addition of around 1 per cent a year to the rate of growth of the Community's gross domestic product for a period of five years or more, if the single market programme should be fully realized. This estimate was well publicized and helped to engender confidence in the programme.

The political and business support for the programme was enough to move it forward at least as fast as could be expected. By the end of 1991, the Commission had presented proposals for all the necessary measures to the Council, which had approved four-fifths of them. The remaining one-fifth included some of the most difficult, including a number on tax harmonization, for which unanimity is required. But those enacted did include such important and complex matters as the provision for complete liberalization of capital movements and the 'passport' for banks to operate throughout the Community. Once enacted, the Directives have to be passed into the laws of member states, some of which have been dilatory about it; and the European Committee for Standardization has found the translation of Community legislation into detailed standards burdensome and time-consuming. But despite such problems, the single market programme gathered strong momentum; and this had a snowball effect, with the single market programme stimulating other policies for developing the Community.

The doubling of structural funds was a first example. The member states with weaker economies, led by Spain, insisted on getting such assistance towards their development to meet the challenge of the single market, securing first acceptance of the principle in the section on 'economic and social cohesion' in the Single European Act, then agreement on the budgetary allocations. It was also argued that the integrated capital market would have to be accompanied by an integrated monetary policy; and this led the Community to consider the project for economic and monetary union. The idea of a Social Charter was promoted by labour interests in the richer member states, where there is fear that the single market could bring with it 'social dumping', or cheap competition from member states where labour legislation is less developed.

The general principle that the removal of barriers in order to free trade needs to be accompanied by the integration of policies for purposes beyond trade liberalization was suggested in the 1960s, with the removal of barriers termed negative integration and the making of common policies beyond that termed positive integration.[12] Examples of positive integration provided in the EEC Treaty were the European Investment Bank and Social Fund for the purpose of what has since been called economic and social cohesion, and the common agricultural policy with its aim of a better life for farmers. The single market programme showed that negative and positive integration need not refer to separate activities, for much of the harmonization involved has to aim not only at the freeing of trade but also at agreement on suitable standards of health, safety, and environmental or social protection. Economic and monetary union likewise combines negative with positive integration; and other projects such as the cohesion policy that have followed from the single market programme also introduce substantial elements of positive integration.

Because positive integration requires value judgements, it is not just a technical but a political activity. It also imposes executive tasks and demands a strong juridical framework. It is therefore likely that a Community developing in these ways will need stronger and more democratic institutions.

If it is true that negative integration brings with it the need for positive integration, a completed single market after 1992 is not likely to rest in stable equilibrium. Either, if the needs for positive integration are not met, it will tend to become less integrated again, as the Community market did in the 1970s. Or the Community will, with more positive integration, move farther towards Union on federal lines. The Maastricht Treaty included a number of steps in that direction. If the new technologies, and the specialization that goes with them, continue to press the European economies towards integration, the cost of resisting movement towards such a Union could be high.

5 Agricultural Policy: Formation, Crisis, Reform

Creating a common market for agriculture was a harder task than for industry. Simple tariffs were not deemed adequate by European states to protect their farmers against the sometimes violent fluctuations in world markets; and they had already devised a variety of complicated forms of price and income support instead. Member states were not ready to let their own supports be undermined by free imports from other member states with differing price systems. If agricultural trade within the Community was, like industrial trade, to be free of tariffs and quotas, the existing national systems would have to be replaced by a Community-wide system of support. Given the importance of the farm vote at the time when the Community was founded, this was a formidable political task.

The British proposal for a Free Trade Area sought in 1957 to evade this task simply by excluding agriculture; but the proposal failed because it was not acceptable to the French. Such a solution could not be contemplated for the Community, for which, in Britain's absence, France was essential as a counterweight to Germany. The French, fearing German industrial strength, were reluctant to open their own industry to German competition. French agriculture was, on the other hand, a strong competitor; and the French saw their potential gains in agricultural trade as an indispensable counterpart to the risks they would take in the industrial common market.

The Community's common agricultural policy can, therefore, be seen as the product of national interest secured by the use of bargaining power. But any such diplomatic success would, in the Community, have been short-lived had it not been part of a general bargain that satisfied all the member countries. For the benefits they all derive from the Community depend on the proper working of its institutions; and these do not work well if they contain representatives from member states that feel seriously aggrieved. It is a cardinal principle of Swiss federal practice that no part of the country should feel that its interests are neglected by the federal system. The Community itself has developed the technique of the package deal to ensure a balance of interests at any phase of its development, and the initial EEC bargain, satisfying French agricultural and German industrial interests, can be seen as the first major example. The bargain might not have endured had either French industry or German agriculture been seriously damaged; but French industrialists rose to the challenge of the common market and the common agricultural policy was arranged so as to satisfy German farmers too. Later on, the agricultural interest was to be pressed to the point where it endangered the Community's equilibrium. But at the outset it was an essential element in the balance. The question was not whether, but how to establish it.

Formation of the common policy

The form of the common agricultural policy was too complex and difficult a matter to be settled in the negotiations for the EEC Treaty. The Treaty provided, in essence, that there should be an agricultural common market without barriers to trade among the member states, that it should be established by the end of the transitional period of 12–15 years from 1958, and that it should be determined by the Council, on a proposal from the Commission, acting by a unanimous vote among the member governments' representatives during the first two stages of the transitional period but by a qualified majority vote thereafter. Thus there was an aim, a deadline, and a procedure, but the hard decisions remained to be taken.

The Germans wanted a policy that was market-oriented and that allowed them to continue importing from the low-cost world markets, with the somewhat contradictory proviso that there should not be too much sacrifice of the high, protected prices that German farmers enjoyed. The French wanted a Community market organization in a form that would enable them to sell a lot to the Germans. These wishes of the two most powerful member states appeared hard to reconcile. But the Community's first Commissioner for agriculture, Sicco Mansholt, identified a first key decision on which he felt they could agree: to base the protection needed for the common price support on the instrument of the variable import levy.

The import levy was familiar to Mansholt, as it was the form of protection used by the Netherlands and he had been the Dutch Minister for agriculture. It secured a stable price for the farmer by making the importer of a competitive product pay a levy to meet the difference between the world market price and the domestic support price. So it would be the level of the Community's support price that would determine how much the high-cost German farmer would be protected, and hence how much he would produce and what share of the German market would be left for imports from France. But that conflict of interests could be resolved later, when the Community's common price level was fixed—as it would have to be when the barriers within the Community were removed and the common import levy was introduced. Meanwhile, Mansholt asked for agreement on the principle of the import levy.

The French and Dutch governments supported Mansholt in this, seeing it as the key to the decisions required to open the Community market to their farmers' exports. The Germans resisted. But the Dutch made agreement on the levy a condition of their acceptance of the Community's passage to the second stage of the transitional period. This could be delayed for up to three years by any member state which could claim that the objectives of the first stage had not been fulfilled; and the Dutch claimed that this would be the case unless agreement was reached on this substantial step towards the common agricultural policy. The Germans were keenly interested in passage to the second stage, which would bring further liberalization of the Community's internal market; and they did not want the Community's political success to be jeopardized. So they finally accepted the levy—but not before the Council resorted to the device of 'stopping the clock' at midnight on 31 December

1961, until agreement was reached after a marathon session lasting until 14 January.

Two more key decisions had to be taken before the common agricultural policy could be put in place: the level at which prices were to be supported and the source of the money to pay for the support.

The price level was another bone of contention between the Germans, who wanted high prices, and the Commission, Dutch, and French, who wanted them lower. The price of wheat was the crux, determining the price of bread and, through its influence on grains for feeding animals, of meat and other livestock products. Two forms of pressure were brought to bear on the Germans. They were much concerned, both for industrial interests and for their good relations with the United States, to secure a successful outcome to the 'Kennedy round' of international trade negotiations, which were to initiate a new phase of liberal world trade. The French government was ready to accept this, but also prepared to make their acceptance conditional on German agreement to a Community price for wheat. This was another example of a major package deal—or rather a further instalment of the Franco-German package deal that lay behind the success of the negotiations to establish the EEC. But de Gaulle was impatient to secure what he saw as France's prime interest in the Community, and disinclined to follow the Community way of doing things by seeking a consensus based on a balance of interests. He preferred the classical methods of power politics. He knew that the Germans set great store on the Community's institutions, which had helped to give them their respected place in the post-war Western system, whereas he felt that the destruction of those institutions would be no great loss, and was certainly in favour of weakening them. He therefore issued threats, in the second half of 1964, that without satisfaction on agriculture France might leave the Community; and he must have felt that this rough tactic succeeded, because agreement on the wheat price was reached before the end of the year.[1] With hindsight it may be doubted whether his tactics paid off. The EEC Treaty provided that until 1966, when the Community passed to the third stage of its transitional period, decisions on agricultural policy had to be taken by unanimous vote in the Council; and the German vote was obtained in 1964 only by conceding a wheat price that was considerably higher than the Commission or the French wanted. This, through its effect on the agricultural price level as a whole, not only helped to protect German farmers from French competition, but was also a cause of the general over-production that was eventually to impose such problems on the Community and its members, including France. Nor was the new price in fact to be introduced until mid-1967, by which time it could have been determined by a qualified majority vote, thus weakening the Germans' ability to exact such a high price—had de Gaulle not by then undermined the principle of majority voting. The high-handed methods preferred by de Gaulle also stiffened the Germans' resolve to resist his next offensive against the Community's institutions, when the third main element in the common agricultural policy, the way in which it was to be financed, came up for decision in 1965.

Money would be needed to support the prices fixed by the Community. Should the price of a product fall below the support level, it would have to be bought and stored. Storage would cost money, and, should it not be possible to sell the stocks later on the Community market for that product, they would have to be exported at subsidized prices or used for purposes that brought a lower return within the Community. The Commission estimated that the Community's customs duties and import levies should at first suffice, with additional contributions from the member states if required. The EEC Treaty provided that the Community should have its own 'resources', i.e. taxes, to finance its budget; and the French government saw this as an important national interest because it would ensure that the cost of the common agricultural policy was borne by the Community as a whole and not just by the member state that produced the surpluses. But the Commission espoused another principle with which the French government of the day did not agree: that since these taxes would pass to the Community without the resulting expenditure being scrutinized by the member states' parliaments, democratic accountability required that the Community budget should be approved not only by the Council, but also by the European Parliament acting jointly with it.[2]

This proposal provoked an epic conflict between the Community and de Gaulle. He was set on securing the common financing of agriculture. France's partners accepted that this was necessary for a Community agricultural policy, but agreed with the Commission that it must be managed by Community institutions that transcended the intergovernmental. But de Gaulle saw this as a threat to French national sovereignty. When his partners failed to submit, he withdrew his ministers from policy-making in the Council, and held to this policy of the 'empty chair' throughout the second half of 1965. This time the Germans and the other four member governments were resolute. They continued Community business; and the French electorate showed, in presidential elections towards the end of the year, that they did not like to see risks taken with the Community. In January 1966, de Gaulle decided to return to normal working in the Community, after sending his ministers to meet their partners in Luxembourg to announce that he would not accept majority votes on 'very important interests': the so-called Luxembourg 'compromise'. While de Gaulle accepted that he could not get the others to agree to any formal weakening of the Community institutions, the Luxembourg 'compromise', which might more accurately have been called the Luxembourg veto, led to the general use of the unanimity procedure in the Council for about two decades, thus consolidating the dominance of the intergovernmental method of operating the Community and diminishing its capacity for action.

When the agricultural common market was introduced in mid-1967, it was at first financed with the help of member states' financial contributions. After de Gaulle resigned two years later, his successor secured the agreement on the Community's own resources as part of the package deal for the first enlargement, conceding in part the institutional conditions that had been anathema to de Gaulle. The customs duties and import levies were supplemented by a tax of up to 1 per cent of the value-added of taxable goods in the Community, which was enough to finance excessive production through the 1970s, leading to the crisis that debilitated the Community until the mid-1980s.

Thus the common agricultural policy was created as required by the EEC Treaty. Unanimous agreement on the three main decisions, the levy, the price, and the financing, was extremely hard to achieve, each time harder than the last, culminating in the conflict over financing that was the occasion for de Gaulle's challenge to the Community in 1965. It was the French interest in the agricultural policy that enabled the Community to survive that challenge. But the settlement at Luxembourg weakened the institutions when it had already become clear that the search for intergovernmental unanimity was an unpromising basis for common action on the scale of the agricultural policy. By making them more intergovernmental, not less, de Gaulle's institutional legacy was a major reason why the policy was not to be reformed until nearly two decades after it had become evident that reform would be necessary. Meanwhile the agri-budgetary crisis did untold damage to the Community.

The sorcerer's apprentice

The single market for other products followed soon after the achievement of the single market for cereals in July 1967. Mansholt and DG VI, the Commission's Directorate-General for agriculture, realized that the price levels which the Council had agreed would stimulate production. Yet the average farmer's holding, at some 13 hectares, was too small to enable him, even with the higher prices, to avoid falling further behind the rising incomes in other sectors in the Community. So long as farms remained so small and so many people therefore continued to work on the land, Mansholt reasoned, they could survive only with prices that were increasingly out of line with world prices, stimulating surplus production that would burden the Community's budget. He concluded that the structure of Community agriculture would have to be rapidly developed, so that fewer people would work on larger, more modern farms, earning much higher incomes.

The Mansholt plan, as it came to be called, was presented to the Council in a Commission Memorandum in December 1968.[3] Its central aim was to reduce the number working in agriculture in the Community by about half in the 1970s, to 5 million by the end of the decade. The main method was to be the modernization of farms, encouraged by Community grants and loans for farm development. For this, the member states would have to accept a big increase in the Community's resources for its structural policy, or for 'guidance' as it is called in the title of the European Agricultural Guidance and Guarantee Fund.

Mansholt put his considerable energy and talent into a campaign to gain support for his proposals.[4] He hoped that his vision of a modern, prosperous agriculture would attract the more dynamic among the farming interests as well as consumers, taxpayers, and others who would benefit. But the farm lobbies were up in arms against the idea of cutting the number of their members in half. Mansholt could argue that more than 5 million had left the land in the preceding decade. But this was one in three of the number at the beginning of that decade, not one in two; it had not cut so close to the hard core of farm people who were most fiercely attached to the land; and it had occurred without being the aim of a specific Community policy that the lobbies could oppose.

The governments were also against him. All, and not least the Germans, were influenced by the lobbies; and the French government, still strongly Gaullist, was keenly opposed to an enhancement of the Commission's role such as the proposed policy would imply. They had accepted that the Community should be responsible for a common agricultural market, because that had been agreed in the EEC Treaty and was the interest of the French government. But there was no enthusiasm among the member governments for handing responsibility for a large part of structural policy to the Community. They wanted to keep it for themselves. The result was the attrition of the Mansholt plan over more than three years of discussions, until the Council decided, in April 1972, to provide only some modest finance for development loans to farmers, incentives for early retirement, and assistance for information and training intended to raise efficiency. The budget for 'guarantee', i.e. for price support, was great and growing; that for 'guidance' remained small.

Not only were the Council's decisions long delayed and quite inadequate when they came. They were also applied unconscionably slowly by the member states. The decisions took the form of Directives, which leave it to the member states to make their own laws to achieve the agreed result; and this often takes a couple of years, with another year before their application begins to have an effect. In this case the decisions were not being applied in France until 1977, five years after they had been taken by the Council; and in Italy there were still no farm development plans at all at the end of 1978, ten years after Mansholt had presented his Memorandum to the Council and alerted them to the dangers ahead if action was not taken.

Not surprisingly, the size of farms changed little in the 1970s, rising by only one hectare to an average of 13.7 hectares. The number working in agriculture did fall by 2.6 million; but in the absence of an effective structural policy and with the cushion of high prices this spontaneous drift from the land was, at half the rate that Mansholt had deemed necessary, not fast enough to resolve the problem he had diagnosed. The poor farmers remained poor. The richer ones prospered, responding to high prices and incomes with a rapid growth of productivity based on technological advance. Production outran consumption. Community production of cereals as a percentage of consumption grew from 91 per cent in 1973/4 to 116 per cent in 1983/4, of meat from 96 per cent to 101 per cent, and of butter from 98 per cent to 134 per cent. Between 1975 and 1984, the Community's agricultural exports grew by 256 per cent, imports by only 14 per cent.[5] This caused disruption in world markets, hitting hard some Third World countries as well as trading partners such as Australia, Canada, New Zealand, and the United States. With Community prices around half as much again as world prices in the early 1980s, the exports were heavily subsidized; and the Community had to finance the growing stocks of products that could neither be exported nor consumed at home. Thus the common agricultural policy had become costly and disruptive of international trade; and instead of assisting the poor it did more to help the rich. The poor farmers suffered while the rich flourished; the high food prices bore hardest on the poorer consumers; and it was mainly the poorer member states that made net contributions to the Community budget for the benefit of the richer.

Had it not been for the entry of Britain in 1973, and the diversion of imports into its large market from its traditional overseas suppliers to the Community farmers, together with the large British contribution to the Community budget, the burden of surplus production would have become intolerable for the Community sooner; and the decision to allocate to the Community budget revenue of up to 1 per cent of value-added also prolonged the period in which the Community could spend instead of reform. The Council was therefore able, despite rising surpluses, especially of dairy products, to sidestep the Commission's exhortations during the later 1970s to pursue a more rigorous price policy. It was not until 1982 that the first serious measures to control expenditure were taken; and it was only in 1988 that a general reform of agricultural and budgetary policy was introduced—nearly two decades after Mansholt had drawn the Council's attention to the need for reform. Meanwhile, the Community had been divided and enfeebled by quarrels over the budget and had fallen in public esteem. It is worthwhile to consider why, when the Commission had so clearly diagnosed the problem, the Community had been allowed to drift so dangerously and so long.

Institutional weaknesses

The Mansholt plan was the work of people who were concerned about the problems of the agricultural common market as a whole. They foresaw that, without structural reform, the common agricultural policy would become untenable. The remedy they proposed was to modernize farming so that rapidly growing productivity would bring farmers adequate incomes without high prices. It was a bold vision. Perhaps they should have put more emphasis on the control of the costs of price support. But this was not what the ministers in the Council, in mutilating the Mansholt plan, proposed. They decided to continue fixing common prices without either a common structural policy or a mechanism for controlling costs. How could ministers act so irresponsibly?

Each minister was responding to the pressures of the political situation in his own member state which were generated by the interests in that state. The ministers' prime concern was not the impending problems of the system as a whole. When, early in 1971, it was time to fix the prices for the coming farm year 1971/2, Mansholt tried to induce them to take his structural reform proposals seriously by linking these to his proposals for prices. But the ministers reacted by merely promising to take some measures the following year, which were in the event only a token of what Mansholt had originally proposed. They had the power of decision; and they were not going to give the Community's needs, important though they might be, priority over political convenience at home. The member states showed the same low regard for the needs of the Community as a whole with their long delays in implementing the Council's Directives.

This order of priorities and its consequences during the 1970s and 1980s demonstrated the contradiction between a common political objective on the scale of the agricultural common market and the intergovernmental method that dominated the taking of decisions to achieve and maintain it. This contradiction has been at its most obvious where unanimous voting has been required, as we saw with respect to the prices and the financing. With the practice of unanimous voting entrenched during the two decades after the Luxembourg 'compromise', prices continued to be fixed by the Council at levels higher than the Commission had proposed, inducing over-production and heavy support costs. Along with this voting procedure went a concern for the special interests of member states that overrode the general interest in the single market, a prime example being the monetary compensatory amounts (MCAs). This is the bureaucratic name for the mechanism whereby special exchange rates for agricultural trade in the Community—also known as 'green currencies'— insulate farmers and consumers from the immediate effects of exchange rate changes. First introduced as a temporary measure in order to protect the German farmers from a cut in their prices that would otherwise have followed from a revaluation of the mark in 1969, MCAs eventually became a general system of border taxes and subsidies that can shield either farmers or consumers from the normal effects of parity changes. They have persisted for over two decades. The single market programme requires their elimination, but that will be hard to achieve without monetary union.

The Council's structure as well as its voting procedures has undermined its effectiveness as a legislature. In no case has the division of the Council into a number of functional Councils, each empowered to enact laws in its own field, caused greater confusion than in agriculture. The Council of finance ministers is responsible for the Community budget. Yet the Council of agriculture ministers, when it fixed the prices, took the decision that determined the size of the predominant part of the budget. Since they had no responsibility for financial matters, it is not surprising that their price decisions were financially irresponsible. The agriculture ministers have been subject to pressures quite other than financial constraints. They are the prime targets for agricultural lobbies, whose influence is particularly strong in election years; and a year seldom passes in which at least one of the member states is not going to have an election. Even if the others did not sympathize with those about to enter an election campaign, with unanimous voting their special interests had to be respected—another cause of higher prices. The agricultural ministries in most member states are close to the farmers' organizations; and the Agriculture Council, as it is usually called, has been advised by a Special Committee on Agriculture, comprising officials from those ministries. Thus farm lobbies, officials, and ministers formed a tight circle, fairly impervious to the influence of other interests such as consumers or taxpayers when decisions were to be taken by the Council. Agriculture ministers in a national context are, of course, subject to similar pressures in making policies; but they have to justify financial implications to the finance ministers in their governments. No such coherence was built into the Community's institutions. The structure of the intergovernmental

Council did not encourage responsibility for the budgetary consequences of agricultural decisions, any more than for the problems of the Community as a whole.

Both the Commission and the European Parliament have been responsive to the agricultural lobbies. But the Commission has, since Mansholt presented his Memorandum on reform in 1969, produced more responsible policies than the Council and proposed more moderate price increases than the Council decided. Before the direct elections in 1979, the Parliament was highly susceptible to agricultural pressures. But since the mid-1980s, it has been more inclined to represent the nine-tenths of the population who are not in the farm sector and thus to check the excesses of the decisions that the Council continued to take until the agri-budgetary reform of 1988. When the Parliament's budgetary powers were determined, however, in the treaties that introduced the Community's own resources in 1970 and 1975, the French government, in a rearguard action of the then retreating Gaullism, insisted that the Parliament's power to enact the budget jointly with the Council did not extend to the agricultural expenditure. Responsibility for the agricultural budget was therefore that of the Council alone. The Parliament, which took a wider view of the Community's interest than the Agriculture Council, had little influence over the decisions.

Common sense indicates that people working in institutions whose responsibility is for the Community as a whole are likely to give a higher priority to its general interest than those whose main work is in the institutions of a member state, devoted to the interests of that state. The interests of the member state and of the Community will often coincide, at least in the longer term. But there will be crucial occasions on which the longer-term general interest and the shorter-term national interest diverge; and it is to be expected that those who work in national government will often be guided by the shorter-term national interest, even if in the long term the national and the general interests would converge. This has been the case with the common agricultural policy. The annual decisions of the Council on price have responded to the shorter-term national interests while leaving the longer-term Community interest— which was also the longer-term interest of the member states—

to look after itself. It is fully understandable that the ministers should be mainly influenced by the context in which they mainly live and work. The fault is not theirs, but that of the Community's constitution which gives so much power to them and so little to the Commission and the European Parliament, where people's main work is in an institution whose function is to produce laws, policies, and decisions for the Community as a whole.

Reform

Despite the defects in its institutions, the Community can take decisions when it has to. The overspending on agriculture could continue so long as the money available to the Community held out. But when, after over a decade of swelling budgets, spending began to approach the limit of the 1 per cent value-added tax plus the customs duties and agricultural import levies, which together comprised the 'own resources', action clearly had to be taken. In 1982, 'price quotas' were introduced to stem the flow of funds into price support for sugar. The full support price became payable only for production required for the Community market; there was a lower price for 'normal exports', or rather for exports that had become normal during the time that they had been dumped on world markets with Community export subsidies; and beyond that, the going price on the world market would obtain. But bringing some discipline into the regime for only one product was not enough. By 1984, the limit of existing own resources was reached.

The first half of 1984 was the time of the French presidency, when Mitterrand assembled a package that included agreement on the Iberian enlargement and on Britain's budgetary rebate. The rebate was the key to a bargain that included British acceptance of the increase in the value-added tax contribution that was necessary to finance the agricultural policy. Increases in own resources have to be approved by all member states (article 201 EEC), and the British government wanted to be satisfied on two counts before conceding its approval: the rebate; and agreement to bring the agricultural expenditure, which was the main cause of Britain's high net contribution, under control. Unfortunately for the Community, the rebate appears to have been the higher priority, for the British government, while ensuring that two-thirds of Britain's net contribution would be reimbursed, accepted decisions on agriculture which failed to ensure an adequate control. Following the price quotas for sugar, a tough quota regime was introduced for milk, which had until then taken a particularly large share of expenditure. From 1984, production of milk beyond quota was subject to a penal levy; and this caused the notorious 'butter mountain' in storage to melt away. It was also agreed that agricultural expenditure should rise no faster than gross domestic product; and this decision was respected in the price decisions for the next farm year. But by 1988, agricultural spending had increased by more than ecu 6 billion, or by 30 per cent since 1984. Once again, the money had run out—indeed, creative accounting was required to finance a good part of that increase. This time, British agreement to more own resources would not be forthcoming without a firm system for the control of expenditure.

The Commission produced proposals for reform of the agricultural policy and the budget in two reports in 1987, known together as the Delors package;[6] and the European Council took decisions on this basis under German presidency in the first half of 1988. 'Stabilizers' were introduced for products accounting for a large part of the budget. After the examples of sugar and milk, these provided for price cuts when an agreed quota was reached, thus reducing the cost of price support and, it was hoped, discouraging farmers from over-production. Some structural measures were taken in addition to these central decisions on price discipline. Farmers were to be paid for leaving arable land to lie fallow, provided that they 'set aside' one-fifth or more of their arable land for five years or more. There was to be compensation for early retirement, and a start was made in providing income support for poorer farmers, related to their need and not their production—in order to avoid stimulating them to produce more. The structural funds, which were to be doubled by 1993, were to include among their objectives the stimulation of new sources of rural employment. Community expenditure on agriculture as a whole was to grow less fast than gross product; its expansion was to be kept within 74 per cent of the rate of growth of GNP. Price decisions were to respect this limit; and if the limit should nevertheless be approached, special action was to be taken to prevent it from being breached.

These measures appeared strong enough to keep the agricultural expenditure under control. So the British government as well as its partners accepted a further increase of the Community's own resources, to 1.4 per cent of value-added together with a new resource related to gross national product, enough to finance the slower growth of agricultural expenditure up to 1992 and the doubling of the size of structural funds. The Community seemed at last to be released from the agricultural incubus that had weighed it down for so long.

This success brought with it some strengthening of the institutions. The prestige of the Commission was enhanced and its capacity was demonstrated to devise proposals that served the Community's general interest while at the same time taking account of the particular problems of member states. In order to protect their agreement to double the structural funds, moreover, the member governments accepted an Inter-institutional Agreement whereby the Parliament would gain influence over the size of the agricultural budget in return for accepting the proposed size of structural funds; and the Council resolved that none of its decisions could require expenditure that had not been authorized in budgetary appropriations, hence determining to bring the agriculture ministers at last under budgetary control.

With quarrels over agriculture and the budget behind it, at least for the time being, and the prospect of the completed single market ahead, the Community was better placed than it had been for many years to consider further steps that could lead towards Union. One such step is economic and monetary union, which was placed on the Community's agenda at the same time as the agri-budgetary reform was agreed, through setting up the Delors committee to recommend the stages by which it could be achieved. But the Maastricht treaty, though it made quite full provision for the Emu, took more modest steps towards federal institutions. It appeared that not enough governments had drawn the conclusions from the experience of the agricultural policy that would lead them to reform the institutions so as to ensure a more adequate performance in establishing and managing its major policies in the future.

The desirability of more effective institutions was again underlined by the new efforts to reform the common agricultural policy, announced in 1990 by Ray MacSharry, the Commissioner for agriculture. With world prices again low and Community production high, surplus stocks and budgetary expenditure were again getting out of hand; and conflict over agricultural trade was undermining the Uruguay round of Gatt negotiations through which it was hoped to maintain a generally liberal system for world trade in the years ahead. MacSharry proposed to do what economists had long recommended: shift the focus of policy from price support towards income support. He suggested sharp cuts of, for example, around two-fifths in the support price for cereals, and farmers' compensation mainly through a greatly expanded set-aside scheme. This would not immediately take the pressure off the Community budget; it would indeed increase the total spending on agriculture for a time. Nor would the price cuts bring the Community level near to world prices or readily resolve the conflict over agriculture in the Gatt. But the longer-term budgetary prospects and the Gatt negotiations would be greatly helped. The Council nevertheless remained dilatory about deciding on the reform, thus prolonging the drain on the budget and endangering the prospect for a successful conclusion of the Uruguay round.

In sum, the Community took almost a decade to establish the common agricultural policy—more, if the time taken to secure its financing on a permanent basis is included; then it took up to two decades to launch a reform on the lines that Mansholt had foreseen would be necessary once the agricultural common market had been established; then, when this proved inadequate, the Council's delay in deciding on a more adequate reform threatened the stability of the world trading system. These inordinate delays, the second of which endangered the future of the Community and the third, that of world trade, were caused, if the reasoning of this chapter is justified, by the dominance of the intergovernmental element in the Community's institutions and the subordinate roles of the Commission and the European Parliament. It would follow that, if the management of such policies is to be more effective in years to come, this imbalance in the institutions will have to be corrected.

6 Industrial and Social Policy

Free market competition is the principal means of promoting economic efficiency and development in the European Community. By opening up the member states' markets to each other, the scope for scale and specialization has been multiplied. Spurred by the more challenging competition, firms have reduced costs and invested and innovated for the future. The way in which the Community has created first the customs union, then the programme for completing the single market in the increasingly complex modern economy, was outlined in Chapter 4.

Because of this complexity, the single market programme is a far cry from the nineteenth-century liberal ideal of laissez-faire. Numerous standards and regulations have to be harmonized for the protection of health, safety, or the environment. But even this does not ensure that markets will not be distorted. Firms can agree to fix high prices or abuse a dominant position in other ways. Governments can give firms subsidies and hence unfair advantage over their competitors in other member states. If it is to have a properly functioning market, the Community must deal with distortions such as these; and this is the logic of its policies for competition and 'state aids'.

While opening the markets and ensuring that they function freely has been the main thrust of the Community's policy for industry, and until Maastricht the EEC Treaty had no specific provision for 'industrial policy', there have also been policies to correct what are seen as inadequacies or undesirable effects of the markets. It is not that the Community has been particularly prone to such intervention. Member states are more so, as witness the Community's efforts to reduce their industrial subsidies. Despite the return to more market-oriented liberal attitudes in the 1980s, all industrialized countries have continued to act in this way, and the choice for the Community has been whether to let its market be fragmented by the different policies of member states or to devise a common policy of its own. It can be strongly argued that imperfections in modern markets justify some actions of this sort, even if it must also be recognized that imperfections in governments may cause such actions to do more harm than good. But this is not the place to tread the well-worn path of that argument.[1] Here we need note only that if the Community did not act in some such cases, the member states would, thus fragmenting the single market.

The most prominent of such Community policies have been directed at old industrial sectors in trouble, where employment has been falling fast. Here, as in steel, textiles, and shipbuilding, the Community has sought to temper the pain for those working in the industry by combining protection against imports (see Chapter 9) with aid from member states and from the EC itself, while at the same time encouraging adjustment towards competitive activity. The previous chapter, on agriculture, showed some of the difficulties that can arise if such a task on such a heroic scale is given to institutions as weak as those of the Community have been up to now. Fortunately, none of the other sectors has presented quite such daunting difficulties as that.

In some fields of technological research, the resources of single member states are not enough to compete with the efforts that can be mounted by countries such as the United States or Japan. Public authorities support such research because the resources of individual firms are likewise not enough, and also because the innovations that result can bring benefits that spread much wider than the organization in which they are made. So the economies of scale may point towards a Community-wide effort to supplement those of the member states; and the Community has undertaken some programmes of this kind.

The Community also has policies that aim to protect the environment or standards of health and safety at work. Pollution from one country can damage the environment of its neighbours; and the products of those who care less about health and safety may undercut the products of those who raise their costs by caring more. Such effects of free markets are often unacceptable to those who suffer them, so the Community tries to prevent them. More controversial are attempts to improve working conditions beyond the limited objectives of health and safety, neoliberals arguing that this makes Europeans uncompetitive and increases unemployment. In Community parlance the whole range of policies relating to the conditions of employees is known as social policy; and how far such policy should go has been a source of conflict in the Community. But some of the industrial policies have been less controversial.

Steel

France has a historic tradition of the use of public power in the economy. There was no question but that the state would have a strong role in rebuilding the French economy after World War II. But at the same time the French wanted to break the vicious circle of low growth and low expectations that had left France less developed industrially before the war than neighbours such as Germany and Britain. This was the context in which Monnet, as head of the French planning commission, developed the system that became known as 'indicative planning'. The planners, working with industrialists, published the production targets that appeared achievable and industry was expected to invest to achieve them. There was no compulsion—no question of Soviet-style imperative planning—but the planners could offer incentives such as low-interest loans to firms that agreed to help fulfil the plan. When the European Coal and Steel Community was established it was natural that Monnet should envisage it pursuing policies of this kind. Since at that time France unquestionably had the leading role, the ECSC Treaty provided for instruments to enable the Community to do so.

The wording of the Treaty gives the flavour of the time. 'To provide guidelines . . . on the course of action to be followed by all concerned', the High Authority was to 'draw up pro-grammes indicating foreseeable developments in production, consumption, exports and imports' and to lay down general objectives for modernization and expansion (article 46 ECSC). But such indications and targets would have been whistling in the wind had the High Authority not disposed of instruments with which to influence the firms. It could impose a tax of up to 1 per cent of the value of production of coal and steel as well as contract loans on the capital markets; and with these resources it could offer cheap loans to firms that were ready to invest in line with the objectives and programmes, and subsidies for technological research. Since the development of the industries would require workers to change their jobs, and since Monnet was concerned that the Community should have a social as well as an industrial policy, thus earning support among workers and the general public as well as industrialists, the High Authority could also provide money for training those who needed new skills and housing those who had to move.

The Treaty also provided for liberal policies to ensure the proper functioning of the market. The coal and steel industries had been famous for their cartels; and, following the example of American Anti-Trust, the ECSC gave the High Authority power, subject to the ultimate authority of the Court of Justice, to prevent abuses by cartels or monopolies, and mergers that would lead to excessive concentrations of power. Since many of the abuses had been reflected in prices, transactions could take place only in line with prices and conditions of sale that the firms had to publish.

The ECSC was founded at a time of post-war shortages, and when memories of pre-war depression and over-capacity were still much alive. So the Treaty provided for the allocation of supplies if there was a 'serious shortage', and regulation of the market in the event of a 'manifest crisis' due to a 'decline in demand' (articles 58, 59 ECSC). The High Authority could not declare that there was a manifest crisis without the assent of the Council, voting by a majority that gave greater weight to the larger producers of coal and steel. But once it had been declared, the High Authority could stabilize the market by imposing maximum production quotas on firms and fixing minimum prices. Thus the Community could impose a fairly strong regulatory system should the market be seriously disturbed.

The removal of barriers to trade within the Community had a substantial effect on the efficiency of these heavy industries, which had been distorted by frontiers that had cut across the logic of production based on iron ore from the Lorraine, coke from the Ruhr, and steelworks that used them both.[2] The industrial policies provided under the Treaty also had significant influence at first. But by the 1960s they became less relevant, for two opposing reasons. The coal industry, declining under the impact of competition from oil, was in crisis by 1958. But the Council rejected in May 1959 a comprehensive plan which the High Authority had proposed to deal with it; and from then on coal was protected by individual member states with subsidies which fragmented the Community market again and outweighed the effect of Community policies. Steel, on the contrary, was prospering in a free market like other manufacturing industries, and had less need of the special industrial policies which the ECSC Treaty had provided for it, but which were not available, or provided to a lesser extent, under the EEC Treaty that applied to other industries. It was not until the 1970s, when steel was hit by a severe recession, that the ECSC Treaty came to the front again. Then in May 1977, the Commission (as the High Authority had become, after the three Councils and executives of the three Communities were merged in 1965 into a single Council and a single Commission) initiated a major episode in the history of the Community's industrial policy when it began to enforce, with the agreement of the Council, a regime of minimum prices for reinforcing bars.

The steel industry had run into difficulty after the oil shock of 1973–4 had led to deflation and recession, at the same time as the Japanese and some newly industrializing countries who could make steel more cheaply were taking shares from the Europeans in world markets. With the high fixed costs of a capital-intensive industry, steel firms incurred heavy losses when production fell. But waiting for bankruptcies to solve the problem by reducing capacity to the level of demand would be a lengthy process. Much of the steel was produced by large firms with correspondingly big resources and borrowing power; and the jobs they provided gave them a political clout that caused governments to subsidize them rather than allow them to fail. That, if it continued unchecked, would be dangerous for the Community, because the more efficient producers, damaged by subsidized competition from other member states, would cease to find the Community of benefit. The spread of subsidization threatened the Community's integration in a number of sectors, and notably in steel.

The minimum prices were extended to other products in 1978. But this was a fragile expedient in the absence of any control of production, because firms would produce in quantities that made the minimum prices hard to hold. When the second oil shock induced a new recession, the Council accepted, in October 1980, the Commission's proposal to declare a manifest crisis; and the Commission introduced a regime for steel that became known as the Davignon plan, after the name of the then Commissioner for industry. In addition to the minimum prices, the Commission imposed maximum production quotas on firms. But this arrangement too would have been insufficiently robust without control over the supply of imports from the saturated world market. Yet whereas the Council could assent to the manifest crisis by majority vote, unanimity was required to ensure the control of imports. The German steel industry had modernized itself ahead of the crisis and the Germans felt that the Davignon regime shielded the less efficient producers in other countries at their expense. They therefore accepted the restriction of imports only on condition that their partners accepted a programme for bringing their subsidies to an end; and the Council agreed, in June 1981, that firms should qualify for state aids only if they were implementing a restructuring programme that would lead to the reduction of high-cost capacity.

This incident exposed a weakness in the Community's crisis regime, compared with the system of recession cartels practised in Japan. There, when a sector suffered from the sort of difficulties encountered by Community steel, the Japanese organized, as the Community did, a regime of minimum prices and production quotas. But while such a regime may ease the pain for the sector, it does little to relieve society of the burden of the high cost of the supported production. The Japanese therefore added an essential element: the firms were allowed to operate the cartel only on condition that they reduced capacity and modernized or diversified production to the point where they were again competitive without special support.[3] Thanks to the Germans' use of their voting power with respect to the import restrictions, the Community from 1981 did require restructuring and capacity reduction as a condition of state aids. But because of the political weakness of the Commission in relation to the governments of the member states, the cuts in capacity were too little and too late to avoid the continuation of the crisis regime until 1988, not far short of a decade after it had been introduced.

The Davignon regime was nevertheless a qualified success. Even with the cushion it provided, closures of steelworks occasioned some serious violence, which could well otherwise have been worse. Trade conflict between member states was kept within bounds. The adjustment to a leaner, more competitive industry that could survive without the regime was eventually made, even if one may guess that the Japanese would have done it more thoroughly and in half the time. Japanese firms are more amenable to such arrangements than the Europeans: less individualistic, not divided by national rivalries, more apt to co-operate with government. Equally important, they have a government with which to co-operate. The weakness of the Community's institutions, with its inter-governmental Council outweighing the Commission, neither being able to act as decisively as a government, raises the question whether the Community should not reconcile itself to less ambitious policies until it has stronger institutions. Even if the experience of agriculture would invite such scepticism, the admittedly less hugely ambitious steel policy may be deemed to have justified itself, although there can be little doubt that stronger institutions would have made it shorter, sharper, and more successful.

The Treaties provide for such market regulation only for steel, coal, and in a different way for agriculture. In other sectors the Community has to rely on its policies to enforce competition and on financial incentives, if it wishes to pursue industrial policies that go beyond the removal of internal barriers to trade (considered in Chapter 4) and the use of tariffs and restrictions on imports from outside the Community (Chapter 9).

Competition policy, state aids

The policies to ensure competition among firms and to control state aids had an important place in the EEC Treaty. By the time that it was negotiated, in 1956–7, Germany had gained economic and political strength and German views about economic policy carried more weight. The German government was committed to the liberal ideas of the social market economy and hostile to the French style of intervention that had influenced the ECSC. The prominence of competition and state aids policy in the EEC compared with other forms of industrial policy reflected this German preference, acknowledged in article 3(f) EEC which affirmed the aim of undistorted competition.

The EEC Treaty gave the Commission a strong position in the competition policy. After the Council had adopted the regulations, on proposals from the Commission, to give effect to the prohibition of restrictive practices and abuses of dominant positions stipulated in articles 85 and 86 EEC, it was up to the Commission to enforce them subject only to appeal to the Court of Justice. Since the Commission deals in this with firms, not governments, and since it can impose heavy fines on firms that break the rules, it is at least as well equipped to act as the cartel offices in member states. It can be strongly argued that such powers would be better held by an independent body that did not also possess, as the Commission does, responsibilities in other fields such as regional, social, or other aspects of industrial policy. But the appeal to the Court is some safeguard; and the record indicates that, even if an independent body might be better placed to exercise such powers objectively, it is much better that the Commission should have them than that nobody should have them at all. In the absence of any such body at the Community level, firms perpetrating abuses across the frontiers within the Community market would probably escape the control of member states' competition authorities—even where effective authorities exist, which is not the case in all member states. As it is, the Commission's record in dealing with restrictions such as price fixing, output restrictions, and market sharing has been described as 'extremely impressive'.[4]

While the EEC Treaty gave the Community competence to deal with restrictive practices and abuses of dominant positions, it did not include mergers that would lead to excessive concentrations of industrial power, as the ECSC Treaty had done. Such concentrations in coal and steel had become acutely controversial in the inter-war period, some being accused of facilitating the arms race and the drift to war; so it was natural that the ECSC Treaty should seek to prevent them. In other sectors, at the time when the EEC Treaty was negotiated, they seemed less of an issue. But firms grew in size between then and the 1980s; and the imminence of a completed single market led to a spate of cross-frontier mergers within the Community in the last years of the decade, which made it more evident that the Community should be able to control them in all sectors, not just in coal and steel. The Council had been sitting on a Commission proposal since the early 1970s. But the Court ruled in November 1987 that the prohibition of restrictive practices (article 85 EEC) could apply where a firm acquires control over another with its agreement (cases 142/84 and 156/84), and could thus lead, by direct application of the treaty, to the Commission acquiring a substantial power of merger control without any framework of specific legislation agreed by the Council. Spurred by this, and with the momentum of the single market programme, the Council agreed in 1989, sixteen years after it had started to consider the matter, on a law that gives the Commission the power to approve or block large mergers in the Community.

The Commission is authorized by the EEC Treaty to allow agreements among firms where they contribute 'to improving the production or distribution of goods or to promoting technical or economic progress, while allowing to consumers a fair share of the resulting benefit' (article 85 EEC). Thus the Commission can set conditions that firms are to meet if their agreements are to be allowed; and when a number of sectors were hard hit by recession and over-capacity in the late 1970s, it occurred to Davignon and the then Commissioner for competition, Raymond Vouel, that crisis cartels could improve production, provided that the minimum prices and production quotas were accompanied by reduction of capacity and modernization. In 1978 the case for a crisis cartel in the man-made fibres sector was being considered by the Commission, and Davignon and Vouel proposed that a regulation to legitimize crisis cartels be presented to the Council for its approval. But the Commission as a whole discarded this idea as likely to lead to a proliferation of restrictions; and the man-made fibres agreement was not approved by the Commission on the grounds that minimum prices and production quotas would not benefit the consumer.[5] It is not out of the question, however, that consumers could obtain 'a fair share of the benefit'; and the Commission was later to look more favourably on arrangements of this sort. The conclusion must be that existing powers offer the scope for a variety of forms of industrial policy, should the institutions of the Community wish to exercise them in such ways.

On paper, the Commission is accorded a similar role in the control of state aids as it has in the competition policy. State aids, that is subsidies or any other form of aid given to firms by member states, are prohibited in principle by article 92 EEC. Once the Council, on proposals from the Commission, has adopted regulations to give effect to this prohibition, the Commission has the power to prevent a member state from giving such aids in any given case, or to require the state to alter the terms of the aid. The Treaty allowed that aids were legitimate in regions with low living standards or high unemployment; and this has led to rules that limit the levels of aid for investments in the more prosperous regions. Casting the net wider, it went on to allow aids 'to facilitate the development of certain economic activities or of certain economic areas', where such aid does not distort trade 'to an extent contrary to the common interest'. This widens enormously the scope for interpretation in what then become political rather than juridical decisions. The interpretation that the Commission has often given is that aids to troubled sectors can be allowed provided that they reduce capacity and promote adjustment into competitive activities. This has been the Commission's policy with respect, for example, to textiles, shipbuilding, and man-made fibres—although until 1978 the main justification of aids to shipbuilding was to match the aids given by Europe's principal competitor, Japan.

The Commission's policy has been sensible and logical. The problem has been to enforce it. In the hard times of the 1970s, state aids grew enormously. If the Commission had prohibited them, it would have incurred the wrath of wide sections of the workforce and endangered the standing of the Community institutions among the public. Outright defiance of member governments' policies would have been risky. Since the Commission needs the governments' co-operation in many matters, including the enactment of its legislative proposals, it was not inclined to provoke them. It may also have feared that, if pushed too far, a government could refuse to respect Community law, with unfortunate consequences for the future of the Community. Even if individual Commissioners were not concerned about their chances of nomination again when the Commission came up for renewal after its four years, the Commission had enough reasons to moderate its rigour with respect to state aids in the 1970s. In other words, its control then was not very effective. The balance of power in relation to member governments is far less favourable to the Commission than in relation to the firms with which the competition policy is concerned. But in the 1980s, with the recovery in the Community's economy and in the Commission's standing, its approach became more robust and it has taken some tough decisions in sectors such as the motor industry, for example with respect to such major firms as Renault and Rover. The control of state aids is a powerful policy instrument, if the Commission's position can be strong enough in relation to the member governments. In the main, this is a political question as to how far the Commission gains the capacity to act as a government for the Community or to what extent member governments succeed in preventing it. But it may also depend in part on how far the Commission is confined to the negative power to prohibit member states' aids and how far it can also offer Community aids for adjustment and development. At least in the field of technological research, its ability to do this has been growing.

Research and development

Monnet was concerned that the Community should not just be able to deal with problems from the past, such as curbing the power of steel barons or weathering a deep recession, but should also help to create a modern industry. The ECSC High Authority had the power to promote research and development and to provide finance for it; and when the relaunching of the Community was being planned after the failure of the Defence Community project, he was more interested in the idea of the European Atomic Energy Community than in the common market. A main consideration was political: the Assemblée Nationale would more readily ratify the former than the latter. But he also saw advantage in building Community structures in new fields where national vested interests were less deeply entrenched. While he was wrong both about the common market, which was a great success, and Euratom, which was a failure, the Community has learnt the validity of his basic proposition the hard way: if it had put less resources into the old agricultural sector and more into the development of new technologies, it could have escaped some of the stagnation and conflicts of the 1970s and early 1980s.

Monnet was wrong about Euratom because it encountered a formidable vested interest: de Gaulle's idea of French military power. The Fourth Republic still existed when the Treaties of Rome were signed in March 1957; and had it continued to exist, the fate of Euratom might have been quite different. But de Gaulle came to power, replaced it by his Fifth Republic, and was determined to cut Euratom down to a small size so that it would have no chance of encroaching on the field he wanted France to occupy: atomic research as the basis for his nuclear *force de frappe*. Euratom continued to run four research centres, with some useful results, but without political significance. In addition to de Gaulle's resistance, the nuclear power plant manufacturers presented national obstacles to collective Community developments. The project which no member state could pretend to finance on its own was however the effort to generate power from nuclear fusion, which the Community has mounted at Culham, near Oxford. This has brought European scientists much prestige and raised high hopes that it may help to solve the world's energy problem in the next century. But the chance of an economic return from the project is no closer than that.

Like the nuclear power industry, 'national champion' firms in other sectors together with member governments ensured that the Community's research policy remained on a small scale and with little effect through the 1970s. But the results of national policies in that decade were disappointing. In the crucial field of microelectronics all the European states were decisively outdistanced by Japan with its programme that resulted in the mass production of chips. With the approach of Japan's fifth-generation computer programme, to be launched in 1981, it was becoming clear that the EC member states, acting separately, would not provide the resources or the framework to enable their information technology (IT) sectors to compete; and this would presage a long period of European industrial weakness.

In 1979 Davignon, as Commissioner for industry, produced a document that analysed the situation of European IT industries. He concluded that fragmentation into national markets was a fatal flaw that had to be overcome. He realized that the member governments and their bureaucracies, enclosed in their national frameworks, would be hard to shift. So he started with the leading IT companies, where consciousness of the danger of their situation was acute and resistance to far-reaching cross-border collaboration was less. He invited the heads of twelve IT companies, accounting for three-quarters of Community production, to lunch in Brussels, told them he had a modest budget to promote co-operation, and asked their advice about what should be done to deal with the situation outlined in his document.[6] They agreed that they would like their firms to co-operate in research, starting at the easy end known as pre-competitive because the results are not close enough to development to be regarded as commercial secrets. This was also easier for Davignon, because the Commission had granted a 'block exemption' for such research with respect to the competition policy, and it could not be impeded as was the case with his idea of crisis cartels.

Davignon's initiative, based on the idea of working as the Japanese Ministry of Trade and Industry was perceived as doing, helping industry to do things that it found useful to do co-operatively, rather than imposing government policies on industry in the European tradition, was off to a good start. The heads of companies continued to meet, and agreed that the division of responsibility for standards in their sector among some sixty standards institutes within the member states was an intolerable defect, fragmenting the market and taking five to ten years to produce a common standard for an industry where the products, and hence some key standards, could become obsolete within a year. They established, by 1983, a Standards Promotion and Application Group, which proposed standards that were accepted by the Commission and adopted by the Council. This was not only an essential element in the single market programme. It has also been seen as the catalyst for a process of merging and co-operating that has changed Europe's IT sector from its cul-de-sac of national champions to a multinational structure that is better placed to compete with the Americans and Japanese.[7] Esprit, as the Commission's programme is called (acronym for European Strategic Programme for Research in Information Technology), has moreover been a success appreciated by industry to the extent that member governments could not ignore. They have accordingly accepted that it be expanded and followed by other similar programmes.

The Commission's success provoked reactions among the more nationalistic government machines, in particular in Britain and France. They countered with the Eureka scheme, launched by Mitterrand in 1985, which relied on inter-governmental organization, outside the Community framework, of projects bringing together different countries depending on where the capacity and the interest was. This did not, however, prevent a build-up of the Community's collective effort, with programmes known as RACE (Research in Advanced Communications in Europe), BRITE (Basic Research in Industrial Technologies for Europe), COMETT (Community in Education and Training for Technology), SPRINT (Strategic Programme for Innovation and Technology Transfer), and BAP (Biotechnology Action Programme). After a confrontation between Presidents Delors and Mitterrand at the European Council meeting in Milan in June 1985, a *modus vivendi* for Eureka and the Community programmes was embodied in the Single European Act, which gave research and technological development a general base in the EC Treaties that it had lacked hitherto, and provided for a multiannual framework programme setting out all the Community's activities in this field. Specific Community actions within the framework programme were to be decided by the Council voting by qualified majority, although the programme as a whole requires unanimity. Its importance depends in part on the size of the Community's budget for research; and this, for the period 1987–92, was reduced from the level of ecu 7.7 billion, which was acceptable to the other member governments, first by resistance from Britain and Germany, then by Britain alone. The decision was moreover delayed for nine months until a British general election was out of the way; then the British government finally accepted a budget of ecu 5.7 billion. This demonstrated once again the delays caused by unanimous voting. The Maastricht Treaty, while strengthening the articles on research and development, retained unanimity for voting on the framework programmes, as also with respect to a new Title on 'industry', which may therefore not bring much change in the field of industrial policy.

Social and environmental policies

Many fear they will be hurt by the freeing of trade. The exposure of high-cost production to competition is, of course, one of the principal purposes; but the pain can be mitigated and the process of adjustment may be speeded if those who work in the high-cost activities are helped to move into more competitive jobs. It was in view of this, and in order to secure the support of trade unionists for his project, that Jean Monnet ensured that the Coal and Steel Community would be able to help people undergoing redeployment with housing and training for new skills.

More generally, when a common market is established the weaker economies may fear that they will be crushed within it by the competition from the stronger; and those with higher pay and social standards may fear undermining by those whose level is lower. Thus when the EEC was established, the French feared that their standards of social legislation could be at risk. They had, for example, a textile sector with many female employees who had gained a right to equal pay, which would have to compete in a free market with textiles from other member states where women were paid less than men. France therefore insisted that the EEC Treaty contain the right to equal pay. Italy, on the other hand, still industrially less developed than the other members, sought help for developing to meet their competition; and the Treaty provided for the Social Fund to facilitate the employment and mobility of workers by training and other means, and the Investment Bank to promote economic development. Later, when Britain joined the Community, it secured the creation of the Regional Development Fund for similar purposes; and Spain pressed hard for the policy of 'cohesion' to accompany the establishment of the single market, which was to double the structural funds between 1988 and 1993 for the benefit of the weaker economies of the Community of Twelve.

People in the richer and stronger economies also have their worries about the single market. The Danes and Germans in particular wanted to protect their standards of legislation relating to working conditions and to the environment. They insisted that the Single European Act stipulate that harmonization of member states' measures should 'take as a base' a high level relating to health and safety at work, and to environmental and consumer protection. The further provision that if a harmonized measure should nevertheless threaten a decline in such standards in a member state, that member would be allowed to refrain from applying it, has not so far led to any fragmentation of the market, because harmonization has set high enough standards to avoid it.

The Single Act also required the Commission to encourage a dialogue between management and labour at European level, reflecting a concept of co-operation between the social partners that prevails in a number of member states, and in Germany in particular. This has taken the form, in the Federal Republic, of the system of co-determination, the best-known aspect of which is the legal right of employees to be represented on the boards of companies. This gave rise to a conflict over the status of workers in the European company statute on which the Council had long been trying to reach agreement, in order to facilitate the development of genuinely European firms. The German unions argued that if employers could choose a European statute that did not provide for co-determination, they would tend to do so, abandoning the German form of company and the obligations towards workers that go with it. British employers were among the foremost who resisted the spreading of the co-determination idea. The result was a lengthy stalemate.

A similar conflict arose over the Social Charter, introduced by the Commission in order to provide reassurance for labour that the single market would be accompanied by improvement in the standards of social legislation (in the sense often used on the Continent of legislation concerning employment conditions). The Social Charter contained provisions with which all member governments agreed, such as freedom of movement for workers, health and safety protection, and the right to join—or not to join—a union. But it also set out aims such as maximum working hours, a 'decent wage', and a right for workers to participation, which Mrs Thatcher's government contested. The Social Charter was approved by the European Council in December 1989, with Mrs Thatcher dissenting. But it was a statement of intentions, not a draft law; and the Single Act, which had provided for the Council to vote by qualified majority on only those measures of social policy that concern the health and safety of workers, had left other measures subject to the unanimity procedure and hence to the veto of a dissenting government.

The eleven governments that had approved the Social Charter wanted at Maastricht to incorporate its principles in the Treaty and to provide for qualified majority voting in the Council, together with the co-operation procedure for the European Parliament, for laws on a number of subjects: not only improvement of the working environment to protect workers' health and safety, but also 'working conditions' more generally, 'the information and consultation of workers', 'equality between men and women with regard to labour market opportunities and treatment at work', and 'the integration of persons excluded from the labour market'. The British government refused to go along with this; and the other eleven adopted the unique device of agreeing, in a Protocol to the Maastricht Treaty which excluded Britain from its effect, to use the Community institutions—but without the participation of the British government in the Council—to take their decisions in the field. Whether such an arrangement would be durable remained to be seen.

Britain did, however, accept the Maastricht Treaty's provision for qualified majority voting in the Council and codecision with the European Parliament for measures to bring about freedom of movement for workers (article 49 EEC). The Single Act had also provided for the free movement of 'persons' in general; and the Maastricht Treaty confirmed this, giving every citizen 'the right to move and reside freely within the territory of the member states', although this was to be achieved by unanimous vote in the Council, after obtaining the assent of the European Parliament. Eight member states—France, Germany, Italy, Portugal, Spain, and the Benelux countries—had already agreed to go farther, with the 'Schengen' agreement, under which they are virtually to abolish controls at their mutual frontiers by 1993, and which is seen as the forerunner for similar action by the Community as a whole. Along with this effort to remove frontier controls goes an endeavour to strengthen the common approach of all member states to tackling crime, terrorists, and drug traffic, and to agree on norms for immigration, including the right of asylum. The section of the Maastricht Treaty providing for 'co-operation in the spheres of justice and home affairs' establishes an intergovernmental framework for this.

Environmental protection is also a field where the Single Act not only guarded against the undermining of standards as a result of the single market, but also gave the Community a wider competence to 'preserve, protect and improve the quality of the environment'. Pollution carried by air or water does not recognize frontiers, so member states have a common interest in its mutual control. As ecological deterioration has become aggravated and public concern correspondingly sharpened, this aspect of Community activity has become increasingly important. Over 200 Directives and Regulations have been adopted relating to most fields of environmental management, including air and water pollution, waste disposal, dangerous chemicals, noise, and wild life. One of the most important was the acid rain Directive of 1988, which committed member states to cut their emissions of sulphur dioxide and nitrogen oxides by stages over fifteen years, amounting to a reduction of 58 per cent for the Community over the period. Another was the reduction of exhaust emissions from small cars. Community quality standards for drinking and bathing water are having a major impact in member states, including particularly Britain. There are noise limits for products such as aircraft, motor vehicles, construction plants, and lawnmowers. In 1985 a Directive required impact assessments to be made of projects likely to affect the environment, before member states' authorities allow development to proceed. A European Environmental Agency is being established to collect data and monitor the state of the environment. The Community is a party to many international environmental conventions. It negotiates on chlorofluorocarbons (CFCs) on behalf of the member states, and it has been argued that it was the EC's approach which, in 1986, broke the international negotiating deadlock on depletion of the ozone in the stratosphere.[8]

The Maastricht Treaty builds on the Single Act by introducing more decisive and democratic procedures for adopting environmental legislation. While measures that are primarily fiscal, that concern land use or significantly affect the pattern of a member state's energy supply remain subject, as under the

Single Act, to unanimity in the Council, qualified majority voting is to apply to all other environmental measures. Apart from this, objectives for action programmes are to be enacted by codecision with the European Parliament and all other legislation by the co-operation procedure.

Taken together, the Community's involvement in social policies in a sense wider than that of employment policy has led towards a concept of a 'people's Europe'; and this was a forerunner of the idea of a European citizenship, conferring rights and imposing duties, which was embodied in the Maastricht Treaty.

7 Monetary System and Monetary Union

Federal governments have three main fields of economic competence: trade, both external and domestic; budget, both tax and expenditure; and currency. With respect to trade, the European Community already has as much competence as a federation. It has a half-developed federal budget; and it has a monetary system which laid the basis for the commitment in the Maastricht Treaty to create a monetary union of federal type. Federalists have, since the 1950s, repeatedly promoted steps towards a common currency and monetary union for the Community; and such efforts have been supported by people with more specific economic or political motives. Against these efforts stood hard facts of economic divergence among the member states and stubborn defence of national sovereignty.

The EEC Treaty itself did not venture far into the fields of monetary or macroeconomic policy. 'Conjunctural policies' and exchange rates were to be seen as 'matters of common concern' (articles 103, 107). Economic policies were to be co-ordinated (articles 105, 145). But the Community was given no instruments with which it could ensure that this was done; and the procedures stipulated for taking decisions in these matters were weak. The Council was to vote on them by unanimous agreement; and experience was to show, as could be expected, that in these questions which lie at the centre of member states' politics, the governments could usually agree only on letting each one go its own way. As an experienced participant has put it: 'In practice, coordination never went much beyond polite ritualistic consultation.'[1] The Treaty also provided for a Monetary Committee, comprising two representatives from each member state (so that there could be one from the finance ministry and one from the central bank) and two from the Commission. The Monetary Committee was to give advice to the Council and the Commission; and this advice has served a useful purpose when the governments have been predisposed to act on it.

Why was the EEC Treaty, which was so decisive about tariffs and trade policy, so weak about currency and monetary policy? France, whose accord was the key to the Treaty's success, was disturbed enough by the prospect of opening its long-protected market to competition from German industry, without having to face the loss of monetary sovereignty as well; and the rejection of the European Defence Community by the Assemblée Nationale was a warning against seeking too great a sacrifice of sovereignty for a second time. In the Federal Republic, Chancellor Adenauer had overridden his Economics Minister, Erhard, who preferred wider international free trade to a European customs union. Erhard enjoyed much support among German finance and business people, and Adenauer could have seen no advantage in trying to face him down on monetary integration without backing from France. In the mid-1950s, moreover, when the EEC Treaty was conceived and signed, international monetary needs were well served by the Bretton Woods system with the dollar at its centre. There was no pressing practical motive for setting up a new monetary system in the Community.

Nevertheless, federalists thought that monetary union would eventually be required, and soon began to press for steps towards it.

Federalists versus de Gaulle

Directly after the EEC Treaty was signed in March 1957, Jean Monnet asked Professor Robert Triffin and Pierre Uri to design an outline for a European monetary system. Uri was one of Monnet's closest collaborators and the main author of the Spaak report on which the Treaty had been based. The Spaak report had suggested that monetary unification would perhaps be required.[2] Triffin was an authority on international monetary questions who had been the architect of the European Payments Union, set up at the time of Marshall aid to restore a system of multilateral payments in post-war Europe. Triffin was to recall that when he then met Monnet, in 1948, Monnet judged the payments union proposal too modest in comparison with the monetary union that he believed would be needed. But Triffin shared the aim of monetary union as an essential element in a political union,[3] and was to become Monnet's constant adviser on monetary matters. Triffin's proposals during the first phase of the EEC's development included a single European currency and a European monetary authority as the last step in founding a monetary union for the Community, with a European reserve fund as one of the first steps.[4]

Monnet's Action Committee for the United States of Europe, bringing together the leaders of all the main democratic parties and trade unions of the six EC member states, adopted Triffin's proposal for the reserve fund and promoted it in the Committee's declarations of November 1959 and July 1961.[5] The Committee criticized the EEC Treaty for failing, with its 'very general provisions', to meet the need for the 'common financial policy' which would be a necessary complement to the common market. It proposed a European reserve fund as the first step towards a European currency and common monetary policy, which would enable the Community to exert its due influence in the international monetary system, as the common commercial policy would in the world trading system. The Committee also pointed out that Britain, which in 1961 first sought membership of the Community, would, if its proposals were adopted, be joining an 'economic and political union'. Monnet, in seeing the prospect of British membership as an occasion to strengthen the Community, was the first to enunciate the policy of 'deepening' at the same time as 'widening', which was subsequently to become embedded in Community thinking about enlargement. The fear that the Community might become weakened through the greater number and diversity of its members was to be met by proposals to strengthen its powers and institutions.

Strengthening the Community in view of prospective British membership was also one of the motives for the Commission's first major proposals for monetary integration, put forward in 1962 in the *Action Programme for the Second Stage*. Similarities between these and Monnet's proposals were not surprising since the Commissioner responsible, Robert Marjolin, was another of Monnet's close collaborators—and also one who 'leant towards' the idea of European federation, even though he felt in the 1960s that the time was not ripe for it.[6] The aim of the *Action Programme*, in addition to offering a framework for prospective British membership, was to set down a path for the Community's development during the second stage of the transitional period on which it was just entering, and through the third stage to the end of that period in 1970. The programme envisaged fixed exchange rates among the member states and a European reserve currency by that date. Meanwhile, some more modest steps should be taken: consultation about monetary policy, mutual assistance to meet balance-of-payments problems, further liberalization of capital movements beyond some measures already decided; and the establishment of committees to facilitate this co-operation, including the Committee of Governors of Central Banks, which was eventually to grow in importance and to play a key role in the monetary union project nearly three decades later.

The motive of meeting the challenge of future British membership was mainly political: an aspect of a more general federalist desire to develop the Community and to build on its early success by filling out gaps in the EEC Treaty such as the weakness of its provisions for monetary co-ordination. There were also economic motives. The first strains in the Bretton Woods system had emerged in the late 1950s, with US payments deficits leading to a weak dollar and a crisis in the gold market in 1960. On top of worries about the future of the international monetary system, consequent revaluations of the Deutschmark and the Dutch guilder in 1961 caused concern for the stability of exchange rates within the Community. Triffin had pointed out that, with growing trade integration, there would be greater need for the co-ordination of economic and monetary policies in order to maintain equilibrium among the member states; and thinking along such lines had led to the new idea of the optimal currency area, suggesting that for highly interdependent economies the benefits of monetary union would be greater than the costs. The benefits would include the removal of foreign exchange transaction costs, the reduction of reserve requirements, the more efficient use of money and allocation of savings to the most profitable uses, and the business confidence resulting from the elimination of the exchange risk; and these would justify sacrificing the right of each state to conduct a macroeconomic policy tailored to its specific needs. Trends such as inflation or deflation would, moreover, spill over from one of the interdependent group of economies to the others, so that joint control over such trends should be in the general interest.[7] While the theorists of optimal currency area were unable to say whether the Community was in fact such an area, their line of thinking added an economic logic to the more practical economic motives for monetary integration, themselves reinforcing the substantial political motives.

An opposite political motive was to stand in the way of steps towards monetary union in the 1960s. This was de Gaulle's insistence on national sovereignty and its effect on the conduct of Community business. The first outstanding example was his veto that unilaterally cut short the negotiations for British entry into the Community in January 1963. The relations between France and the other member states were upset to the point where much in the *Action Programme* had to be shelved. In the Federal Republic, moreover, Erhard replaced Adenauer as Chancellor in that year. He was oriented towards the international economic and monetary system and to the United States rather than towards France and the European Community; and unlike Adenauer, he had no rapport whatsoever with de Gaulle. If monetary integration required French leadership and Franco-German understanding, in these circumstances there was little chance of either.

Monetary difficulties pressed on the Community again in 1963 and the following year, with balance-of-payments crises in Italy. Interest in monetary integration was renewed. The Committee of Central Bank Governors was established in

1964; and in 1965 the Commission adopted fixed exchange rates as an objective.[8] In this it had the discreet support of the Monetary Committee and, more significantly, of the Banque de France and of de Gaulle's finance minister, Valéry Giscard d'Estaing.

This did not reflect any change of heart on the part of de Gaulle himself. His opposition to federal elements in the Community remained intransigent. Anticipating the passage from unanimous to majority voting in the Council for many important decisions when the Community moved in 1966 to stage three of the transitional period, he withdrew his ministers from the Council in July 1965 in order to squash the federalist-inspired proposal for financing the Community budget; and at the same time as he returned them early in 1966 on the understanding that France would not be bound by majority votes on matters that the French government regarded as important, he replaced Giscard as finance minister by Michel Debré, a militant opponent of all things federal, who was later to lead the opposition in France to the Community's first major monetary union project. Monetary union was not destined to progress while de Gaulle was President of France. The federalists would have to sit it out until his departure.

The first sign that this was impending came with the student rebellion of May 1968, followed by workers' militancy that led to wage rises of around 20 per cent. Violent speculation against the franc ensued; and it was with a weakened French economy and money that de Gaulle resigned in April 1969.

Giscard was again finance minister in the new French government. Not long before, he had reiterated his proposal for a common currency, to cure the Community of the instability that resulted from the weakness of the franc, as well as the dollar, and the consequent strength of the mark.[9] By August 1969, the franc was devalued and the mark was allowed to float upwards. Not only did this offend those who valued currency stability, and there were many of them in France. It also led to the imposition of the border taxes, called monetary compensatory amounts, on trade in agricultural products within the Community. Since farm prices were fixed in common in European units of account, they would rise in France when the franc was devalued and would be cut in Germany as the mark appreciated. But the Germans insisted that their farmers should not be paid less in terms of marks; and the French wanted to avoid the inflationary impulse of higher food prices in francs, when they were struggling to get the inflation that followed the events of 1968 under control. So the monetary compensatory amounts were introduced. Although they seemed necessary for France's anti-inflationary policy, this new barrier within the agricultural common market, which had been seen as a principal French interest in the Community, was a heavy blow for the French: another motive for French support for monetary union, which would render any such border taxes unnecessary in the future. On top of this, the prospect of a new British effort to join the Community in the wake of de Gaulle's departure renewed French thoughts about deepening the Community in order to prevent damage through dilution. In short, there were strong reasons to turn French policy round from blocking monetary integration to promoting it.

Emu blocked by economic and political divergence

In 1969 Georges Pompidou became President of France and Willy Brandt Chancellor of the Federal Republic. Both were disposed to relaunch the development of the Community after it had been frozen by de Gaulle. The day after Brandt became Chancellor, Monnet wrote to him suggesting that the time was ripe to transform the Community into a monetary and political union and to enlarge it to include Britain.[10] Brandt was a long-standing supporter of federal ideas. But he also had a more specific motive for wanting to strengthen the Community. He was initiating his Ostpolitik in order to improve relations with the Federal Republic's neighbours to the East and with East Germany in particular, and he knew that this could worry those, particularly in France, who recalled the power games that Germany had played between East and West before World War II. He therefore wanted to complement his Ostpolitik with a Westpolitik that would strengthen the Federal Republic's relationship with the West, and with France and the Community in particular. Deepening and widening the Community as Monnet proposed would serve this purpose perfectly. Closer ties between France and Germany were also in the Gaullist tradition to which Pompidou adhered; and he was much less averse than de Gaulle to strengthening these ties in the context of the Community.

Pompidou, Brandt, and the other heads of government of the member states met at The Hague in December 1969. Brandt's major proposals were monetary union and enlargement. While enlargement to include Britain was less welcome to France so soon after de Gaulle, Pompidou accepted it provided that it was combined with deepening in the form of monetary union, and completion of some unfinished business of interest to France in the form of a regulation for the joint financing of the common agricultural policy. For monetary union he had the French motives, economic and political, mentioned above; and for finance minister he had Giscard, who could be relied upon to promote the project. Italy and the Benelux countries were also in favour. So the aim of monetary union was adopted by the summit meeting at The Hague.

Meeting soon after, in February 1970, the Council agreed without much difficulty that there should be a common currency at the final stage of monetary integration. But there was sharp division about the steps towards it. The French wanted to move to the permanent fixing of exchange rates without much stress on co-ordinating economic policies beforehand. Once exchange rates were locked in this way, they argued, economic policies of member states would have to be adjusted so as to bring the relationship between their economies into equilibrium. The Germans, on the contrary, saw such definitive monetary integration as the end of a process in which the economies would be brought into equilibrium by the harmonization of economic policies; otherwise the locking of exchange rates would put the relationship between economies under too much strain. With their aversion to inflation, consequent on their two post-war hyper-inflations in this century, they feared in particular that a premature monetary link with more inflationary economies would undermine their ability to prevent it. In order to provide a strong enough framework for an effective monetary union, moreover, Dr

Schiller, the German finance minister, affirmed that the EEC Treaty would have to be amended to provide for majority voting on these matters in the Council and, for the sake of democracy, a transfer of powers to the European Parliament.[11] Such federal ideas about institutions had been anathema to de Gaulle; and his successors were not yet ready to accept them. Unable to agree among themselves, the ministers set up a working group to analyse the different suggestions and 'identify the basic issues for a realization by stages of economic and monetary union', as the project had come to be called in deference to the German insistence on co-ordination of economic policies to accompany the monetary integration.

The group was chaired by Pierre Werner, Prime Minister of Luxembourg, and contained the chairmen of the relevant Community committees, including Bernard Clappier, then Chairman of the Monetary Committee, formerly Robert Schuman's *directeur de cabinet* when Monnet persuaded Schuman to launch the proposal for the European Coal and Steel Community, and since then another of Monnet's close associates. The Werner report, as the document presented by the group to the Council in October 1970 was called, defined economic and monetary union as comprising irrevocable convertibility of the member states' currencies, free movement of capital, and the permanent locking of exchange rates or, which would amount to the same thing, the replacement of the member states' currencies by a single currency. While this was to be achieved no later than 1980, the report was prudent on the subject of institutions, no doubt with the intention of avoiding trouble with the Gaullists. It went no farther than to envisage a 'Community system for the central banks' and a 'centre of decision for economic policy', on the grounds that a 'deeper study of institutional questions' was not in the group's terms of reference. Presumably Clappier, and Giscard with whom he must have been closely in touch, hoped this was vague enough to placate the Gaullists. But Debré was implacable. By the time the Council met to consider the report in November 1970, he had fomented enough opposition in France to the prospective loss of national sovereignty to prevent Giscard from accepting the report's conclusions. The French policy at the Council meeting was to agree to the modest steps assigned to the first stage of the Werner plan and to leave the questions of institutions, powers, and treaty revision until later —a policy closely replicated by the reluctant British when the Delors report on economic and monetary union was presented to the European Council in 1989. France's five partners resisted this line. The Germans and the Dutch wanted to start with steps towards economic policy co-ordination rather than with the narrowing of the margins of exchange rate fluctuation which was the central element of Werner's stage one; and none of the five wanted to limit the agreement to that small step, postponing *sine die* decisions on the larger monetary and institutional reforms. But French participation remained essential and French refusal an insuperable obstacle. In March 1971 the Council agreed in principle on the establishment of economic and monetary union by stages; but stage one was to be tried on an experimental basis and there was no commitment to the rest.

The experiment was not a success. The attempt to keep the member states' exchange rates closer together coincided with aggravated turbulence in the international monetary system which again put upward pressure on the mark. By May, the Germans wanted to float again and they suggested that the others float with them—an idea not unlike that which later underlay the Exchange Rate Mechanism of the European Monetary System. But France and Italy refused, both because they wanted to safeguard their exports by keeping their exchange rates down and because of their policy preference for exchange controls rather than floating to deal with turbulence. So the German mark floated without them. By August the dollar, weak and under constant pressure, also floated and the Bretton Woods system, based on a stable dollar at its centre, came to an end.

The Community had a second try in 1972. The Council agreed in March that member states' currencies would stay within a band of 2.25 per cent, or 1.125 per cent on either side of their dollar parity, compared with a band of 4.5 per cent to which other members of the IMF adhered. This was called the 'Snake in the Tunnel', depicting a narrower band moving up and down within a wider one. But speculative pressure was again too strong. The pound, which had joined the Snake in anticipation of British entry into the Community, left it again within a few weeks; and the French franc was floated by January 1974. The Snake became reduced to the currencies of the Federal Republic and half a dozen small neighbours, not all of them members of the Community. France made a third attempt to join in 1975, but this again lasted only a few months.

The ambitious goal of economic and monetary union had been placed in question by politics: divergences of economic philosophy and of attitude towards a federal reform of the Community institutions. The Snake had been seen as a first step towards it; and that was thwarted by the economics of the 1970s. The turbulence of the early 1970s, culminating in the oil shock of 1973–4 when the price of oil more than quadrupled, led to highly divergent performances by the different member states. Germany soon got its inflation under control. At the other extreme Italy, together with Britain, by now a member, combined high inflation with massive payments deficits. Not only was monetary integration frustrated, but the question was posed whether divergence would impede further integration of any sort within the Community.

One result was a new wave of thinking about optimal currency areas. One view, taken by some neo-classical economists, was that divergent performance was due essentially to differing macroeconomic policies; the convergence required for economic and monetary union was, therefore, a matter of political choice, and an optimal currency area would be one in which the governments were ready to decide on policies that would bring stability. Another view was that the divergence was caused by differing economic structures, particularly in the labour markets. Factors such as the strength and behaviour of trade unions built different propensities to inflation into the economies; and so long as this divergence remained significant, monetary integration could not take the form of a permanent locking of exchange rates or common currency.[12]

This thinking led to a proposal to move towards monetary union by developing a parallel currency,[13] which would be launched alongside the member states' currencies both for official use, as a reserve and means of settlement, and for use in the private markets for money and capital. As its importance grew the economies would adapt to it until it could eventually replace the existing currencies as a single Community currency. The idea was taken up by the Commission in 1975;[14] and when the European Monetary System was established in 1979, the European Currency Unit (ecu) began to perform some of these functions. Its further development was among the measures proposed in 1990 for the transitional period in establishing the economic and monetary union; and the Maastricht Treaty assigned this task to the transitional European Monetary Institute.[15] The focus of the next phase of monetary integration which started in the late 1970s with the European Monetary System was, however, not the parallel currency but an exchange rate mechanism.

Jenkins, Schmidt, Giscard, and the EMS

Roy Jenkins, a former British Cabinet minister, became President of the Commission in 1977, when the Community was in a stagnant state and there was much pessimism about its future. He perceived a need to 'break out of the citadel or wither within it', and in order to break out he sought a theme around which he 'could help to move Europe forward'.[16] Inspired by Jean Monnet's example,[17] he sought it among the problems that pressed on the governments of the day, which included unemployment, inflation, and divergence; and his solution was to introduce a bold proposal on to the agenda, in the form of economic and monetary union (Emu).

Jenkins launched the idea publicly in his Jean Monnet Lecture in October 1977, enumerating the expected economic benefits and envisaging that it would 'take Europe over a political threshold'.[18] Reactions from the experts, the media, and the politicians were almost uniformly sceptical. A significant exception was the Belgian government, currently taking its turn in the presidency of the Council. The Belgians, instigated by Jenkins, got the European Council in December

1977 to reaffirm its commitment to the objective of Emu and to approve the idea of making progress in that direction. These would have been empty words without the genuine commitment of major member states, and of the Federal Republic, as the Community's leading monetary power, in particular. But Helmut Schmidt, the German Chancellor, who had merely expressed a 'mildly benevolent scepticism' in December, told Jenkins in February that he wanted a major step towards monetary union. He had in mind a European monetary bloc based on a common reserve pool.[19]

Schmidt's conversion was crucial to the establishment of the European Monetary System (EMS), and hence to the drive towards Emu a decade later. The impact of the idea of Emu on his thinking should not be neglected. He had just written the introduction to the German edition of Monnet's *Memoirs*, in which he mentioned the Action Committee's early declarations in favour of it; and he later acknowledged the influence of Jenkins on his thinking about Emu.[20] But the idea would have remained just that without the political and economic grounds in which it could germinate. Politically, Schmidt was much concerned about what he saw as the failure of American leadership under President Carter, whom he regarded as incompetent. This had painful economic consequences for the Federal Republic. Large American payments deficits through 1977 weakened the dollar, which fell by one-tenth between October 1977 and February 1978, and again by another tenth by the autumn of that year. As usual, the weak dollar was reflected in a strong mark, which was bad for German exports; and, to add insult to injury, the US Administration pressed the Germans hard to reflate, so that the German economy would act as a 'locomotive', drawing world demand upwards behind it and thus helping to correct the US payments deficit. The Germans were, as ever, sensitive to the danger of inflation; and Schmidt saw the Americans' pressure as an attempt to shift the responsibility for solving their problem on to the Germans, whose supposed fault was to manage their economy in a prudent manner. In response to this pressure, Schmidt told the Bundestag in January 1978 that Germany could accept the role of locomotive only if it was shared with others. These others would be Europeans and in particular France, whose President, Giscard d'Estaing, Schmidt was wont to call 'my friend', or even 'my only friend'.[21]

Schmidt and Giscard had worked closely together since Schmidt became finance minister in 1972 and both moved from that position to become Chancellor and President respectively in 1974. The political fortunes of both were prospering in 1978, with Giscard in particular being liberated from dependence on Gaullist support following elections in March of that year. When Schmidt then sought Giscard's backing for his proposals for monetary integration it was, given Giscard's long-standing commitment to the idea, readily forthcoming. In April, in the European Council in Copenhagen, they together promoted a project for a reserve pool in a European Monetary Fund, and for greater use of the ecu's forerunner, the European Unit of Account.

The British Prime Minister, James Callaghan, was almost alone in expressing serious reservations about the idea, and work on designing the EMS went ahead. It became clear that consensus would focus on exchange rate stabilization rather than a reserve pool; and the Exchange Rate Mechanism (ERM) was at the centre of the EMS when its structure was agreed by the European Council in Brussels in December 1978.

EMS and Exchange Rate Mechanism

Behind the detail of the ERM was a radical new departure: parities could be changed only by 'mutual agreement' of the states participating in the ERM together with the Commission. Although a member state could pull out of the ERM if it saw fit, so long as it continued to participate this would be an unprecedented transfer of monetary autonomy. Control over the exchange rate had been at the core of monetary sovereignty, and the participants were to take a big step towards sharing it.

The day-to-day management of exchange rates was to be bounded by a 'grid' in which margins of fluctuation were not to exceed plus or minus 2.25 per cent of the central rates, defined in relation to the ecu, which was itself a weighted average of the EMS currencies. From this starting-point, a band was to be calculated for each pair of participating currencies, and if the limits of the band were reached, the authorities responsible for each of the currencies in question were to intervene in the market in order to keep the difference between them within the band. But the governments of states with the weaker currencies, such as France, Italy, and the UK, were averse to this grid system, on the grounds that it favoured the strong currencies, in particular the mark. Intervention on behalf of weak and strong currencies was, they argued, asymmetrical. Intervention by the weaker countries, using foreign currencies to buy their own when it reached the bottom of a band, would be limited by their foreign exchange reserves, and before these were reduced too far they would have to raise interest rates, thus deflating their economies; whereas the stronger countries could continue selling their own currencies and piling up their reserves indefinitely, without being obliged to reciprocate by reducing their interest rates.

The governments with weaker currencies therefore sought alleviation in various forms. One such was the divergence indicator, which was intended to trigger changes in policy by both partners when divergence between a pair of currencies reached three-quarters of the permitted band; those with weaker currencies hoped that this would shift more of the burden of policy adjustment on to the stronger countries, and on to Germany in particular. A second device was the wider band of fluctuation, of plus or minus 6 per cent, secured by Italy, and subsequently, when they entered the ERM, by Spain then Britain, although the Italians applied the normal limits of 2.25 per cent in 1990. Britain, for its part, chose to remain outside the ERM, with the proviso that it could 'enter at a later date'—in the event over a decade later. Credits were also to be available for countries that had to intervene heavily to support their currencies; and loans with interest rate subsidies were to be provided for Italy and Ireland, the two member states which at that time claimed a need for development assistance.

Although the EMS had been strongly promoted by Giscard and Schmidt, and did enter into force in March 1979, it encountered resistance in the most powerful member states. In France the Gaullists, still concerned about sovereignty, and the farmers caused the starting of the system to be delayed for three months, during which the French government sought concessions from its partners regarding the monetary compensatory amounts. But no such concessions being forthcoming, the French demand was dropped.

In Germany, Schmidt faced powerful opposition. The Christian Democrats were hostile. So was the financial sector in general; and Karl Otto Pöhl, Schmidt's own nominee as Vice-President of the Bundesbank, expressed his 'fundamental reservations' about possible inflationary implications. The Bundesbank fought, successfully, to reduce Schmidt's reserve fund idea to a minimalist European Monetary Co-operation Fund, with three-monthly swaps of ecus against one-fifth of the member states' gold and dollar reserves, instead of definitive transfers which could eventually be used for intervention. The European Council did agree to establish the European Monetary Fund by 1981, with full use of the ecu as a reserve asset and as a means of settlement; but the second oil shock came in 1979, and the resulting instability in the international monetary system intervened to deter the governments from carrying out what they had agreed. But apart from this, Schmidt did overcome his opponents in Germany, partly by spending an estimated 200 hours in 1978 persuading people that the EMS was desirable, and partly by keeping his cards very close to his chest until the project was well and truly launched. This he did by ensuring that its development through the spring of 1978 was entrusted to only three people: Dr Schulmann, the economic adviser to his own office; Bernard Clappier, by now Governor of the Banque de France; and Kenneth Couzens, Second Permanent Secretary at the UK Treasury, who, given the cool British attitude to the project, did not participate fully. By the time that what became a Franco-German project was launched, its German opponents, and the Bundesbank in particular, could secure modifications to it but not prevent it.

One of the British arguments against the EMS at that time was the fear that it would be deflationary and exacerbate the de-industrialization which was already causing concern. This could be compared with the worries expressed in France and

Italy, except that when the pound became stronger the British turned the argument on its head and resisted entry into the ERM on the grounds that it would be inflationary. A second argument was that the EMS could upset the wider international monetary system and annoy the Americans. Such also was Callaghan's orientation when he sided with the Americans and against Schmidt about the locomotive role for Germany, rather than working with Schmidt to seek a European response to the Americans' concerns. A third argument, frequently used in Britain regarding initiatives to develop the Community, was that the Continentals would talk about it but not do it. The flavour of this attitude was caught by the unguarded remarks of Couzens to the press after the meeting of the European Council in Bremen at which the proposal prepared by Clappier and Schulmann had been generally approved: 'the Treasury remains sceptical to the point of contempt', he was reported to say, 'of most of the detailed content of the Franco-German scheme', which showed 'the danger of allowing enthusiastic amateurs to dream up schemes for monetary reform'.[22]

Callaghan nevertheless then grasped the political significance of what was happening, and British officials worked hard on the technical preparations for the EMS, though without commitment about eventual participation. Such commitment would have been politically difficult for Callaghan, who was faced with a House of Commons resolution signed by 120 Labour MPs, rejecting 'any attempt by the EEC, its institutions or its member states to assume control of domestic policies through a new monetary system for the Community': an attitude which was later to underlie some of the explanations Mrs Thatcher was to give for keeping the pound out of the ERM through the 1980s.[23] The hostility of those Labour MPs was strongly enough reflected in the Cabinet and the Labour Party to put full membership of the EMS out of court for Callaghan. The most he could achieve was participation in the EMS but not in its key element, the ERM. When the project ran into difficulties at the European Council in Brussels in December 1978, where it was accepted but sidetracked by the issue of the monetary compensatory amounts, Jenkins found British officials 'almost gloating that things had fallen apart'.[24]

Once again, they underestimated the forces that have carried the Community forward. The EMS was established three months later, with results that helped to transform the prospects for the future of the Community.

The EMS in the 1980s

The Exchange Rate Mechanism of the EMS helped to stabilize the participants' exchange rates in the 1980s. Their variability in the period 1979–85 was half what it had been in 1975–9, and it halved again in 1986–9, both for the nominal rates on which exchange dealings are based and for the real rates that discount the effects of differing rates of inflation. Both exchange rates and interest rates became less volatile, partly because policies became more credible to those dealing in the markets, but partly also because France and Italy damped down potential volatility by retaining exchange controls. Misalignments, that is more durable deviations from exchange rates likely to ensure longer-term equilibrium, also appear to have been reduced.[25] The need for realignments, or changes of parities within the ERM, consequently declined. There were seven realignments between 1979 and 1983, only four from 1983 to 1989.

This new stability would not have been achieved without a convergence of macroeconomic policies. The EMS was launched at a time of growing consensus in western countries that the priority for monetary policy should be to prevent inflation. The participants in the ERM were thus aligning their policies on those of their partner with the strongest economy and currency, the Federal Republic. France was an exception for a couple of years after the arrival of a Socialist government under President Mitterrand. But its expansionary policy led to payments deficits of a size that demanded a response. Two types of policy were proposed. One was to take a step back from European integration by restricting imports and floating the franc out of the ERM. The other, advocated by Jacques Delors, who was then the French finance minister, was to apply a restrictive macroeconomic policy and thus remain within the ERM. President Mitterrand, valuing the relationship with the

EC and with the Federal Republic in particular, was persuaded that the franc should stay in the ERM; and French policy too converged on that of the Federal Republic.

The convergence of policy was accompanied by a growing habit of co-operation among the monetary authorities of the participating countries. The central banks worked closely together with respect to their interventions in currency markets in order to keep the exchange rates within the bands. The parities from which the bands were defined were the responsibility of the finance ministers, not the banks; and by 1989 it could be said that parity changes, decided by the finance ministers at weekend meetings in time for the markets to open again on Monday morning, had become 'truly multilateral decisions'.[26] Thus the participants were sharing sovereignty in practice over one of the most fundamental decisions of economic policy.

This did not apply to Britain, which, like Greece and then Portugal, remained outside the ERM throughout the 1980s. Mrs Thatcher had said at an early stage that the time was not right for the pound to enter; and the time continued, in her view, not to be right throughout the decade, and it was not until October 1990 that Britain finally participated. The private markets in the City of London were not so hesitant about another product of the EMS, the use of the ecu for private transactions. London was among the leaders in developing such use, which made the ecu one of the four or five most used currencies in certain sectors of the international markets, such as bonds and inter-bank transactions. The UK Treasury had also helped to build up the ecu market by issuing ecu 2.8 billion of Treasury bills by early 1990, thus contributing a significant share of the ecu 16 billion of bills and bonds issued by the British, French, and Italian public authorities, together with a small bond issue by the Federal Republic's state development bank.

But it was the success of the ERM in stabilizing exchange rates and converging policies that offered a basis for the renewed efforts which began in the late 1980s to move by stages to a single currency or to the permanent locking of exchange rates. The other main elements of economic and monetary union, freedom of movement for capital and a single market for financial services, had by then already been set in train by the Single European Act.

The Single European Act and a single financial market

The Single European Act did something for the exchange rate element in monetary integration. It brought the EMS, which had been set up alongside and not as a part of the Community, within the scope of the treaties, thus consolidating its juridical status; and it made economic and monetary union a formal treaty objective. But its main contribution to Emu was in the freeing of capital movements and the integration of the markets for financial services.

The Act, as we saw in Chapter 4, embodied a commitment to complete the single market by the end of 1992, and made it feasible to enact the necessary laws by stipulating majority voting in the Council for most of the measures required. The single market programme also eased the process of legislation by reducing the harmonization of laws and regulations to the minimum needed for health, safety, and consumer protection, and relying beyond that on the mutual recognition by member states of each other's standards and regulations. In the field of financial services the equivalent of mutual recognition is 'home country control', whereby a firm providing such services anywhere in the Community will be subject to the laws of the member state in which it is registered. Community legislation is introduced only to the extent that such laws do not meet the minimum standards deemed essential by the Community institutions.

The legislation necessary to complete the single market for financial services was nevertheless complex and apt to be resisted by member states with their own entrenched regulations and institutions. Many were sceptical that it would be possible to obtain the two-thirds weighted majority in the Council required to enact the measures. But enough had been achieved by 1991 to make it likely that the legislative programme would be completed by the end of 1992. A significant example was the second banking Directive, passed in

1989, in order to allow credit institutions legally established in one member state to establish branches or offer services directly throughout the Community: the 'European passport' for banks, which will enable them to provide an integrated Community-wide service. Progress had likewise been made with legislation for insurance and securities services.

The financial sector could not, however, be seen as integrated if exchange controls were to prevent the transfer of money from one member state to another. The EEC Treaty had established the aim of abolishing obstacles to free movement of capital (article 3); but the specific provision for this had referred only to the movement of capital 'to the extent necessary to ensure the proper functioning of the common market' (article 67). The Court of Justice had later ruled that this provision was not 'directly applicable': that is to say, the Court itself could not decide whether the exchange control regulation in question was necessary for the common market; the Council would first have to enact a measure defining the principles on which such necessity should be judged.[27] This the Council had failed to do; and many exchange controls remained in place, particularly in France and Italy, where they had been seen as a means of damping down pressures for devaluing the exchange rates. The Single European Act brought the free movement of capital into the single market programme to be completed by 1992 (article 13 SEA).

Exchange controls had been regarded as key instruments of macroeconomic policy in France and Italy, as well as in southern member states that had joined the Community in the 1980s, so their removal was widely expected to be one of the hardest tasks confronting the single market programme. But Jacques Delors, by now President of the Commission, did not delay in proposing, once the member governments had signed the Single European Act, that the complete liberalization of capital movements should be accelerated. He doubtless sensed that the climate of opinion among French policy-makers was ripe for this, and that the integration of capital markets could be a catalyst for a revival of the economic and monetary union project. Directives enacted in 1986 and 1988, together with those agreed in 1960 and 1962 when the Commission made its first attempts to promote monetary integration, did indeed provide for full freedom of capital movements by July 1990, with a delay allowed to the Community's weaker, peripheral economies.

By the time Delors took the initiative over exchange controls, governments that had previously insisted on the need to maintain them were ready to respond, partly because the balance-of-payments deficits that had worried them in the early 1980s were much reduced and because the new stability within the Exchange Rate Mechanism had made them more relaxed about the risks to their exchange rates. Radical innovations in the financial markets had moreover diminished the effectiveness of such administrative controls and raised the cost of attempting to enforce them; and the more dynamic operators in those markets were eager to be part of the global village which the international financial community was rapidly becoming, and which threatened to leave them on the sidelines if they were hampered by restrictions. Governments gave weight to their interests because a dynamic financial sector was seen as an essential part of a modern economy, owing both to its growing size and to the importance of the services that it provides to the rest of the economy. The Cecchini report estimated the direct savings in the financial sector from the reduction in prices of financial products due to the competition that would follow the opening of markets at ecu 22 billion, or about one-tenth of the total economic gains from completing the single market; and if the effect of the consequently lower interest rates on the rest of the economy was taken into account, this was expected to bring further gain of a similar order of magnitude, comprising some 1½ per cent of Community gross domestic product in all.[28] These estimates reflected the ample incentive for the more competitive firms in both finance and industry to support the completion of the single market for financial services and the abolition of exchange controls.

Thus the Single European Act succeeded in setting the Community on course for the integration of financial markets that is one of the main components of economic and monetary union. The removal of exchange controls also released pressures for the completion of the other element: the single currency or permanent locking of exchange rates. When there is, as happens from time to time, disturbance in the financial markets, capital flows from one member state to another will be bigger if there is no exchange control; and this will put pressure on the exchange rates. Thus the stability achieved in the Exchange Rate Mechanism may be threatened if the participants' macroeconomic policies are not co-ordinated to counteract this risk. Such co-ordination is another element of Emu; and the integration of capital and other financial markets reduces the autonomy of the member states' policies, so that the gains from joint control may be greater than any loss from the sacrifice of the right to take independent action. If autonomy is to be thus reduced, the question arises whether it would not be wiser to confront the danger of unstable exchange rates more directly by moving to the permanent renunciation of the right to change them. Exchange rate stability had proved popular among the participants in the ERM. Why not, instead of risking the loss of this advantage as capital markets became integrated, go on to abolish any such risk once and for all? It was economic arguments such as these that, combined once again with political motives, helped to place the Emu project at the top of the Community's agenda by the end of the 1980s.

Emu and the Delors proposals

On top of the general economic arguments for complementing the free movement of capital with the permanent fixing of exchange rates was a particular argument that appealed to France and Italy. These countries had, by 1988, got their inflation rates down fairly close to the German level. Having successfully aligned their policies on those of Germany, they were less inclined to accept that Germany had the right to lead them in co-ordinating macroeconomic policies: they had learnt their lesson and no longer wanted the teacher's tutelage.[29] A single currency would not be managed by the Bundesbank, which, through the strength of the mark, dominated the EMS, but by common Community institutions in which all participants would have their due influence.

The role of the Bundesbank in the EMS was but one aspect

of a growth in the Federal Republic's strength and assertiveness which was causing increasing worry in France. The idea of containing German power within a common European framework, rather than attempting to balance it in a system of separate sovereign states, embodied the same political logic as in 1950, when Monnet had initiated the Schuman plan. Now it was the Emu project that seemed apt to integrate the Bundesbank more firmly in a Community setting, and doubtless with yet more significant implications for political integration. France became strongly committed to the project, and the more so as the prospect of a united Germany playing a powerful role in Eastern Europe came nearer to realization.

When Delors called in 1986 for early steps to free the movement of capital, he started a process which could lead to monetary union. By 1988 he was ready to launch the Emu project; and he made it increasingly clear that he saw this as a major step towards a federal Community. With firm backing from France, he was able to ensure that it was on the agenda for the meeting of the European Council under German presidency in Hanover in June 1988. That meeting agreed to set up a committee, chaired by Delors and including the central bank governors of the member states, to study and propose 'concrete stages leading towards' the objective of economic and monetary union which had been confirmed 'in adopting the Single Act'. The resulting 'Delors report'[30] proposed the establishment of Emu in three stages. In June 1989, the European Council agreed that stage 1, in which all member states would enter the ERM and economic and monetary cooperation would be intensified, would begin in July 1990; and in December 1989, under French presidency, it was agreed that an Intergovernmental Conference (IGC) would be convened in December 1990 to draw up the necessary treaty amendments.

The Delors report's definition of Emu was similar to that of Werner: complete liberalization of capital transactions and full integration of financial markets; total and irreversible convertibility of currencies; the elimination of margins of fluctuation and the irrevocable locking of exchange rate parities. The report noted that the locking of parities did not necessarily imply the replacement of the member states' currencies by a single currency, but recommended that it should replace them as soon as possible after parities were locked. With complete liberalization, integration, and convertibility, the member states' currencies would, with permanently locked exchange rates, anyway be no more than the 'non-decimal denominations of a common currency'.[31] In its own document on Emu, published in March 1990, the Commission also came down in favour of the single currency on the grounds that it would be more definitively irrevocable and would eliminate any remaining costs of changing currencies.[32]

Delors was much more explicit than Werner about the Emu's institutions. The Community's money would be managed by a European System of Central Banks (ESCB, called in the Commission's report Eurofed), with a policy-making Council comprising the central bank governors and the members of the ESCB Board that would be responsible for overseeing the execution of the Council's policy. The Council would, like the Bundesbank, be independent from instructions of governments. It would be committed to the objective of price stability but, subject to that priority, bound to support the EC's general economic policy. Operations to implement the Council's policy would be undertaken by the central banks of the member states; and the Council would have to account for its activities to the European Council and the European Parliament.

The British government agreed to stage 1 as proposed in the report, and hence to entry into the ERM, which was as we saw indeed effected before the end of 1990. But its initial concept of the further stages was one of freely competing currencies of member states, managed by their monetary authorities and without an ESCB. This was widely seen as an attempt to prolong stage 1 indefinitely rather than to proceed with stages 2 and 3 as envisaged by the report. Its subsequent proposal for promoting a hard ecu, which would always be as strong as the strongest among the member states' currencies, as a parallel currency was seen as an attempt to prolong stage 2, although it could also be envisaged as a way of moving towards the single currency without necessarily prolonging that stage.

Stage 2 would, according to the report, start when the treaty amendments entered into force. The ESCB would be established and would increasingly co-ordinate the member states' monetary and economic policies, thus making it possible to diminish changes of the exchange rates. For stage 3, exchange rates would be locked and powers over monetary policy would be transferred to the new institutions. The ESCB 'could participate in all aspects of international monetary management', although it remained likely that decisions on the parity of the Emu's currency in relation to other currencies would be taken by the Council of economic and finance ministers. The Emu would become a major actor in the international monetary system.

The Delors report was much influenced by the policy of the Bundesbank, as the most powerful of the central banks represented in the committee. That policy was set out clearly by Karl Otto Pöhl, by now President of the Bundesbank, in a paper that was annexed to the published report.[33] He insisted that the Community should have power to limit the budget deficits of member states in an Emu, because they would, if allowed on the scale that had recently been practised by some members such as Italy, present an inflationary threat to the Community as a whole. The proposal to limit deficits was adopted in the report. But it was opposed by some as an infringement of member states' fiscal sovereignty, and also on the grounds that the markets should be the judge as to whether to lend money to a government, on condition that the governments were not allowed special privileges in the markets and that the central banking system was not allowed to print money to cover their deficits. The Commission, in its document of March 1990, took up these two conditions; but it also tried to steer a course between Pöhl and his critics, by recommending that the member states should be bound by legislation which they themselves would enact to curb excessive deficits.

The Bundesbank's policy also contributed to the Delors report's coolness towards the promotion of the ecu as a parallel currency during stages 1 and 2. The Commission's document was more positive, not only about the role of the ecu as the currency of the completed Emu, but also about its development during the transitional period.

The concerns of member states with the weakest economies contrasted with those of the Bundesbank. It was the governor of the Irish central bank who wrote a paper for the Delors committee making the case for resource transfers to the less-developed regions in an Emu, analogous to the policy of 'cohesion' designed to help the weaker economies to adapt to the single market, which had resulted in the agreement to double the Community's structural funds by 1993; and Delors himself also contributed a paper on the subject.[34]

Emu: interests and motives for and against

The momentum that the Emu project had gained by 1990 owed much to the strength of the French commitment, motivated, as we have seen, by a particular desire to replace the Bundesbank's tutelage by a common Community control over monetary policy, and in general to strengthen the Community framework for the containment of German power. Thus, as in 1950, the French transmuted their German policy into a European policy; and this European policy was now shared, for differing mixes of motives, by some other member states, in particular Belgium, Italy, and Spain. This federalist orientation was shared by a big majority in the European Parliament, by most of the political party groups represented in it, and by such eminent politicians as Giscard and Schmidt. It was also shared by the Commission, whose President, Delors, played a leading part in promoting the project.

The Emu project also enjoyed strong support from industry and finance. Business leaders established an Association for the Monetary Union of Europe, whose President was the President of Philips, and Vice-President the Chairman of Fiat. In addition to the gains from the liberalization of financial markets, estimated in the Cecchini report at over ecu 40 billion a year, the monetary union was expected to save at least ecu 15 billion in the transaction costs incurred in changing money from one currency to another.[35] Although this saving may not be so welcome to banks, for which those transactions are a significant source of business, they too are well represented in the Association. More important for industry than the saving of transaction costs is the greater certainty with which longer-term plans could be made for investment and trade within the

Community. As with the single market, this 'dynamic effect' is likely to be greater than the more immediate 'static effects'. Industry is also motivated by remaining fears that currency upsets could disrupt the single market programme, while monetary union would remove that risk altogether.

For the private financial sector, Emu can be seen as a framework which should enable European firms to be competitive players in the international financial system. At the level of public policy, Emu should give the Community a bargaining power in relation to the dollar and the yen analogous to that which the common tariff secured in the field of trade. American budgetary, exchange rate, and interest rate policies have caused discomfort to Europeans and others in recent years, and Emu could be expected to give the Community more influence over US policy-making, as well as in the international monetary system and its institutions.

These interests and motives, both economic and political, were enough to account for the momentum of the Emu project. There were also forces that resisted it. There were fears that the weaker economies would lose out if tied so closely to German monetary power, mirrored by Germans' fears that they would catch inflation from their partners. While attuned to the need for more co-operation, finance ministries and central banks contained people who were ill-disposed to part with their powers over macroeconomic policies, and there were those in politics who shared their reluctance. The most outspoken of these was Mrs Thatcher, who explicitly espoused de Gaulle's view of the Community and resisted the sharing of sovereignty such as Emu would require. She had less power than de Gaulle to prevent progress towards monetary integration in the Community, as the success of the Exchange Rate Mechanism without British participation had demonstrated. But she and the government of her successor, John Major, both hoped that their proposal for developing a non-inflationary 'hard ecu' as a parallel currency might enable them to divert the other member states from their intention to create Emu with a single currency and federal bank. The ability of a British government to weaken its partners' commitment to Emu depended however on how far Germany was committed to the project.

The policy of the Bundesbank was in principle favourable to Emu, but hesitant about specific steps of monetary integration before the other member states should become as proficient as Germany in preventing inflation. Support in Germany for political union of the Community remained substantial, however; and as Germany accomplished its own unification the German government stressed the importance of political union, in order to maintain the stability of the European system. Political union also appealed to the French government, concerned to anchor the new Germany within a stronger Community. As both projects appealed to most member governments, the IGC on political union was linked with the IGC on Emu, comprising a more attractive package for Germany than Emu on its own. Whatever the doubts among Germans, the Maastricht Treaty demonstrated the German government's commitment to the project.

Emu was included in the Maastricht Treaty in a form not far different from that outlined in the Delors report. The European System of Central Banks (ESCB), comprising the European Central Bank (ECB) and the member states' central banks, is to have price stability as its primary aim and is to have complete independence in pursuing it. During stage 2 of the transition, to begin in January 1994, a European Monetary Institute is to prepare the ground for stage 3 and for the establishment of the ECB before that stage starts, perhaps by 1 January 1997 and not later than 1 January 1999. The participating countries' exchange rates will then be fixed irrevocably, leading to the introduction of 'a single currency, the ecu'. In order to participate, member states have to fulfil quite stringent monetary and budgetary conditions; those that fail to do so cannot participate until they comply. In order to help the weaker economies to meet these conditions and to face the prospect of Emu, it was agreed at Maastricht to expand the cohesion policy. Britain alone insisted on a special exemption from Emu, allowing it to stay outside unless the British government and parliament decide to join. Once participating, member states must avoid excessive government deficits, or the Council may decide by a qualified majority to impose penalties, including fines.

It remains possible that Emu would be confined, at least for some time, to a small group of countries that meet its high monetary and fiscal standards. But while the story of efforts to promote monetary integration in the Community shows that the obstacles should not be underestimated, this element of the federal idea has shown resilience; and all the member states except Britain are committed to it by the Maastricht Treaty. It is reasonable to expect that by 1999, if not before, the Emu together with the single currency will be in place; and that all the member states will eventually participate.

8 European Budget and Public Finance Union

The Community's budget has been at the centre of conflicts that have accompanied the development of the Community, for two highly political reasons.

First, the budget has been an arena for struggles about the distribution of gains from integration. France saw the expenditure on agriculture as a way of ensuring that the French agricultural interest was satisfied, offsetting that of German industry. Then Britain fought to secure refunds to compensate its heavy net payment into the agricultural part of the budget. Then the Community's weaker, peripheral economies sought aid through the budget to help them meet the competition of the stronger economies in the single market to be completed in 1992. These distributional motives have played a big part in giving the budget its significant economic weight, reaching some ecu 66 billion for 1992.

Secondly, the budget has been a focus for conflict over the powers of the different institutions: over who controls the size, pattern, and management of the expenditure. Here the issue has been the relative power of the member governments and of the Community institutions. Some, in what has been termed the 'nationalist approach', have wanted to keep power in the hands of the governments. Others, preferring the 'federalist' approach, have held rather that 'new forms of representation and legitimation should be built up alongside the national governments and parliaments', and that the role of the European Parliament over against that of the Council should therefore be enhanced.[1] It is with respect to the budget that the federalist approach has come closest to realization.

Own resources, Monnet, and de Gaulle

Jean Monnet had concluded from his experience of international organizations that the Community would be hamstrung if it depended on the financial contributions of the member governments, which they might unilaterally reduce or withhold from one year to the next. As the architect of the ECSC Treaty he insisted that it should have its own resources of revenue; and the Community was empowered to levy a tax directly on the value of the production of coal and steel. The Treaty set a limit of 1 per cent of that value, which could however be exceeded if the Council accepted by a qualified majority a proposal by the High Authority for a higher rate.

Monnet, in his speech at the inauguration of the High Authority in August 1952, underlined that the Community obtained its financial resources 'not from the contributions of states', but from 'levies directly imposed' on production, citing this as one of the characteristics that made the institutions 'federal'. Altiero Spinelli, who helped him draft the speech, doubtless sharpened this point with his knowledge of the origins of the US constitution, which was given federal taxing powers precisely because the preceding confederal system was being bankrupted by the failure of the states to pay their contributions.[2] The underlying idea was later to be formalized by the theory of fiscal federalism, in its principle of congruence or correspondence, which stipulates that each level of government should have its own sources of revenue, whether separate taxes or parts of shared taxes, sufficient to match its expenditure responsibilities.[3] Like many aspects of the ECSC, 'own resources' have remained a basic principle for the Community ever since, underlying the process of developing its budget.

The ECSC Treaty also kept the control of the administrative budget out of the hands of the member governments. The budget was to be agreed among the Presidents of the four main institutions: the High Authority, the Parliamentary Assembly, the Council, and the Court of Justice. Thus the member governments were represented in the process of approving the budget by the President of the Council; but the Commission and the Parliament were likewise represented, foreshadowing the co-legislation by Council and Parliament on a budget proposed by the Commission, which was later to govern the adoption of part of the EC's budget—with the Court's role becoming, however, a more normal one of ultimate judicial authority.

The EEC Treaty of 1957 gave the Commission, for the execution of the budget, the strong independent status that had in general belonged to the High Authority in the ECSC. Thus article 205 EEC provided that 'The Commission shall implement the budget . . . on its own responsibility'. But in adopting the EEC budget, the Parliament's role was only consultative. Adoption was to be the sole responsibility of the member governments' representatives in the Council, even if it was to be done by qualified majority, thus avoiding the blockage of a single government's veto (article 203 EEC). While own resources were envisaged, moreover, they could not be introduced until the member states had unanimously ratified the arrangements for levying them; meanwhile, the Community would have to get by with contributions from the member states (articles 200, 201 EEC).

This mixture of intergovernmental and federal elements was to prove explosive. Eventually, in the 1970s, the own resources were introduced and the European Parliament's role strengthened, but not before the Community had suffered a severe crisis over these matters in the mid-1960s.

The budget to pay for the common agricultural policy was seen by de Gaulle as a powerful French national interest, and by the Commission and the federalists as an important step towards a federal Community. Both wanted it to be introduced as soon as possible. In December 1964 the common price for wheat was agreed; and since this was the key decision in constructing the agricultural policy, the Commission proposed that the own resources to finance the price support should come into effect at the same time as the common wheat price, that was to say in July 1967.[4] The Commission therefore proposed a financial regulation to govern the expenditure of such resources on agriculture from that date. At the same time the Germans, following the logic of the original Franco-German bargain on agriculture and industry, claimed that the establishment of the agricultural common market should be balanced by equivalent progress on industrial trade, which would be completion of the customs union by the same date. The Commission proposed that this should be reflected in the allocation of both agricultural import levies and customs duties as own resources from July 1967. Since these own resources of the Community would no longer pass through member states' budgets and would thus escape control by their parliaments, the Commission also proposed that the Parliamentary Assembly, as the European Parliament was still called, should exercise some control over the EC's budget.

This federalist proposal was a direct challenge to de Gaulle's concept of national sovereignty. Until then the Commission had avoided provoking him. But the majority of Commissioners felt that this was the time to take a stand. French policy had been so negative about almost everything other than the agricultural policy and the finance for it, that they felt de Gaulle might put the Community on ice once these had been agreed; and they believed that the French interest in the agricultural policy was so strong that he would swallow the pill of parliamentary powers if linked with the agricultural and financial decisions. The Commission was firmly backed in this by the Dutch parliament, which had bound the Dutch government not to accept any proposal for EC own resources that did not provide for control by elected representatives. So the Commission put the parliamentary powers into its package.

De Gaulle's counter-attack has been described in Chapter 1. He was evidently not going to accept any building up of federal institutions, infringing what he saw as the exclusive legitimacy of member states and governments. The Commission and the other member governments had to accept that the agricultural policy would be financed by member states' contributions, which member states' parliaments could approve, until he had left the scene. They would just have to wait until then.

Own resources and European Parliament's powers

In 1969 de Gaulle resigned and the Commission revived its proposals for own resources and for the strengthening of the European Parliament's control over the budget. The French still saw the own resources of the Community as a major French interest, so Georges Pompidou, de Gaulle's successor as French President, went to the Community's Summit meeting in The Hague in December of that year determined to secure 'completion' of the Community's programme in this respect. Such completion was agreed, along with widening to include Britain and other applicants, and deepening in the form of economic and monetary union. The arrangements for own resources were rapidly agreed and set down in a Treaty signed in April 1970.[5] The Community was to have the agricultural levies and customs duties as proposed in 1965. But the cost of the agricultural policy had grown so that this was no longer enough to pay for it, and the Community was also allocated a share in the value-added tax (VAT) that was levied in all the member states. The Community's share was up to 1 per cent of the value added by businesses producing or trading in the goods and services that were included in the VAT's 'base'. Defining the base was a most complex matter, since it differed from country to country in the Community and many thousands of products were involved. In order to allow time for the agreement on this and its administrative consequences, the Community's share of VAT was to be paid only at the end of a transitional period lasting until the start of 1978—which was eventually stretched to 1980. Thus member states were continuing to pay national contributions to the Community budget for over two decades after the EEC Treaty, stipulating that own resources should be introduced, had come into force.

The political choice of own resources had nevertheless been quickly made in the first months of 1970. The question of who was to control their expenditure was not so easily resolved. The French government, in this early post-de Gaulle period, was still reluctant to give powers to the European Parliament, while France's partners wanted it to have such powers and the Dutch were particularly insistent. The French, less intransigent without de Gaulle, were however ready to concede something for the Parliament, provided that the bulk of the expenditure, most notably that on agriculture, remained under the control of the governments. This they secured through the device of dividing expenditure into two categories: compulsory and non-compulsory expenditure (NCE). The compulsory expenditure was to be that 'necessarily resulting from this Treaty or from acts adopted in accordance therewith' (amendment to article 203 EEC). The argument was that when, for instance, the ministers in the Agriculture Council decided on agricultural prices, these prices became part of Community law and must be supported as such, whatever the cost to the budget might be. So the Parliament could have no right to alter the budget for agriculture. The French foreign minister defended this idea in the Assemblée Nationale as a means of preserving the sovereignty of the Council and preventing change in the allocation of powers among the Community institutions— arguments repeated in the 1980s by the British government in resisting greater powers for the European Parliament. Since agriculture then accounted for some nine-tenths of Community expenditure, and this was seen in France as a very important national interest, the definition of agricultural expenditure as compulsory was the French ministers' central demand. But they sought to include a number of other headings under the 'compulsory' part of the budget.

The Dutch and the European Parliament wanted, on the contrary, to reduce the scope of compulsory expenditure. It amounted, after all, to a licence for ministers from spending departments to take decisions regardless of the budgetary consequences; and the uncontrolled expansion of agricultural expenditure was subsequently to show the danger of such a concept. The scope of compulsory expenditure was later reduced. It now comprises only spending for agriculture and for fulfilling the Community's international obligations. But the Parliament sought further to gain leverage over the compulsory as well as non-compulsory expenditure, through a right to reject the budget as a whole.

The European Parliament, although it then had few formal powers, was not lacking in influence over the arrangements the Community was making for the budget. The Council's proposals for giving the Community own resources and amending the budgetary procedures laid down in the treaties would have to be ratified by all the member states. Ratification was not likely to be forthcoming from the Dutch and some other parliaments if the principle of parliamentary control over resources which belonged to the Community, and thus escaped the control of member states' parliaments, was too blatantly ignored. Faced with this sanction, and with the Dutch government itself strongly supporting the giving of powers to the European Parliament, the governments agreed in April 1970 to provide for the Parliament to share power with the Council in approving the non-compulsory part of the budget. For the compulsory expenditure, the Parliament could propose 'modifications' but the Council could normally overrule them; and for the budget as a whole, the Parliament was to be consulted and, if the text of the treaty amendment was liberally interpreted, might be construed to have the right to reject the budget as a whole. The Parliament held that this was not good enough, and the President of the Council, who was in the first half of 1970 Belgian and sympathetic to the Parliament's case, declared that the Council would consider proposals about it from the Commission, which the Commission undertook to submit within two years.

The Commission set up an expert group with Georges Vedel, a distinguished French lawyer, as its chairman, to study the constitutional implications of greater powers for the European Parliament. The Vedel report proposed a general right for the Parliament of co-legislation with the Council, and likewise a share in the nomination of the Commission's President.[6] Following the Commission's proposals, a second Treaty on the budgetary procedures was adopted in 1975, sharpening up somewhat the Parliament's powers to amend the budget and strengthening its claim to be able to reject it as a whole. The Parliament's capacity to supervise the process of Community spending was also enhanced. It was given the power to grant the Commission a Discharge for the implementation of the budget, i.e. to approve—or not—the way in which the Commission had spent the money. So seriously was this taken that a Commissioner for the budget was later to suggest that the Commission might be obliged to resign if Discharge was refused.[7] At the least, the Commission was required to take action on the comments with which the Parliament accompanied its grant of Discharge.

The 1975 Treaty also established the Court of Auditors,

responsible not only for ensuring propriety but also for judging whether 'the financial management has been sound' (article 206a EEC). This followed the revelation by the Parliament's Budget Committee in 1973 that some 100 million units of account of expenditure could not be accounted for. The annual reports of the Court of Auditors were to provide much material that would assist parliamentary scrutiny of Community spending.

The Treaties of 1970 and 1975 have been considered in some detail, not only because they ensured that the Community would have its own resources, or, in plain words, its own tax revenue. These treaties, together with the EEC's founding treaty, resulted in what amounts to a federal relationship among the institutions for the enactment of the Community budget, as far as the non-compulsory expenditure is concerned. For this, the European Parliament has the right of co-legislation with the Council: this part of the budget cannot be enacted without the Parliament's approval, and the Parliament has the edge over the Council in case of disagreement. For the budget as a whole, the Council has always used the procedure of voting by qualified majority, even when, following de Gaulle's *démarche* at Luxembourg, all Councils save those dealing with the budget were proceeding only by unanimity. The Commission has the sole right to propose the draft budget and to execute the budget when it has been approved: the Commission acts, in fact, like a government. Questions of lawfulness are, of course, referred to the Court. This is how legislature, executive, and judiciary interact in a federal system of government; and, since 1975, the non-compulsory expenditure has grown to the point where it was expected to exceed ecu 20 billion in 1992, or about one-third of the total budget.

This system for the non-compulsory expenditure has on the whole worked well. But the procedures for the part of the budget designated as compulsory expenditure remained severely defective. There was no parliamentary control; and the doctrine of expenditure 'necessarily' resulting from acts adopted in accordance with the Treaty was to give the Agriculture Council scope for the unchecked spending which nearly brought the Community to grief. Nor did the legislative branch of the institutions—Parliament and Council—have any authoritative way of treating the budget as a coherent whole, with the various spending Councils having autonomous legislative power, and the Parliament lacking powers over tax and compulsory expenditure. The Community has come closer to achieving some coherence. But it was to suffer grave budgetary crises before it brought itself to the point of doing so.

The idea of a federal budget

In the mid-1970s, the Commission had cause to be concerned about the future of the Community. The great project for economic and monetary union had been shelved and its offshoot, the Snake in the Tunnel, had been reduced to an exchange rate club of Germany and a few small countries, following the French departure from it in January 1974. Sharply differing inflation and deficits, following the oil shock of 1973–4, posed the question how integration could proceed among such divergent economies; and Britain, reopening the issue of membership through the referendum organized for mid-1975, posed an additional question of political divergence. The Commission wanted to know how the budget could help to make the Community more cohesive and capable again of contemplating a project such as Emu. It asked Sir Donald MacDougall, a much-respected British economist, to chair a group to 'examine the future role of public finance at the Community level in the general context of European economic integration'. The group started work late in 1974 and its report was published in April 1977.

The report considered the question of the budget in the light of the principles of fiscal federalism.[8] It examined the criteria for assigning functions to the different levels of a multi-tier government: in the Community's case, EC, member states, regions, and local government. One criterion for assigning functions to a higher level was externality, when the costs or benefits of an activity spill over from one area of the body politic to another. Thus wind or rivers may carry pollution across frontiers, so there is a cross-frontier function of pollution control and perhaps of compensation to perform. Another criterion is indivisibility, or economies of scale: nuclear fusion research facilities are too costly for any member state to afford and cannot be divided into smaller units; so the Community itself finances one. A third criterion is the desire to provide citizens with a minimum standard of services or of prosperity, which is reflected in the Community's 'cohesion' policy of resource transfers to the regions with weaker economies. Against these criteria for transferring functions to a higher level are those that favour keeping them closer to the citizens: democratic control and flexibility; innovation, comparison, and competition among different units of government; and the advantages of political homogeneity within the smaller communities. The term subsidiarity has since been used for the principle of keeping functions with the smaller units of government where there is no major advantage in transferring them to bigger ones.

The report applied these principles for assigning functions, with respect to the three main aims of public economic policy: stabilization, or the use of macroeconomic policy to secure price stability and high rates of economic activity and employment; allocation, or the use of microeconomic policy instruments to favour the efficient use of resources; and redistribution.

The Community budget would not play much part in stabilization so long as it remained small and, complying with the EEC Treaty, balanced. This would be the function, rather, of the Emu, with its monetary policy and any co-ordination of member states' budget policies.

Allocation, in the market economy, is mainly the function of the market, although public policy incurs some costs in ensuring a level playing field, for example through competition policy. Public expenditure has arisen, however, at the Community level in, for example, the allocation of resources to technological research based on economies of scale; and big resources have, of course, been allocated to agriculture, in large part for distributional motives.

It was, indeed, in redistribution that the MacDougall group saw the main purpose of the Community's budget, as a condition for enabling the weaker economies to participate fully in economic integration and eventually in an economic and monetary union. It envisaged expenditure on structural, employment, and regional policies to help the weaker regions, and transfers to offset the impact of cyclical fluctuations on particular regions. The report estimated that ecu 10 billion, or 0.7 per cent of Community GDP, should reduce the difference of incomes between richer and poorer regions by some 10 per cent, which 'might be judged an acceptable start'. This compared with a reduction of about one-third in the difference between the regions within five existing federations studied by the group. But there were reasons why the Community should be less ambitious, at least at first: there was less propensity to migrate between the member states and hence less pressure to harmonize income levels; and, without direct taxes and benefits to individuals, the Community lacked some of the most powerful instruments of redistribution of incomes among the regions of federal states.[9]

Following its analysis, the group considered budgets of three different orders of magnitude. A budget of the size in fully developed federal states such as the United States or the Federal Republic of Germany, amounting to 20–25 per cent of GDP, was not considered. With the existing budget of 0.7 per cent of GDP in the Community in the mid-1970s as the starting-point, the group defined first a 'pre-federal' budget for a Community with a single market and further steps towards monetary union. This budget could amount to 2–2½ per cent of GDP. The next type of budget considered would be for a 'small public sector federation', with monetary union but without defence responsibilities; and this could amount to 5–7 per cent of GDP. By the late 1980s, when the Emu project became active again, the Commission appeared, however, to take the view that Emu would require no more than the sort of budget that the MacDougall report defined as pre-federal. Finally, the report estimated that defence competences could add some 3 per cent of GDP, bringing the total to 7½–10 per cent.[10]

As a source of finance for an expanded budget, the group was attracted by a share of VAT with a progressive key, which would cause the richer member states to pay a higher percentage of VAT than the poorer ones.[11]

While few of the group's recommendations were accorded early implementation, the report's thinking has had influence on the later development of the budget. First, however, there were some nasty problems to be overcome.

The British budget question

The British budget question, or BBQ as it came to be known in the Commission, took up unduly much time and political energy from the mid-1970s to the mid-1980s.[12] With their large imports of foodstuffs, the British paid heavily for the common agricultural policy, through levies on their imports from outside the Community and high prices for imports from within it; and British agriculture, as a small though efficient sector, brought in less benefit from the price supports than the agricultural sectors in the other member states, which comprised a larger part of their economies. The net budgetary cost of the agricultural policy to Britain was estimated at about ¾ per cent of GDP when studies were done before Britain joined the Community.[13] This was one reason why the Treaty of Accession provided for seven years of transition before the EC's budgetary system would apply in full to Britain. It was hoped that, by 1980, the share of agriculture in the budget would have been reduced and the bias against the British thus alleviated. But in case this should not be sufficient, the British during the entry negotiations secured a declaration from the Community that if unacceptable situations should arise, 'the very survival of the Community would demand that the institutions find equitable solutions'.[14]

In line with the thinking that was to inform the MacDougall report, Edward Heath, who as Prime Minister had driven the entry negotiations through to a successful conclusion, persuaded the Community's Paris Summit in October 1972 to agree to the idea of a regional development fund, hoping that it would be big enough to go a substantial way towards solving the problem of the bias in the agricultural budget through payments to Britain's economically weaker regions. But while the establishment of the fund was being negotiated, the Community ran into difficulties. The oil shock evoked defensive attitudes. The Germans became weary of their role as 'paymaster' of the Community, stemming from the original Franco-German bargain on agriculture, followed by the rise of the German economy to be the richest in the Community and hence the biggest contributor of VAT. The British themselves, after Heath's government had been replaced by a Labour government early in 1974, turned their attention to 'renegotiating the terms of entry' rather than to securing a large regional fund. So the fund started on a small scale, with 300 million units of account in 1975 rising to 500 million in 1976 and in 1977; and although, after the European Parliament had succeeded in getting it declared non-compulsory, the fund's budget rose to ecu 2.4 billion in 1984 and ecu 3 billion in 1988, the net benefit was destined to go to the poorer member states, Greece, Portugal, Spain, and the Irish Republic, rather than to Britain. By 1975, then, Britain was set for a decade of conflict in the Community over special refunds from the budget to deal with the British budget question.

The Labour government's 'renegotiation' was not effective. The Community did agree in March 1975 to refund any excess gross contributions to the budget. But the complicated formula that was agreed brought no significant results. Then, with full incorporation in the budget system looming close ahead, the Labour government sought to use the negotiations to establish the European Monetary System in 1978 to reopen the budget question. The Commission was asked to carry out concurrent studies of such questions alongside the establishment of the EMS, with the result that a paper on the subject was presented to the first meeting of the European Council attended by Mrs Thatcher as the new Conservative Prime Minister, held in Dublin in December 1979.

Valéry Giscard d'Estaing and Helmut Schmidt, who between them were leading the Community at that time, came to the meeting with a low offer which Mrs Thatcher could hardly accept. She, for her part, gave a foretaste of the posture she was to adopt in the Community by repeatedly asserting that she wanted her 'money back'. Britain had just cause to seek redress, because the net contribution to the budget was as big as had been foreseen before entry. Agricultural spending continued to dominate the budget and the regional fund was a puny counterweight. Nor, with the bad economic conditions of the 1970s, was there a clear benefit from membership for British industry. But instead of promoting the development of the Community, the British government was inclined to block such development until its budgetary demands were satisfied. With curbing public expenditure at home a priority, the government could hardly have been expected to pursue an expansionary policy for the Community's budget; but that need not have precluded a more positive policy in other areas, such as completion of the single market, which was later to receive such strong British support. As it was, many in the other member states felt that Britain wanted to reduce the Community to little more than a free trade area; and that discouraged them from striving to find solutions for Britain's problem.[15] At the same time the other member governments were disappointingly reluctant to act on their commitment to respond adequately to an 'unacceptable situation'. The result was five years of patched-up arrangements for refunds accompanied by serious impediment of the Community's development.

It was not until the Community was faced with financial necessity that the logjam was broken, during the French presidency in the first half of 1984. Agricultural expenditure had expanded through the 1970s and early 1980s until the 1 per cent of VAT, together with the customs duties and import levies, did not suffice to finance the Community's budget. By 1983 the money was running out, and it was clear that the limit to the Community's share of VAT would have to be raised if the commitments under the agricultural policy were to be met. But once again, ratification by all the member states was required if the scope of own resources was to be enlarged. British assent was necessary, and would not be forthcoming without a satisfactory answer to the British budget question. Behind that necessity, moreover, lay a perception that the Community would not recover its dynamism unless an answer was found. The bargain that was reached was an increase of the VAT limit to 1.4 per cent, together with a refund for Britain of about two-thirds of its net contribution, based in fact on the difference between the percentage of the Community's total

VAT receipts provided by Britain and the percentage of expenditure allocations that Britain received. The European Council at which this deal was approved, at Fontainebleau in June 1984, also undertook to ensure that the growth of agricultural expenditure would be controlled in future. But instead, the spending rose faster than ever; and, with the net contribution from VAT at no more than 1.25 per cent when the refund to Britain was deducted from the 1.4 per cent limit, the budget was again deep in crisis by 1987. Own resources had to be increased again in 1988, accompanied by a renewal of the mechanism agreed for Britain at Fontainebleau and, this time, a more thorough reform of the Community's budgetary arrangements. But the British refund will not remain permanently unchallenged; it is likely eventually to be subsumed in a more general system of burden-sharing. Meanwhile, the beginnings of such a system were initiated as part of the reform in 1988, to deal with the problem of the weaker economies on the Community's periphery.

Cohesion

The agricultural policy demanded by France and the refunds demanded by Britain were somewhat peculiar forms of redistribution, which generated fierce conflicts around the Community's budget. The Community has also developed forms of redistribution that fit more readily into the pattern found by the MacDougall report to be typical of federal systems; and these have caused less aggravation in the Community's politics.

Already in the EEC Treaty, the European Investment Bank and the Social Fund were established in order to meet the demands of Italy, which, as the weakest economy in the Community at that time, wanted the opening of its market to competition from stronger economies to be accompanied by some help for its development. The European Development Fund, included at the same time in the Implementing Convention for the association of overseas countries and territories, was designed to secure the help of other member states in sharing the cost of development aid for French colonies, as they then were, in Africa; and it may thus be said that this too was a form of redistributional policy. When the EMS was founded in 1979, low-interest loans, subsidized from the Community budget, were provided for Ireland and Italy, on the grounds of their monetary weakness and development needs. Then when Greece entered the Community, in 1981, its Treaty of Accession included a provision for 'unacceptable situations' such as Britain had secured less formally in its entry negotiations; and the Greeks took advantage of the negotiations for Iberian enlargement, which would have to be ratified by all member states including Greece, to ensure agreement that the Community budget would finance Integrated Mediterranean Programmes (IMPs) for the benefit of development in the Mediterranean parts of the Community.

The accession of Spain and Portugal, in January 1986, coincided with the conclusion of the negotiations for the Single European Act, with the single market programme at its centre. With strong support from Spain, Portugal, Ireland, and Greece, President Delors argued that the Act should include a commitment to accompany the completion of the single market with a policy of 'economic and social cohesion' designed to reduce disparities between regions and the backwardness of least-favoured regions, in order to help the weaker economies to face the challenge of open competition. The Act required the Commission to submit to the Council proposals for the future of the structural funds: the Social Fund, the Regional Development Fund, and the Guidance Section of the European Agricultural Guidance and Guarantee Fund. This the Commission did; and, in connection with the reform of the budget in the first half of 1988, it proposed the doubling of the structural funds in order to fulfil the obligations undertaken in the Single Act. The European Council, under German presidency, agreed to double the budget for the funds, increasing it progressively to that level by 1993. The size of the combined funds was then to be equivalent to about $\frac{1}{3}$ per cent of the Community's GDP. This compares with the $\frac{2}{3}$ per cent of GDP envisaged by the MacDougall report for a pre-federal Community; but the structural funds are more closely tailored to the promotion of development than, for example, the unemployment assistance which was a major item of expenditure recommended in the MacDougall report. Payments from the structural funds should, moreover, amount to 5 per cent of the GDP of Greece, Portugal, and the Irish Republic, and to 1½ per cent of Spanish GDP, comparing, in the first three cases, not unfavourably with the 3–10 per cent of gross regional product usually channelled, according to MacDougall, to the receiving regions of existing states.[16]

Agreement to a cohesion policy on this scale was far from a foregone conclusion. The British government in particular, with its scepticism about public expenditure and about many aspects of Community development, could have been expected to resist. But in the Single Act, the principle of cohesion was linked with the completion of the single market to which Britain was strongly committed; and in the 1988 budgetary reform, when the doubling of the funds was agreed, the British government was concerned not to lose support for the payment of its refunds. The allocation for cohesion was, indeed, an element in a comprehensive package which each member government had some reason to approve; and for similar reasons the Maastricht Treaty again gave a fair wind to cohesion expenditure.

The budgetary reform of 1988

With world prices for agricultural products low and surplus production in the Community continuing unchecked, the cost of storage and of export subsidies soared and the extra revenue from the 1.4 per cent VAT limit agreed in 1984 was quickly spent. By 1987 no less than 1.9 per cent VAT would have been needed to balance the budget without resort to devices that pushed the costs into future years. Advances paid to member states to cover their costs in implementing the agricultural policy were paid two months later than previously; and even if this practice was to be continued, it brought the budget only a once-for-all gain. Stocks in store which had halved or more in value were still accounted at the original price, and no provision was made for the day of reckoning when they would have to be disposed of. More revenue was required and, this time, agricultural spending really did have to be brought under control. The mechanism for the British refund was due to lapse, five years after it was agreed at Fontainebleau in 1984; and the commitment to the policy of cohesion also had to be respected. A comprehensive reform of the budget, bringing these elements together and, because of their importance, having implications for the relationship between the institutions, was clearly indicated. It was undertaken, on a proposal from the Commission and under German presidency in the European Council, in the first half of 1988.[17]

The trigger for the reform was, once again, the interest of France and other agricultural exporters in securing more own resources for the Community to pay for the agricultural policy. This time Spain and the other countries with less-developed economies were also pressing for more resources to finance the policy of cohesion. Britain was intent on a bargain that would include the renewal of its refunds. Germany, having its turn in the presidency of the Council, wanted to succeed in dispatching the Community's business and maintaining its dynamism. President Delors likewise sought success in problem-solving, as well as an opportunity to move the Community in a federal direction. The reform was based on Commission proposals which were given his name, as the Delors package. The mix of motives among the member governments and the Commission was powerful enough to ensure significant improvements in each of the three dimensions of Community budgetary policy: revenue, expenditure, and control.

The Community's existing sources of revenue had two drawbacks: they were slower-growing than GDP; and they were regressive. The yield from customs duties had fallen as tariffs were cut through international trade negotiations. Agricultural imports had fallen as the agricultural policy induced self-sufficiency for the Community, thus reducing the scope for import levies. The base of goods and services on which VAT was calculated declined as member states grew richer and a bigger share of national incomes was saved or applied to purposes such as education and health, which were largely outside the VAT base. Thus the Community budget was squeezed by the relatively slow growth of its own resources. Secondly, these indirect taxes bore harder on the poor than on the rich. Tariffs and levies are highest on items such as food and clothing, which take a larger part of the spending of those with lower incomes; and, just as VAT contributions hit the poorer countries harder, so they do the poorer people. The Commission wanted to move towards a less restrictive and regressive revenue system.

As a moderately progressive new tax, the Commission proposed the logical complement to VAT: a tax on the difference between the gross national product and the VAT base, which would reverse the incidence of VAT and bear more heavily on the rich than on the poor. This was too much for some among the richer, however, and in particular for Italy, where a new calculation of gross product, including an estimate of the informal economy which escapes the taxman and the national statistics, showed the average Italian to be richer than the average Briton. The European Council decided, therefore, that the 'fourth resource', as it was called, should be neutral in relation to incomes, and related it direct to GNP (though as a concession to the poorer, any part of the VAT base which exceeded 55 per cent of GDP, which does not apply in any of the richer countries, was to be excluded from the calculation).

In order to escape from the constraint of revenue growing slower than gross product, the Commission proposed and the European Council agreed that the total revenue could rise so as to finance expenditure of 1.2 per cent of Community GNP by 1992, while commitments, which are bigger than appropriations for payments because they include the budgets for some multi-year programmes, could in that year be as much as 1.3 per cent of GNP. Thus while the VAT limit was kept at 1.4 per cent, no such limit was applied to the fourth resource, which could be levied at whatever percentage was needed to finance the balance of expenditure beyond what the other three taxes could afford, while, of course, respecting the global limit of 1.2 per cent of GNP for the four taxes combined.

The European Development Fund and the British refund are not included in the budget, and together amount to about 0.11 per cent of GNP. Total Community expenditure could, therefore, reach 1.31 per cent of GNP by 1992. Although borrowing and lending are, moreover, generally included in the budgets of states, the loan transactions of the European Investment Bank, the ECSC, Euratom, and the New Community Instrument, which was introduced in 1979 to support policies against unemployment, low investment, and divergence, are not included in the Community's budget. While the budget still falls short of the 2–2½ per cent of gross product envisaged by MacDougall for a pre-federal Community, the difference between that and the limit set for total expenditure in the financial perspective has narrowed significantly.

The revenue agreed by the European Council allowed for Community expenditure to increase by over 14 per cent a year from 1988 to 1992. Within that total, agricultural expenditure was to rise much less fast, its growth being limited to not more than 74 per cent of that of Community GNP, and hence to some 2–3 per cent a year.

The rapid expansion of the budget was no longer to be mainly for agriculture, but rather for the structural funds, the allocations for which were agreed by Parliament and Council in April 1989 to rise from ecu 7.8 billion in 1988 to over ecu 14 billion in 1992 (the doubling being over the longer period 1987–93), with some ecu 1 billion a year later to be added to provide for the needs of East Germany. Agriculture and the structural funds were to take up over four-fifths of the total budget in 1992. But there was also some scope for expansion in new policies as well as in the other existing policies. These latter included in the 1988 budget a dozen headings: Integrated Mediterranean Programmes, Portuguese industry, other regional and social policies, energy, environment, transport, innovation and the internal market, research and investment, information and culture, development (other than European Development Fund), administration, refunds to member states. The largest of these items was research and investment, with not far short of ecu 1 billion.

As a firm framework for the containment of agricultural expenditure and the expansion of the structural funds, the European Council agreed a 'financial perspective' which set out the allocations under six major headings for each year from 1988 to 1992. With the cost of agriculture contained as intended, non-compulsory expenditure would rise to one-third of the total budget by 1992. But sceptics, recalling past experience, might well ask whether the intention would be fulfilled. Aware of the problem, the European Council made a serious effort to provide the Community with a proper system of budgetary control.

Agricultural spending was to be checked by the system of stabilizers, reducing prices if production exceeds an agreed threshold. Member states undertook to supply the Commission with regular and up-to-date information about their expenditure, product by product. If the Commission perceived a danger of overspending, it was to ask the Agriculture Council to strengthen the stabilizers; and if that Council failed to take strong enough action, the Commission was to call a joint meeting of the Agriculture and Finance Councils, where the finance ministers' interest in budgetary discipline should be brought to bear. If that too was not enough, the Commission was to use its own management powers. This reinforcement of the Commission's budgetary powers was strongly backed by the British government, which had usually looked askance at a strengthening of the Commission, but in this case favoured the most rigorous control over expenditure. Despite these new procedures, however, the Commission's ability to control laxity in the Council could still be seen as an open question; and part of the answer might be found in the new role of the European Parliament that ensued from the budgetary reform.

With the decision to double the structural funds taken, and the member governments obliged to ensure that it was realized, the Council had to make sure that the Parliament would not use its power to amend the budget for non-compulsory expenditure to upset the arrangement. Not that the Parliament has been hostile to the cohesion policy or the structural funds: on the contrary, it has strongly supported them. But in case the Parliament should be tempted to transfer funds from structural to other headings, either because of any unexpected shortage of revenue to finance all items of non-compulsory expenditure or in a trial of strength with the Council, the Council sought a firm commitment that the Parliament would accept the allocation for the structural funds. The Parliament in turn demanded a commitment from the Council that the allocations for agricultural support would not exceed the amounts foreseen in the financial perspective. The result was that the Inter-institutional Agreement concluded between the Parliament, Council, and Commission to regulate their relationship with respect to the new budgetary arrangements provided that the Parliament would accept the allocations in the financial perspective while the Council accepted the Parliament's control over the total of compulsory expenditure: neither Parliament nor Council could alter the objectives of the perspective without the agreement of the other. Thus the Council accepted that, until 1993 at least, the Parliament could veto any proposal for expenditure on agriculture beyond the allocations then agreed: a significant step towards parliamentary control over the compulsory expenditure. The Council, moreover, agreed that payments beyond the appropriations were not to be made until the budget or financial estimates had already been properly amended.[18]

The reform as a whole was the result of a serious display of resolution by the Community institutions. But its effectiveness in hard times was not immediately tested, because higher world prices helped to cut the agricultural costs, by some ecu 1 billion in 1989; and the subsequent return to rising costs had not yet begun. With the Community economy growing faster than expected, revenue was more buoyant than the perspective assumed. So the new procedures for control did not have to be used to deal with difficult problems. On the contrary there was money available to spend on new policies, the outstanding example being the response to an entirely new challenge, in the movement of Central and East European countries towards market economies and pluralist democracies. The first allocations for helping this process were for aid for Hungary and Poland. The Parliament raised the sum agreed by the Commission and Council in the second half of 1989 from ecu 200 million to ecu 300 million; and the Council accepted, with the Parliament, the corresponding increase in the allocation for the relevant heading in the financial perspective. In June 1990, both Parliament and Council went further, agreeing to reserve ecu 850 million in 1991 and ecu 1 billion in 1992 for co-operation with Central and Eastern Europe.

In favourable circumstances, then, the budgetary reform of 1988 worked well enough. It did, moreover, shift the budget in modest but significant ways in the direction of a more federal system, with respect to revenue, expenditure, and institutional procedures. But the reform related essentially to the period until 1992, and to a Community which was completing the single market but not yet embarking on a project for economic and monetary union. It is necessary to consider the future of the budget beyond 1992.[19]

Beyond 1992: a public finance union?

The question of redistribution is again posed in 1992. The Maastricht Treaty declared the intention to make the Community's taxation less regressive and gave a new impulse to the cohesion policy of assistance for the poorer regions, which now include Germany's five eastern Länder. Aid for Central and Eastern Europe too must be considered. The pattern of Community expenditure will also be affected by the reform of agricultural policy and by spending on new policies stemming from Maastricht. All these elements must be combined within a 'financial perspective' for 1993–97. In addition, there may well be proposals to reconsider Britain's rebate, which has been paid outside the budget.

Maastricht provided for a Cohesion Fund to be set up before 1994, to help finance environmental projects and investment in trans-European transport networks in member states with less than 90 per cent of the average Community GNP. A new Title on trans-European networks was introduced into the Maastricht Treaty, with respect to energy and telecommunications as well as transport networks, allowing for financial contributions from the Community. The potential scale of such projects had been indicated by proposals from member states' railways for a network of high-speed trains to cost some ecu 90 billion.[20] Maastricht also opened the way to more Community expenditure on the environment in all member states.

The establishment of the Cohesion Fund and 'review of the size' of the structural funds agreed at Maastricht was a result of growing pressure from the lower-income member states, led by

Spain, for help towards the adjustments required to prepare for economic and monetary union. The grounds for this were explained by Maurice Doyle, the governor of the Irish central bank, in his annex to the Delors report.[21] Just as was argued with respect to the single market, he held that as integration proceeded, so should the role of regional policy increase: that economic and monetary union would be sustainable if cohesion was promoted by such a policy. President Delors, in his own annex, gave reasons why regional policy might not have to be so costly as was envisaged in the MacDougall report.[22] New technologies had brought products for which transport costs were lower, thus reducing one of the disadvantages of the periphery, while telecommunications and capital mobility were eroding the advantages of the centre. The results could be seen in the troubles besetting some central regions such as North-East France, Wallonia, and the Ruhr, and the dynamism of outlying regions such as Bavaria, Puglia, the Rhone Valley, and parts of South Wales and Scotland. While cohesion would still cost money, it is better spent on infrastructure which helps economic development than on straight financial transfers among member states, such as are practised among the German Länder. The Delors report itself noted that structural policies might have to be strengthened after 1993, in the process of creating the economic and monetary union.[23]

The British rebate has been a straight financial transfer of an *ad hoc* nature; and there have been suggestions that it should be placed in the context of a more general arrangement. One such proposal was already made in the Padoa-Schioppa report in 1987, for transfers among the member states which would ensure that each state's net balance in relation to the EC budget would be inversely related to its income per head: the richer states would then become net contributors and the poorer states net recipients.[24]

The cost of any such mechanism would be reduced if the incidence of EC revenue and expenditure were less regressive. Thus a reduction of agricultural expenditure in favour of structural and other budget headings would help to change the balance for Britain and Portugal, while also making room for expenditure focused directly on the poorer states as a whole.

The Commission, as we saw, tried to introduce a progressive tax in 1988, though it had to be content with one that was broadly neutral. The MacDougall report suggested that VAT contributions be adjusted by a key which would increase the percentage contributed by the rich and reduce that of the poor; and one of its authors later proposed a surcharge on member states' income tax, which would leave them completely free to fix their own tax rates while ensuring that they contributed to the EC budget in progressive proportion to their citizens' incomes.[25] The distributive effects of a new energy and carbon tax may also eventually have to be taken into account. Such a tax has been proposed by the Commission in order to reduce the damage caused to the environment by too much consumption of energy, particularly of carbon fuels.[26]

The economic and monetary union project also raises the question of the role of the EC public finances in stabilization, or macroeconomic, policy. The EEC Treaty stipulates in article 199 that the revenue and expenditure shown in the budget shall be in balance. Without treaty amendment, therefore, the budget balance could not be used as a policy instrument. With EC expenditure only a little over 1 per cent of Community GDP, or some 4 per cent of total public expenditure in the Community, it is in any case the member states' budgets and public sector borrowing requirements that will play the main part, alongside monetary policy, in macroeconomic policy within the Community. But it is possible for the Community to use its borrowing powers to stimulate investment, and thus to make a public finance contribution to macroeconomic policy.

This had already been done when the New Community Instrument was launched in 1979 to borrow money from the international capital market in order to promote investment and employment as well as convergence. Even if without the same intention, the Community's borrowing under its powers relating to the ECSC, Euratom, and the European Investment Bank has had similar effects. The Albert–Ball report to the European Parliament in 1983, noting that these four instruments were raising some ecu 10 billion in that year, suggested that the EC could stimulate investment and hence the dynamism and competitiveness of the Community economy through a programme of expenditure of ecu 15 billion a year for three years on research and development, regional development, and investment in infrastructure in the Community and the Third World, financed by money raised in those ways.[27] The Commission, in its document on economic and monetary union in March 1990, likewise noted that the Community could borrow for investment projects in such a way as to support 'a desired thrust of the concerted economic policies of member states'.[28]

In addition to the functions of the budget in allocation, redistribution, and stabilization, issues of coherence and democracy remain with respect to its control by the EC institutions. The Inter-institutional Agreement of 1988 contributed to both coherence and democracy by giving the European Parliament some new influence over the total of 'compulsory' expenditure; and the Maastricht Treaty enhanced its powers of scrutiny over the Commission's conduct of expenditure. But the Parliament will certainly continue to press for full budgetary codecision, including the same powers over the agricultural and other 'compulsory' expenditure as it has over the 'non-compulsory' budget. Similar arguments would apply to bringing the European Development Fund and the British rebate within the budget, as well as subjecting the Community's borrowing and lending operations to parliamentary scrutiny.

The lack of coherence and control over the budget has been exacerbated by the incoherence of the Council, with the laws passed by the Agriculture Council in particular, when it fixes prices and other terms for farmers, having taken precedence over budgetary discipline. The question whether EC law relating to the budget, or other legislation, is to prevail was answered by the Council, though not in a definitive way, in June 1988 when it accepted that no law passed by one of the Councils and requiring expenditure could be implemented until the budget or financial estimates had been amended to allow for it.[29] This decision needs to be entrenched if the Council is to play its due part in good housekeeping for the Community.

The Maastricht Treaty will affect the distributive impact of the Community budget significantly and the financial perspective for 1993–97 will have an important influence over the size and pattern of revenue and expenditure during that period. But many issues regarding the budget will still remain to be determined: enough, perhaps, to justify a new MacDougall report to show how the Community could develop what has been called the 'public finance union' component of the economic and monetary union.[30]

9 From Common Tariff to Great Civilian Power

The economy of the EC is equivalent to that of the US in its production and somewhat greater in its external trade. It is much greater than the economy of any other country in both. But if it is to bring its weight to bear in defending its interests or shaping the international economic system, the Community must have an external policy; and the experience of the Community's external relations shows that this common policy becomes truly effective when it disposes of a common policy instrument.[1]

The original Community, the ECSC, designed as the framework for a new Franco-German relationship, was not given the main tool of external trade policy, that is a common external tariff. The project for a European Defence Community, responding to the challenge of Soviet military power, was on the contrary intended to integrate the basic instrument of the member states' security policy by creating a European Army. But after years of indecision French politicians decided they would not go so far, and the project was shelved in 1954. The Community's first effective instrument of external policy was, then, the common tariff of the EEC, which was within a few years to make the Community a power in the international trading system equivalent to the United States.

The common external tariff

To give the EEC a common external tariff was not inevitable. Following the example of the ECSC, there was no mention of it in the memorandum from the Benelux governments which was the starting-point for the negotiations to create the EEC; and the German Minister of Economics, Ludwig Erhard, backed by German industry, would have wished that the Federal Republic keep its own low tariff for its trade outside the Community.[2] But the French preferred a customs union complete with common tariff. They feared, with their long protectionist tradition, that their own protection would be undermined by competition coming through Germany and Benelux with their lower tariffs. They also began to see the common tariff as cement to bind the member states together politically, providing a base within which France could regain its influence that had been impaired by the events of World War II. The federalists who composed the Spaak report on which the EEC Treaty was based also had their reasons for preferring a customs union, with common tariff, to a free trade area in which each member state would keep its own tariff.[3] They wanted a level playing field, in which competition would not be affected by differing tariffs among the member states; and they saw the common tariff as an instrument that would give the Community bargaining power in international trade negotiations. Such power could be used for liberal or protectionist ends. Their inclination was liberal. They proposed, in conformity with the Gatt rules, that the common tariff was to be no higher than the average of the member states' tariffs (there were four, not six of these, since the Benelux countries already had their own common tariff); and the EEC Treaty duly provided for a tariff along these lines, to be introduced by aligning the member states' tariffs on it in three steps during the 12–15 year transitional period. They also envisaged that the bargaining power would be used as a means of getting the tariffs of the Community's trading partners down; and this too was to occur in the event. Over a century earlier, Friedrich List, promoting the project for a German customs union, wrote that 'without a common tariff system . . . political nationality was robbed of its most solid foundation'.[4] While the authors of the Spaak report did not express themselves in such terms, their idea of making the Community an actor in the world trading system can nevertheless be seen as a step in the direction of political union.

For the French government, the common tariff became a weapon in their rivalry with the British for European leadership. The British were faced by a dilemma. Outside the customs union, their exports to the Continent would be threatened; inside it, their imports from the Commonwealth would decline. Because they resisted union with the Continent at the expense of Commonwealth ties, they devised the proposal for a European free trade area that would enable them to get the best of both worlds: free trade with the Europeans but without a common external tariff would not get in the way of the free entry to the British market that most exports from the Commonwealth to Britain then enjoyed under the system of Commonwealth preference. Politically, the dilemma would be neatly circumvented. The economic effects were also expected to be favourable. According to the Anglo-Saxon economics of the time, the choice between customs union and free trade area revolved around the concepts of trade creation and trade diversion. Trade creation was the replacement of high-cost domestic production by lower-cost imports when a tariff was removed, and would thus raise efficiency and welfare. Trade diversion, on the contrary, replaced low-cost imports from the rest of the world by higher-cost production from another country within the area where tariffs were being removed. At least for the member states that had the lower tariffs, a free trade area would cause less diversion than a customs union that forced them to raise their tariffs against the rest of the world.[5] So the customs union acquired a protectionist connotation, reinforcing for the British the political arguments against it. Econometric calculations were later to show that trade creation within the Community in the 1960s was about ten times as large as trade diversion.[6] Doubtless liberal pressure for lower tariffs was one significant reason. But meanwhile, the British attempt to breach the Community's common tariff by means of a free trade area was thwarted. The French feared that if the British were vouchsafed free trade without the commitment to a common agricultural policy, the German commitment to that crucial part of their bargain with France would be weakened; and the federalists thought that the wider and looser scheme would undermine the Community's common institutions and instruments. The return to power of General de Gaulle during the course of the free trade area negotiations gave a new edge to French reluctance to give Britain a privileged relationship with the Community, and he broke off the negotiations in November 1958. When Britain approached the Community in 1961 in order to seek full membership, the common tariff was already evoking a reappraisal of US–EC relations.

Towards the end of June 1962, Jean Monnet's Action Committee for the United States of Europe called for a partnership of equals between a united Europe and the United States.[7] A week later, on 4 July, President Kennedy, making a 'Declaration of Interdependence' at Philadelphia, said 'We do not regard a strong and united Europe as a rival but as a partner'. The first embodiment of this idea was his proposal for trade negotiations in which the EC and the US would be the principal parties. His Trade Expansion Act, enacted by Congress in October 1962 with the main purpose of securing cuts in the Community's external tariff, gave the President power to negotiate tariff cuts of up to 50 per cent, setting a time limit at mid-1967. The Kennedy round of trade negotiations in the Gatt ensued.

Such negotiations concern complicated conflicts of interest, and the Kennedy round was no exception. The Americans wanted tariffs to be cut by a given percentage across the board, while the Community wanted the highest tariffs, of which the US had more than the EC, to be cut more deeply than the rest. The Americans wanted concessions on agriculture from the Europeans, who in turn objected to the Americans' protectionist treatment of their chemical industry. With all the Gatt participants and several thousand tariff positions involved, these conflicts would anyway take time to resolve; but they were further complicated by sharp differences within the Community itself.[8]

Gaullist France was contesting American leadership while France's five EC partners were inclined to support American policy. Germany and Benelux were liberal whereas France and Italy were more protectionist. The Germans saw their interest in industrial trade while the French wanted to secure the markets for their agriculture. Conflict over the Community's institutions and de Gaulle's tactic of the empty chair blocked the Community's decision-taking capacity for half a year in the middle of the Kennedy round negotiations. But the negotiations were nevertheless concluded just before the deadline of mid-1967 with the unprecedented success of cuts which reduced the tariffs of industrialized countries by an average of about one-third. The Community was evidently too important to its members for them to risk failure in what was, with the common agricultural policy, one of its two main projects of the 1960s. The Americans were determined to keep the Atlantic relationship in working order. Behind these political motives, the stronger industries on both sides of the Atlantic saw their future in wider open markets, beyond the confines of the EC or the US; so they were demanding success from their politicians.

Had the Kennedy round failed, the world might have slid back to the protectionism that had blighted the international economy in the 1930s. Instead, the way was cleared for continued expansion of world trade, with the prospect of some immediate economic benefits and of more significant longer-term dynamic effects.[9] Politically, the success of the Kennedy round helped the Community to come through the 1960s in a condition that made its further development possible; and the Commission's reputation was enhanced. Although the Council acted to keep it on a tight rein, the Commission was able, by exploring appropriate compromises with the negotiating partners, to make it hard for the Council to renege on them. Given the satisfactory conclusion, the merit of the Commission's measure of independence was demonstrated. Above all, the Kennedy round vindicated the decision to give the Community its common external tariff by showing that the idea of partnership was feasible, despite considerable difficulties. One of these was what was seen on both sides of the Atlantic as de Gaulle's anti-American policy. Another was the process of a change in relative power, painful for the country whose superiority is being reduced, and clearly recognized by an American observer at the time:[10]

The dominant position of the United States in Gatt evaporated with the implementation of the Rome Treaty. . . . The Common Market is now the most important member of Gatt, and can determine in large measure the success or failure of any attempt to liberalize trade. When Europeans instruct Americans in the realities of the new international economic situation they are demonstrating the change in relative power that has taken place.

While EC–US relations were later to suffer from an American reaction to changes in power relations, in the form of a harder-nosed diplomacy, the Kennedy round nevertheless had a lasting effect. The process of tariff cutting was to continue through successive Gatt rounds, until tariffs were well below half their original levels; and the concept of partnership, embodied in this practical demonstration, can still be seen as a valid option in the 1990s. For the Community itself, this use of its common tariff had established its position as an equal of the United States in the world trading system, causing it, as an emergent union without security competences, to be visualized as 'the first of the world's civilian centres of power'.[11]

Non-tariff distortions

Although the Kennedy round went far to establish a low-tariff international trading system, many forms of protection with instruments other than tariffs remained. For trade among the advanced industrial countries of the Organization for Economic Co-operation and Development (OECD), agricultural protection was the most important. We have seen in Chapter 5 how the Community, with massive protection for its farmers through import levies and support through export subsidies, has turned from being a big net importer of key agricultural products to being one of the world's largest exporters; and this has disrupted the trade of OECD countries such as Australia, Canada, New Zealand, and the US, as well as of some less-developed countries. Some other European countries are even more protectionist in the field of agriculture, and the US has also protected its farmers heavily. The Uruguay round of Gatt negotiations, still in difficulties at the end of 1991, has been the first with a serious prospect that agricultural protection would follow that of industry in becoming subject to some form of international control.

The Swedish economist Gunnar Myrdal, writing in the mid-1950s, predicted that international integration would be prevented by what he called national integration: the efforts of governments to improve their citizens' welfare by intervention in the economy.[12] Such measures would, he thought, disrupt or distort international trade, even if unintentionally. If he was right, the regional integration within the EC would have the same effect on wider international economic relations. The experience of the Kennedy round and of the opening of markets to trade in manufactures among the advanced industrial countries proved him wrong. The interest of the more dynamic sectors of the economy in wider markets which would give them space to develop new technologies was strong enough to overcome the tendencies towards protection, whether on the part of the EC or of other advanced industrial economies. But with respect to agriculture, where intervention is much heavier, his idea has proved abundantly justified, not least as far as the EC is concerned.

Myrdal's idea has also found some justification in the treatment by advanced industrial countries of their imports from other parts of the world. Imports from less-developed countries of many products, such as textiles and shoes, in which they have a comparative advantage, are tightly restricted by quotas. The same applied to the Community's imports from Eastern Europe, though this began to change rapidly in 1990 as the reforms there gathered momentum. Within the OECD group, Japan's success in exporting a wide range of manufactures has been met by the demand that the Japanese apply voluntary export restrictions (VERs), with the threat that other action will be taken if they fail to do so. With the recessions and stagflation of the 1970s, such instruments of protection multiplied.

While quotas restricting mutual trade among the EC member states are not allowed, other forms of protection such as subsidies, preferential public procurement, and divergent standards or regulations were severely distorting and obstructing the Community's internal trade. Hence the single market programme, to complete the necessary legislation by the end of 1992. But this programme raises the question whether it will, like the common tariff on manufactures, lead to a wider liberalization of international trade, or whether, like the agricultural levies and subsidies, it will instead provoke international disintegration.

The general interest in liberal trade is harder to bring to bear against protectionist pressures in the case of non-tariff distortions than of tariffs, because there is no formula for liberalization as simple as that of cutting tariffs by up to one-half. Even that formula led to a most complex negotiation. When standards, regulations, or state aids in a variety of forms are involved, the complexity, and hence the scope for lobbies to secure special treatment, is yet greater. But there are principles that can help in resisting them. For services such as banking and insurance, home-country treatment is such a principle: that services supplied by third-country firms are treated in the same way as those supplied by local firms. The EC's second banking Directive of 1989 applies this principle to banks, provided that their country of origin applies the same principle in its treatment of Community banks. Since the Community's rules give banks more scope than do those of the other two major financial powers, the US and Japan, this Directive did something to allay fears that the single market would become a pretext for the building of a highly protected 'Fortress Europe'. Insulation from the world market would work against the interests of the more dynamic elements in financial services as well as in industry, and this should help to countervail the pressures for protection.

Since the Community's single market is backed by Community law enforced by the courts, it is more solidly based than the results of wider international negotiations. It has been suggested that 'the Community provides an example of effective international law-making that at some point might be replicated at the global level',[13] but meanwhile, the Gatt is the best available framework. In its Tokyo round of negotiations, completed in 1979, codes were drawn up to guide behaviour with respect to subsidies and public procurement. In the Uruguay round, non-tariff distortions moved to the centre of the stage. The agenda included services and textiles, safeguards against 'disruptive' imports, intellectual property, and methods of resolving disputes. But it was the conflict over agriculture that proved the most intractable.

With American negotiators constrained by a more protectionist Congress, the Uruguay round lacked the strong US leadership that gave such an impulse to the Kennedy round. Although the Community's own internal agreement on the principle of shifting its agricultural policy away from price support reduced a major obstacle to agreement in the Gatt, there was still great difficulty in closing the gap between the EC and the US over agriculture, and hence in reaching agreement on a conclusion of the round that would provide a liberal framework for the international economy in the years to come.

Lome Convention

The tariff-cutting in Gatt negotiations is based on the most-favoured nation (mfn) principle: reductions accorded to one participant are extended to all. The aim was to establish a generally liberal system rather than to proliferate bilateral deals. The Americans, who had been much irked by the Commonwealth preferences introduced between the two world wars, were insistent on this principle, which underlay the Gatt rounds in which the Community demonstrated its equality with the US as a trading power. But the EC, from the starting-point of French imperial preferences, was to use its common external tariff to develop a network of preferences which included the big majority of its trading partners. The full mfn tariff is levied only on imports from the US, Australia, Canada, New Zealand, South Africa, Japan, republics of the former Soviet Union, and a very few other countries. Most-favoured nation has become least-favoured nation; and the EC has used its tariff in this way as a powerful instrument of policy towards the rest of Europe and the Third World.

When it was agreed that the EEC would be a customs union, the French and their five partners were faced with a trilemma. The tariff-free entry into France from the French empire (as it then was) could have remained as an exception, as was indeed agreed for imports from East Germany into the Federal Republic; but France wanted a better deal for its colonies. Or the common tariff could have been imposed on the imports into

France, as was later to be the fate of imports into Britain from Australia, Canada, and New Zealand, when Britain joined the Community. But this was unacceptable to France. The French insisted, instead, on extending the preference in favour of their colonies to imports into the whole of the Community. The Germans and Dutch, more concerned about trade with other less-developed countries and reluctant to become involved in supporting French colonies, resisted this idea. But Guy Mollet, the French Prime Minister, told them that the Assemblée Nationale would not ratify the EEC Treaty unless these preferences were agreed.[14] Without France, the EEC could not have been established. So France's five partners accepted, and Part IV was added to the EEC Treaty, providing for favours to 'Overseas Countries and Territories', mainly French colonies and mainly in Africa, though there were also a few such associates of Belgium, Italy, and the Netherlands, and a few in the Atlantic and the Pacific as well as Africa.

Part IV provided, then, that no tariffs would be imposed on imports from these associates into the whole of the Community. Exports to them from the Community would at the same time enjoy 'reverse preferences', that is to say any preferences that were already granted to such exports from France, Belgium, Italy, or the Netherlands would be extended to exports from all the Community countries. France also persuaded its partners that the Community should create a European Development Fund, with a budget of $581.25 million for aid to the associates in the first five years, to be renewed for subsequent periods. Thus the Community put together a package of trade preferences and aid for these associated countries.

With the coming of independence for the French colonies, the package was renewed in the form of the Yaounde Convention for successive periods, until this was replaced by the Lome Convention in 1975, following the accession of Britain to the Community. The Yaounde associates were joined, under the Lome Convention, by the Commonwealth countries in Africa, the Caribbean, and the Pacific (hence the term ACP used for the Community's partners in this Convention); and most of the remaining countries of Africa south of the Sahara have also acceded to it, together with Haiti and the Dominican Republic, bringing the total of ACP partners to over sixty.

The provisions of Part IV were extended during the course of the Yaounde and Lome Conventions. First, a joint Council of Ministers and Committee of Ambassadors and a Joint Assembly were established, reflecting the independence secured by most of the Community's partners in the 1960s. Then the Lome Convention removed the reverse preferences, which most of the ACP countries regarded as a relic of the imperial order that caused them to buy more expensive goods from the Community rather than cheaper goods elsewhere. In view of the importance of sugar exports for a number of small Commonwealth countries in the Caribbean and the Pacific, the Community agreed to import 1.3 million tonnes of sugar from them at the high prices guaranteed to EC farmers. There is by now preferential access to the EC market for most of the ACP exports of products that are subject to levies under the common agricultural policy. The aid has been increased with each renewal of the Lome Convention at five-year intervals, to reach ecu 12 billion for the period 1990–5 covered by Lome IV. This aid comes not only from the European Development Fund but also from the European Investment Bank and five funds for particular purposes. Two of these, Stabex and Sysmin, are to provide compensation for countries that lose significantly from falls in commodity earnings (Sysmin for minerals, Stabex for other commodities); and there is structural adjustment aid, refugee aid, and emergency aid for disaster relief. Since debt became such a heavy burden for many ACP countries in the 1980s, over 90 per cent of the aid under Lome IV will take the form of grants.

Thus Part IV of the EEC Treaty, designed originally mainly to resolve the problem of preferential entry into France from a dozen of its colonies, has developed incrementally into a complex structure of trade and aid support for almost the whole of Africa and a score of small countries, mostly islands, in the Caribbean and the Pacific. But although many see the Lome Convention as a model for relations between advanced industrial and less-developed countries, its effectiveness in stimulating development is far from clear. Imports into the

Community from ACP countries of tropical products such as cocoa, coffee, and tropical hardwoods have certainly benefited, but largely through diversion of trade from other less-developed countries, in Asia and Latin America. The aid has surely been helpful and some sugar exporters would have suffered severely without the guaranteed sale of sugar at high prices. Yet the response of the ACP countries to the tariff-free entry for manufactures into the EC has been disappointing. It seems that the lack of an industrial culture has prevented most of them from taking advantage of his opportunity. Rather than an engine of development, then, the Lome Convention appears to have acted as a system of life-support. Politically, it has eased the post-imperial transition to a new relationship between ACP countries and Europeans, which could have been more difficult if preferences had remained anchored only to the former imperial powers.

The effects of the Yaounde and Lome Conventions on Asians and Latin Americans were negative. Trade diverted towards the ACP countries was diverted away from them. The Asian countries of the Commonwealth were excluded from the Lome Convention when the ACP Commonwealth countries were able to adhere to it, evidently because some of the EC member governments were not willing to accept the competition from developing countries that could export manufactures, giving the impression that the Europeans preferred to associate with suppliers of primary products in a form of neo-colonial relationship rather than with countries that showed a capacity for industrial development. The Community was also discriminating against almost all the large countries of the Third World which could be expected to become great industrial powers in the next century: Brazil, China, India, Indonesia, Mexico. All this added up to a case for extending preferences beyond the ACP countries to the developing countries of Asia and Latin America: hence, for the Generalized System of Preferences (GSP).

The Generalized System of Preferences

It was soon after the signature of the first Yaounde Convention that Third World countries began to propose that the advanced industrial countries should grant them generalized preferences, without discrimination in favour of one or other group in the Third World. There were arguments in favour of a positive response by the Community. Such preferences should promote prosperity and stability in the Third World, and hence its potential as a growing market and a reliable source of primary products. While industries in the Community would resist imports of manufactures such as clothing and footwear produced with cheap labour, such imports would improve life for many of the poorer consumers. The Community would gain friends that would be useful for a new and politically still developing organization. For the Dutch and Germans, generalized preferences would be a move towards the wider concept of relations with the Third World that had caused them to resist Part IV of the EEC Treaty. The British, when approaching membership of the Community in the early 1970s, had strong grounds to support the GSP proposal, because it would help to ease the problem posed by the common external tariff for imports that had hitherto entered the UK market tariff-free from the Asian members of the Commonwealth.

A small group of officials in the Commission skilfully exploited the potential support for the GSP in the member states. As had been done in the Kennedy round, they discussed possible solutions with their negotiating partners which the EC member governments then found it difficult to repudiate.[15] They used the window of opportunity offered by the negotiations for British accession to promote the GSP as a solution to the problem of the Asian Commonwealth; and the EC decided to adopt its GSP just as those negotiations were completed. So it was that the EC, despite the handicap of its heavy inter-governmental decision-making process, introduced its GSP before the US or Japan. The system was installed initially for a decade beginning in 1971 and was renewed for a further decade, each time with a break half-way for reconsideration of the rules. It was renewed annually for 1991 and 1992, pending conclusion of the Uruguay round.

The GSP provides for tariff-free entry into the EC for manufactures and semi-manufactures from less-developed countries. But there are limits to this liberality for products described as 'sensitive', where competition based on low wages is painful for European industry. The tariff-free entry is limited to quotas determined by the Community for a substantial number of such products; and textiles are largely excluded from the GSP, being controlled by quotas negotiated under the Gatt's Multi-Fibre Arrangement. Some agricultural products are included but, in order to curtail the impact on farmers in the EC and the ACP, the tariffs are not eliminated but imposed at reduced rates. Least-developed countries receive exceptional treatment: no quota limits on tariff-free entry of manufactures, and zero tariffs for some agricultural products. As with the Lome Convention, the EC's partners are not required to grant reverse preferences.

Not surprisingly, it is the newly industrializing countries that have benefited the most from the GSP, along with consumers in the EC who have been able to buy their cheap manufactures. But the other, less-developed countries have also been able to benefit from an EC programme of aid parallel to that for the ACP countries, though less generous, reaching a level of some ecu 1 billion a year in the late 1980s.

In recognition of their importance, the Community has negotiated co-operation agreements with some of the larger Asian and Latin American countries, such as China, India, Brazil, and Mexico, as well as agreements with some regional groups such as the South-East Asian ASEAN, the Gulf States, and the Central Americans. There are regular meetings to discuss problems of their relations with the Community; but, except perhaps in the case of Central America, where the Community has tried to encourage economic integration and the peace process, the results do not appear to be very significant.

Mediterranean preferences

Just as, from the modest start with Part IV of the EEC Treaty, the Community developed preferential systems for almost the whole of Africa, Asia, and Latin America, so it has evolved preferential arrangements for almost all the countries around the Mediterranean.

It started with Greece. The Greeks wanted access to the newly established EEC and applied for association with it in mid-1959, soon after the negotiations for a free trade area had been terminated. The EC for its part, wanting to strengthen its position in relation to the British-led Efta group and to establish itself as an actor in international economic relations, was keen to conclude such an agreement, which was therefore done in time for the association to come into force in 1962 on terms quite favourable to Greece. The aim was a customs union between Greece and the Community, with a transitional period of twelve years for the EC but as much as 22 years for Greek tariffs that protected sensitive products. Some Greek agricultural products were to receive intra-Community treatment at once, others later. Financial assistance was to be provided for Greece. A Council of Association, comprising representatives of the Commission and of the governments of EC member states and Greece, could decide by unanimity on anything required to fulfil the aims of the agreement. The ultimate aim was Greek accession to the Community, which was in fact achieved in 1981, after a period in which it had been precluded because Greece succumbed to a military dictatorship.

The Turks, whose exports to the Community were competitive with those of Greece, followed the Greeks in seeking a similar form of association. Here again an agreement was concluded and association came into force in 1964. It was largely similar to that with Greece, although there was no clear commitment to eventual membership, and the transitional period to complete a customs union was still more extended, being set at 22 years in a protocol to the agreement in 1970. Some aspects of the agreement were suspended during a period of military rule. But with a democratic government again functioning, Turkey applied in 1987 for accession to the Community, which delayed until 1990 before making clear its view that the application was premature.

At the other end of the Mediterranean, the door was opened for Morocco and Tunisia by a Declaration of Intent attached to the EEC Treaty to negotiate for association with 'independent countries of the franc area'. Both countries took advantage of this to negotiate free access to the EC market for industrial products and tariff preferences for agricultural products; and by 1972 they had been followed by almost all other countries bordering on or close to the Mediterranean. The other Arab countries included Algeria, Egypt, Jordan, Lebanon, and Syria. With the inclusion of Arabs, the Community could hardly refuse Israel. As European countries, Cyprus and Malta obtained association. Yugoslavia, European but Communist, was accorded a co-operation agreement because of its political choice of separation from the Soviet bloc. Spain, while still under Franco's dictatorship, was not eligible for EC membership, but negotiated an agreement for preferences reducing tariffs on manufactures by 60 per cent. Thus only Albania and Libya remained, by their own self-exclusion, as Mediterranean countries without a preferential agreement with the Community.

This web of agreements had grown incrementally and *ad hoc* through the 1960s, with the Community finding it hard to refuse each new applicant what its neighbours had received. By 1972, the Commission was pressing for a 'global approach' to provide an orderly framework for the agreements; and although no formal global framework such as the Lome Convention was established, by the end of the 1970s they had much in common. All provided tariff-free entry for manufactures into the EC market, though there were ceilings for some products beyond which tariffs would be imposed. Tariffs were at reduced rates for most agricultural products. There was no reciprocation through reverse preferences, except for Cyprus, Malta, and Turkey, which had agreed to move to customs unions with the Community, and Israel, which had agreed to a free trade area. There was in all cases an element of financial aid and other co-operation, in the fields of science and technology, problems of migrant labour, and the environment in particular. In short, apart from the absence of a global framework, the Mediterranean agreements have much in common with the Lome Convention.

As has been found among the recipients of GSP, only the countries with an industrial culture have benefited from the free entry for manufactures. This is almost identical with the list of countries that were able to offer reciprocity, that is, Cyprus, Israel, Malta, and Turkey, with the addition of Yugoslavia. The Mediterranean exporters have benefited from the preferences for agricultural products, partly through the diversion of trade from similar American and Australian products, partly through trade creation in competition with the Community's own Mediterranean farmers. The accession to the Community of Spain, however, with its great potential for such production, caused the Mediterranean trade partners to fear that Spanish farmers would displace their exports. The Community gave assurances that the traditional flows of trade would not be disrupted, but this did not allay the fears of the exporters. The web of agreements has doubtless been of help to the Community's political relations with the Mediterranean countries, though it has done little to set at rest European worries about the dangers of political instability in the region.[16]

Efta

When the EEC was founded many in Britain saw it as a protectionist grouping that would split the European economy. But it has in the event not only enlarged its membership from six to twelve, but also been the catalyst for an area of free trade covering the whole of Western Europe.

When the negotiations for a free trade area of all the OEEC members were brought to a halt in 1958, a truncated free trade area was set up by seven countries: Britain, Denmark, Norway, Sweden, Austria, Switzerland, and Portugal. Finland and Iceland later became members of the European Free Trade Association (Efta), as it was called; and Britain, Denmark, and Portugal left it when they joined the Community. The six remaining members of Efta (it was only in 1991 that Liechtenstein joined, making seven) stood aside from the Community for motives which included fears about dilution of neutrality, insistence on national sovereignty, and long-standing democracy.

When Britain negotiated accession to the Community, it posed the condition that all the Efta countries should secure industrial free trade with the Community when the accession took place. Otherwise, the British government explained, the House of Commons would not accept the accession treaty. Although the British negotiating position was weaker than that of France when it posed a similar condition with respect to the French colonies, since France was essential to the Community whereas it had proved itself capable of doing without Britain, the British nevertheless had cards to play. France's five partners wanted Britain to join, and the Community would have suffered difficult times if the negotiations had broken down; and the Federal Republic in particular wanted to restore its trade links with Efta countries. These were traditionally strong with the Scandinavians, Austrians, and Swiss, and Efta had succeeded in diverting some of their trade with Germany to Efta members, particularly Britain. Contrary to the Community's experience, where trade creation was ten times trade diversion, it was estimated that not far short of half the increase of trade within Efta due to the removal of tariffs was trade diversion, much of it from Germany.[17] Thus for economic as well as political reasons, the Community agreed to the principle of industrial free trade with Efta countries.

Here again, the Commission made good use of the window of opportunity between mid-1971, when the enlargement negotiations were concluded, and the end of 1972 when Britain, Denmark, and Ireland entered the Community. Some of the EC member governments wanted to insist on a measure of harmonization of Efta countries' policies with those of the EC before free trade would be allowed. But this would have made the negotiations complex and long, risking delay beyond the target date of end-1972 and, worse still, the general economic and political disruption caused by the oil shock at the end of 1973. The Commission managed to persuade the member governments to confine the agreements to relatively straightforward free trade areas with each Efta country, thus ensuring that free trade would extend over the whole of Western Europe: within the EC; within Efta; and between the EC and each Efta country under the six free trade agreements.

Although the EC, enlarged to twelve members, accounts for nine-tenths of the population of Western Europe and Efta for only one-tenth, the Efta countries are rich and collectively comprise the EC's biggest trading partner. Both sides have gained from the trade creation that has followed this widening of the market; and political relations within Western Europe are certainly better than they would have been had no such economic accommodation been reached. The EC's single market programme, however, disturbed the equilibrium that held through most of the 1970s and 1980s. Efta countries feared that their trade would be damaged unless they participated with the Community in the removal of non-tariff distortions. Austria applied for full membership in 1989 and it seemed likely that other Efta countries would follow, as did Sweden in 1991. The EC, worried lest accession negotiations with Efta countries might disrupt the 1992 programme, sought negotiations with them collectively to deal with their concerns about the single market by creating a 'European Economic Area' (EEA) which would enable them to participate in it as far as possible. The wheel had come full circle and harmonization was seen as necessary now that the focus was on non-tariff distortions rather than tariffs. The problem for the Community was to give the Efta countries enough say in the EC legislative process relating to the single market without undermining the Community's autonomy; the problem for Efta was the Community's view that the single market requires agreement on laws, and then their enforcement, in ways that are not compatible with the national sovereignty on which Efta countries had insisted hitherto. Political agreement on the EEA was reached in October 1991, but the Court of Justice challenged the legitimacy of the arrangement whereby difficulties were to be settled by a tribunal comprising three of its members and two judges from Efta states, thus pre-empting the ultimate authority of the Court in interpreting Community laws. However this problem is resolved, it seems likely that other Efta countries will, like Austria and Sweden, conclude that full membership of the Community would be preferable. As suggested towards the end of Chapter 3, the security constraint that has inhibited some of them has become less significant. The same may be said of Central and East European countries in considering how to link themselves with the Community.

Central and Eastern Europe

Soon after the end of World War II, the Soviet Union came to be seen in Western Europe as a hostile superpower, dominating its smaller neighbours in Central and Eastern Europe and preventing western countries from having a normal relationship with them. The EC's six founder members reacted to Stalin's use of force by negotiating the treaty for a European Defence Community, which as we have seen was shelved in 1954. For some time Soviet policy was aimed at preventing further development of the Community; and this resulted in a refusal to recognize the Community until the late 1980s. Through the Gaullist and early post-Gaullist periods, the EC member states kept commercial policy towards the East as far as possible in their own hands, preferring to negotiate direct with the eastern countries rather than to conduct a common Community policy. But the EEC Treaty provided for the common commercial policy to be completed after the end of the transitional period, and late in 1974 the Commission was authorized to offer the negotiation of trade agreements to all the state-trading countries.

It was fifteen years before an agreement was finally reached between the EC and the Soviet Union in 1989. The Soviet refusal to recognize the Community's institutions with their federal characteristics was one reason. The bad relations caused by the Soviet intervention in Afghanistan in 1979 and repression in Poland in 1981 were another. The Soviet attempt to give the Council for Mutual Economic Assistance (Comecon) a big role in the negotiations was yet another, because this would have given the Soviet Union an extra leverage over Comecon's other members in Central and Eastern Europe and was thus unacceptable to the Community, which was concerned rather that they should have more autonomy.

Behind these political motives lay the economic fact that neither the EC nor the Soviet Union had much to gain from trade negotiations with each other. Trade with the Community was important for the Soviet Union, being a source of equipment which transferred technology and producer goods that helped to keep Soviet industry functioning. But the exports with which the Soviet Union earned the money to buy these things were preponderantly oil, gas, and other primary products, which encounter no tariffs or quotas on entering the Community market. It followed that the Soviet Union could have few significant demands to make of Community commercial policy. To the EC, the Soviet Union's command economy, in which production and trade were largely regulated by quantitative instructions from the planners to the enterprises, presented negotiators with a problem which was never satisfactorily solved. Either the western partner, in this case the Community, would seek concessions in the form of quantitative targets, which would have infringed both the Soviet planners' autonomy and the free market principle on which the EC economy was based, or the Community negotiators would have no demands of significance comparable to a tariff reduction in negotiations among market economies. Thus trade negotiations offered neither the EC nor the Soviet Union an economic incentive sufficient to overcome the political obstacles.

Until the Soviet policy was changed by Mikhail Gorbachev, the relations of the other European members of Comecon with the Community were constrained by Soviet power. Stalin set up Comecon in 1949 in response to the American initiative of Marshall aid, but that was a formality; he bent the other member states to his will by bilateral control. Nikita Khrushchev wanted to reflect the establishment of the EEC in a supranational Comecon, but his proposal of 1962 was rejected by Romania on grounds of national sovereignty, and covertly resisted by Hungary and Poland. Leonid Brezhnev, following his suppression of the Prague Spring in 1968, sought to ensure stability in Central and Eastern Europe through economic integration under Comecon's Comprehensive Programme decided upon in 1971; and it was in this phase of Comecon's development that the Soviet Union tried to get more control over the external trade of the other member states by insisting that the Community's offer of trade negotiations be answered by Comecon rather than by its member states, which would themselves negotiate about trade only after Comecon had agreed a framework with the EC. Given the Community's resistance to such a reinforcement of Soviet hegemony, this occasioned the delay of a decade and a half before the Central and East European states could conclude agreements with the EC, with economic implications that were more serious for the smaller members of Comecon than for the EC or the Soviet Union itself.

These smaller Central and East European countries—Czechoslovakia, Hungary, Poland, Bulgaria, and Romania—depended much less than the Soviet Union on exports of energy and raw materials to the Community, and much more on agricultural products competitive with those of the Community and on low-technology manufactures, competing with EC industries that were already hard-pressed by imports from the newly industrializing countries. East Germany's situation was easier, because it had free access to the market of the Federal Republic under a Protocol to the EEC Treaty. But the other Central and East Europeans were hard hit by the Community's protection of its sensitive sectors. They were allowed to negotiate with the EC about its protection of particular sectors such as agriculture, steel, and textiles; but Soviet policy prevented them from embarking on general trade negotiations until Comecon as a whole should reach an agreement with the EC.

Under Gorbachev the deadlock was broken. The Soviet Union accepted the EC's condition that negotiations about trade were a matter for the EC and Comecon's member states, not for Comecon itself. A Joint Declaration of mutual recognition was signed by the EC and Comecon in 1988, providing for regular discussions between the two organizations; and the EC reached trade and co-operation agreements with Hungary, Poland, and the Soviet Union in 1989. These provided for the removal by 1995 of the quotas still imposed by the EC specifically on imports from these countries, though with a safeguard clause as protection against market disruption. But these were quite modest concessions, limited by the difficulty that the EC still found in dealing with command economies. During 1989, however, it became clear that this constraint was disappearing in Poland and Hungary as they moved towards pluralist democracy and market economy, followed rapidly by East Germany and Czechoslovakia; and the

Soviet Union, Bulgaria, and Romania were taking steps in the same direction, together with Yugoslavia which, although not a member of Comecon, had retained a system that gave the Communist party a monopoly of political power and failed to achieve adequate economic reform.

The Community responded rapidly to the radical changes in Central Europe. It accepted that the accession of East Germany to the Federal Republic would bring the whole united Germany into the EC without the need for prior changes in the treaties, although some transitional measures were required to ease the accommodation of East Germany with certain Community laws and policies. When the Poles and Hungarians decided to establish pluralist democracies and market economies, the Community gave them GSP treatment from the start of 1990, removed most of the remaining quotas restricting its imports from them, and allocated substantial sums of aid; and these benefits were extended to the other East European countries as they too embarked on their reforms. In April 1990, the Community declared itself ready to negotiate association agreements with Central and East European countries taking steps towards pluralist democracy and market economy; and by the end of 1991 it had concluded 'Europe Agreements' with Czechoslovakia, Hungary, and Poland, providing for a phased programme to industrial free trade; financial and technical assistance; and institutions of association in which political as well as economic matters could be discussed.

The Community's response to the Central European changes was swift and comprehensive, partly because of the strong political motive to support these new democracies, but also because the Community's long experience with preferential and association agreements gave it many precedents on which such action could be based. The response to the disintegration of Yugoslavia and the Soviet Union has been harder to devise. The war in Yugoslavia presented the Community with an unprecedented problem. The new Russia's reforms were launched in the face of enormous economic and political difficulties, in the context of conversion of the highly centralized Soviet state into a loose association of republics; and other republics were hardly better placed. By the end of 1991 the Community was delivering significant food aid and technical assistance, but on a scale dwarfed by the problems. Yet relations with Russia in particular are so crucial to the future of the Community that designing a suitable policy is one of the greatest challenges for it. Given the highly charged political and security elements, much will depend on how far the Community can combine its external economic policy with a more integrated common foreign policy.

Foreign policy co-operation or common foreign policy

No sooner were the negotiations to found the first Community, the ECSC, under way than the proposal for a European Defence Community, and hence for a common foreign and security policy, was made. With the US insisting on a German contribution to the defence of the West, following the Communist aggression in Korea, Monnet applied the same logic to military as he had to industrial power: Germany and France, with other European countries, should be contained together within a Community framework. But much more than coal and steel, armed forces were at the heart of national sovereignty: hence Monnet's conclusion that federation would have to become an immediate objective.[18] But that federal project failed, partly because of fierce Gaullist opposition. After de Gaulle came to power, inheriting a Community whose federal characteristics he abhorred, he attempted to initiate co-operation in foreign policy among the member states on an intergovernmental basis. But the Fouchet plan, as the project was called, likewise foundered after negotiations in 1961–2, because it provoked sharp opposition among France's five partners: partly because of a cleavage between de Gaulle's policy towards the US and theirs; partly because federalists objected to the stress on intergovernmental at the expense of Community institutions. So it was not until after de Gaulle's departure that the member governments started to organize foreign policy co-operation.

The Community's Hague Summit in December 1969, which launched the process of enlargement and the project of monetary union, also asked the foreign ministers to report on how to achieve 'political unification', in the sense of foreign policy co-operation. The result was the Davignon report,[19] on the basis of which the Council decided in October 1970 to hold regular meetings of foreign ministers and senior foreign affairs ministry officials, calling the procedure European Political Co-operation (EPC). The EPC had an early success in the first round of the Conference on Security and Co-operation in Europe (CSCE), concluding with the Helsinki Final Act in 1975. Among other things, the EPC put human rights on the agenda, which surely contributed to the ferment that eventually led to the political changes in Central and Eastern Europe. But differences over matters such as sanctions against South Africa stood in the way of common policies; France and Britain in particular resisted co-operation in certain areas in which they felt they had a special interest; and Greece, in the first years after joining the Community in 1981, was responsible for no less than three-quarters of all the cases of unilateral action. Yet the intensive exchange of information, constant meetings, and efforts to harmonize views exercised a drip effect, and by the time that the Single European Act was negotiated the member states found it worthwhile to formalize the EPC procedures in the treaty and to create a small EPC secretariat in Brussels. When the Single Act came into force in 1987, it also provided that the EPC could include the 'political and economic aspects of security', and that the European Parliament should be 'closely associated' with the EPC. A further provision of the Single Act that may strongly influence the development of external policy is the 'assent procedure', whereby the European Parliament's assent is required before association agreements can come into effect and before the Council can act on an application for membership.

The flow of information among the member states' foreign ministries has attained a very considerable volume. The annual programme of EPC meetings had included four for the foreign ministers, twelve for the foreign ministries' political directors, and some hundred working groups on particular subjects. Outside the Community, the ambassadors of the Twelve in each capital have meetings; the President for the time being of the Council, or the troika of present, preceding, and succeeding

Presidents, makes visits where discussions are thought to be useful; and there have been regular contacts with a score of countries and groups, including the Soviet Union, Hungary, Poland, and Yugoslavia; China, India, and Japan; ASEAN, and the Central American and Gulf groups of states. Common positions or declarations are produced at the rate of more than one a week.[20] But beyond the exchange of information and the expression of common views, common action requires common instruments to be effective. These exist in the Community's instruments of external economic policy, and are sometimes used in co-ordination with the EPC's positions, for example where the trade and aid instruments are employed in the relationship with ASEAN or Central America. Most importantly, the Community responded to the great changes that began in Central and Eastern Europe in 1989 with a powerful common policy towards that area, using the instruments of external economic policy available to it in a comprehensive way, with the specific aim of helping the establishment of market economies and pluralist democracies. In 1990, it gave economic support to the United Nations action against Iraq after the invasion of Kuwait, rapidly imposing sanctions and following this with aid for Middle East states whose economies were hit by the blockade and the refugees. But here, as in relation to the subsequent war in Yugoslavia, the Community's lack of defence competences restricted the part that it could play.

With the notable exception of its policy towards Central Europe, the Community could hardly be said to have established 'a European foreign policy', which the Single European Act stipulated that the member states 'shall endeavour to formulate and implement'. The EPC became 'a major procedure for foreign policy-making', but the question remained whether it could evolve as a 'federal foreign policy'.[21] Various proposals were made to move it in that direction. The Tindemans report on European Union, presented to the European Council in 1975, proposed that the Council should vote by majority in this field.[22] The European Parliament, in its Draft Treaty on European Union in 1984, proposed that the assent procedure, which was under the Single European Act to give it the right of codecision for association and accession, should be extended to all international agreements made by the Community, and that the Commission should be responsible for the preparation of foreign policies, as it is in other fields of Community competence. The Maastricht Treaty does extend the assent procedure to all agreements that establish institutions or have substantial budgetary implications. The Treaty provides not only for 'systematic cooperation', continuing along the lines of the EPC, but also for 'joint action' on foreign policy, which the Council may decide within guidelines set by the European Council. France, Germany, and other member states would have accepted the progressive introduction of qualified majority voting on this but Britain resisted; the outcome was that the scope and aims of policies would be subject to the unanimity rule but that the Council could agree unanimously what aspects of implementation could be decided by qualified majority. The framework for the common foreign and security policy (CFSP) has been set up as a separate wing alongside the Community; the Commission and Parliament are not given powers that they have in the Community and the Court of Justice is to have no role at all. The Commission is, however, to be 'fully associated' with the work of the CFSP, with the right, which it shares with the member states, to make proposals to the Council. The Parliament is to be consulted and regularly informed, can put questions or make recommendations to the Council, and is to hold an annual debate on the policy.

With the predominance of the unanimity procedure and the denial of the normal roles to the Commission, Parliament, and Court, the institutional framework for the CFSP is weaker than that of the Community. But the effectiveness of the policy depends also on that of the instruments at its disposal. Those of trade policy already belong to the Community, as do the resources that the Community is allocated for aid; and when used by the Community institutions boldly enough in support of a foreign policy aim, the example of Central and Eastern Europe shows that they can be quite powerful. Economic and monetary union with a common currency will extend the Community's influence into international monetary and macro-economic policy. The Community will then dispose of the economic instruments which are the major basis for the foreign policy of, for example, Japan. But the question remains how policy based on the Community's economic instruments is to be related to that based on security instruments, hitherto the prerogative of the member states.

International events have been pressing most of the EC members towards closer European co-operation on security. With arms reduction and the disintegration of the Warsaw Pact then the Soviet Union, American expenditure on defence in Europe is declining, raising the question of how Europeans will take more responsibility for their defence in a Continent and a world where many uncertainties remain. Desire for a stable political framework for the united Germany is also a motive for strengthening the security element in that framework. Thus most of the EC member states feel the need for a more integrated system centred on Western Europe. This feeling lies behind the moves towards Franco-German co-operation in, for example, the joint brigade of soldiers from their two armies; and former Chancellor Helmut Schmidt has proposed reviving the concept of a European Army.[23] It has also motivated the provisions in the Maastricht Treaty for common security alongside those for common foreign policy.

Maastricht provided that the CFSP is to include all questions of security, including the 'eventual' framing of a common security policy, which 'might in time' lead to a common defence. The common policy would allow for the 'specific character' of member states' security and defence policies, for example Irish neutrality, and would respect their Nato obligations; and in the field of defence, so sensitive for national sovereignty, there would be co-operation by unanimous agreement only. The Western European Union is to be an integral part of the European Union established by the Maastricht Treaty, which may request it to carry out decisions and actions with defence implications. The members of WEU, comprising all the Union's members save Denmark, Ireland, and Greece—with Greece, following Maastricht, likely to join—declared at Maastricht that they would strengthen the WEU with these aims in mind, thus developing 'a genuine European security and defence identity and a greater European responsibility in defence matters'.

This relationship between WEU and the Community was a compromise between the British government, which wanted to keep them apart, and the French, German and a number of other governments which wanted them closer together. The way towards eventual merger was kept open by the provision that the relationship would be reviewed in 1996, two years before the WEU treaty is due to expire, in the light of the aims of 'ever closer union' and of the effectiveness of institutions. If member states are persuaded that Community or federal institutions would be more effective than the intergovernmental system, and make treaty amendments accordingly, these institutions would acquire full responsibility for foreign and security policy; and to the extent that they moved beyond co-operation to integration of armed forces, would dispose of all the main instruments of that policy. Meanwhile, the common foreign and security policy will involve the complex and sometimes frustrating task of co-ordinating policy based on Community economic instruments with that based on member states' security instruments.

How far the attempt succeeds to create a common foreign policy based on security as well as economic instruments depends not only on these internal dynamics but also on external pressures and the performance in reacting to them or anticipating them. Growing interdependence in the international economy has led the EC and the US, as the two greatest economic powers, to understand the need for organized collaboration. There are regular meetings at presidential level. The Commission has meetings twice a year with the US Administration, there are joint meetings of representatives of the European Parliament and the US Congress, and an EC–US treaty has been suggested as a framework for closer collaboration. While the single market and economic and monetary union, as well as the development of an EC security competence, could cause strains in the relationship, they could also induce the EC and the US to realize Jean Monnet's vision of an Atlantic partnership, as the EC's common tariff and the ensuing Kennedy round at first promised to do.

When the economic and political changes in Central and Eastern Europe began to gather pace in 1989, it was agreed that the EC Commission should take the lead in co-ordinating the actions of the EC, the US, and other OECD countries to support them. Already, in their early stages, these changes brought the Community closer than it had been before to a common foreign policy with important achievements to its credit, thus giving more conviction to the case for strengthening the policy-making capacity. The development of policy towards the Community's eastern neighbours, and Russia in particular, will be critical in determining the future of the common foreign and security policy.

While the use of the common tariff to negotiate liberalization on a most-favoured nation basis in the Gatt gave the Community its capacity for common action in relation to the advanced industrial countries, it was the combination of preferential tariff reductions and economic aid that gave it that capacity in relation to the Third World. A common currency would add to the instruments with which the Community can continue to develop its policy towards less-developed countries, building up its relationship not only with the Mediterranean and ACP countries, but also with the Asians, Latin Americans, and countries of the Middle East, including in particular the larger powers within those regions.

The EC has used an apparently modest set of instruments to create a network of relationships with all parts of the world. This has enabled it to conduct an external policy which defends the collective interests of the member states and also identifies common interests with its partner countries, which can be developed in common institutions of association or in wider international organizations. A combination of internal and external forces has been pressing the Community towards a strengthening of its instruments and institutions that could make a reality of its declared intention to establish a common foreign policy; and the arrangements provided in the Maastricht Treaty for the CFSP are a result. If the weaknesses in these arrangements are overcome and the policy becomes successful, the Community will, in the coming century, be one of the great powers in a multipolar world. Although it may well continue to acquire increasing competences in the field of security, its multinational character and international situation are likely to prevent it from becoming a military superpower. Thus it may remain legitimate to regard it as a very great civilian power. Given also its own experience as an emergent multinational polity, it may fulfil Jean Monnet's hope that, if the European Community, endowed with federal institutions, succeeds, it could be 'a useful example to the world' of how to establish prosperity and peace.[24]

10 The Building of a Union

Steps

This book has shown how a score of substantial steps have taken the Community from its first manifestation in the ECSC up to the point it has reached today. In the 1950s the three big steps were the founding of the three Communities: ECSC, EEC, and Euratom. In the 1960s the customs union was completed ahead of timetable, the common agricultural policy was put in place, and the Kennedy round negotiated. The 1970s brought in Britain, Denmark, and Ireland; and despite the problems that ensued from this and from the stagflation that began in 1974, the Community's institutions and policies were significantly strengthened. The amending treaties of 1970 and 1975 gave the Community its own tax revenue and the European Parliament power over non-compulsory expenditure, making the institutions in effect federal for the latter part of Community activity; direct elections were introduced; the foreign policy cooperation (EPC) and the European Council were established. The European Monetary System was created and industrial policies developed. New relationships were initiated in Europe, with the association with Efta countries, and in the wider world, with the Lome Convention and the generalized and Mediterranean preferences.

Although the 1980s started on a low note, with the Community hamstrung by the British budget question, and the entry of Greece among the few achievements, big steps were taken in the second half of the decade. Following the European Parliament's Draft Treaty on European Union and the Commission's single market programme, the Single European Act committed the member states to complete the single market by the end of 1992, gave the Community some additional competences, and further strengthened the institutions. The budgetary reform sharpened control over the budget and the agricultural policy, and doubled the scope of the structural funds. The reforms in Central and Eastern Europe gave a new impulse to the Community's external policy. The Community entered the 1990s with East German entry, with other major developments in its Central and East European policy, and in 1991 with agreement on the Maastricht Treaty providing for economic and monetary union and some elements of political union.

These, together with numerous smaller steps, have brought the Community far towards a federal European Union. Over trade, it has the powers of a federation: externally, the common tariff and the common commercial policy; internally, the power to create the single market, along with a modest industrial policy and the common agricultural policy. The free movement of capital, integration of financial markets, and the Exchange Rate Mechanism paved the way for the agreement on Emu at Maastricht. Community expenditure, rising by 1992 to nearly 1½ per cent of gross domestic product, is substantial—not far short, according to some, of what will be needed when Emu is established. There are significant powers over environmental and social legislation. Monetary union will complete the Community's set of instruments for external economic policy, which is to be related to general external policy through the common foreign and security policy. The Maastricht Treaty offers a basis for security co-operation, the other main element of a federal Union's external policy, while remaining short of the control of armed forces required for a federal state.

The institutions that exercise the Community's powers, unlike those of most international organizations, have, apart from the Council, the federal characteristic of a direct relationship with citizens of member states. The juridical system is, indeed, broadly federal. The Commission is an independent executive, though its independence is circumscribed by the Council and its network of supervisory committees. The Commission also has the right to propose laws, as governments do, to the legislature; and it has, by the same token, the capacity of political initiative, which it has used in launching the EMS, the single market programme, the agri-budgetary reform, and the project for economic and monetary union. The directly elected European Parliament has a power of assent over accession, association, and some other international agreements; power to approve the appointment of the Commission, backed by the power of dismissal; equal power with the Council for non-compulsory expenditure and 'codecision' for some legislation; and substantial influence over the whole budget and much other legislation. The Council votes by majority for most single market legislation as well as for the budget, agricultural policy, commercial policy, and a number of other matters. But its diplomatic methods of decision-making behind closed doors are those of the ministerial committee of an international organization, and its predominance over the Parliament in legislation and detailed control over the Commission are not suited to the house of states in a federal Union.

In growing from six to twelve, the member states have come to contain nine-tenths of the population of Western Europe. But with a number of European countries to the East, as well as the North and South, still outside it, the Community has some way to go before it can fully justify the name of 'European' Union.

Results

The original aim of the Schuman declaration has been realized. France and Germany have been reconciled and war within Western Europe appears impossible. The Atlantic alliance has been one major cause. But the Community has been another. Power politics has been replaced by civilian politics among the West European states. The rule of law prevails in economic relations among their citizens; and there are the beginnings of representative government in the Community's legislative process and in the control of the executive. The majority of citizens show strong support for the Community and for its development into a federal European Union.

The aims of the Economic Community have also been substantially fulfilled. First the customs union, then the single market have provided scope for the specialization and scale needed to make European firms competitive, and thus laid the basis for the prosperity experienced by Community citizens in the 1960s and foreseen by the Cecchini report for the 1990s. Monetary union is expected to offer a further phase of dynamic effects on investment, technology, and competition.

While the main instrument for allocating resources in Western economies, the market, has thus been transformed, the Community has done less to ensure price stability and full employment as well as growth of productivity and external balance through what are known by economists as stabilization policies.[1] The EMS and in particular the Exchange Rate Mechanism have contributed to the convergence of policies and the reduction of inflation and of exchange rate fluctuations among the participating countries; but the economic and monetary union project reflects a judgement that a more solid arrangement is needed. The European Investment Bank and the New Community Instrument are among the methods whereby the Community has tried to supplement the action of the market in creating employment; but unemployment has remained higher than in Japan or the United States.

Distribution, the third main aim, along with allocation and stabilization, of economic policy, is also less developed in the EC than in federal polities. The agricultural policy has redistributed substantial resources, initially from Germany to France, latterly from Britain and Germany to various other member states; but apart from its help to Ireland and Greece and the contribution from Germany, this degenerated into a redistribution from the poorer to the richer and caused sharp conflict in the Community. Following earlier and minor attempts at redistribution through the Social and Regional Development Funds, the Community has moved towards a more significant distributive policy with the doubling of the structural funds, under the cohesion policy, to reach ⅓ of 1 per cent of GDP by 1993. But this is far less than the transfers normal in federations.

Its common tariff made the Community the equal of the US in trade negotiations; and the use of the tariff for preferential or free trade arrangements improved relations with other West European countries and with many in the Third World. The

European Political Co-operation enhanced the weight of Community countries in external policy, for example in the Conference on Security and Co-operation in Europe, though without approaching the combined strength that could stem from a common external policy. Central and East European countries have been attracted to the Community partly because of the preferential treatment that it can offer; but more important is the example of prosperity and democracy.

Most countries throughout the world are, indeed, impressed by the Community; and most of the Community's citizens are pleased with it. But in most member states, governments and citizens express the desire for the Community to be further developed in the federal direction. This would involve completion of the Emu and bringing responsibility for the common foreign and security policy by stages from the intergovernmental into the mainstream Community institutions. It would reform the institutions to make majority voting the general rule in the Council, to enable the Parliament to share legislative power with the Council on equal terms, and to give the Commission more independent executive competence. Citizens would be guaranteed fundamental rights and freedoms, and member states the power to control their domestic affairs according to the principle of subsidiarity. Membership would eventually be extended to include all democratic European countries wishing to join.

There is substantial support for these developments. But they are far from being assured. To judge the likely outcome, we need to assess the forces for and against.

Forces against federal Union

The experience recounted in preceding chapters shows that nation-states can powerfully resist moves towards federation. France led by de Gaulle was the prime example, with his defence of the 'Europe of states' against the federalists' 'myths, fictions and pageants'.[2] Among academics, this approach was reflected in the 'realist' school, with their view of the immutable status of the nation-state and the unreality of proposals to transfer sovereignty to common institutions, and hence their stress on intergovernmental co-operation. The Gaullist policy succeeded in blocking, first the project for a European Defence Community, then the practice of majority voting in the EC Council; and it continued to influence French policy after de Gaulle's demise.

Harold Macmillan, in attempting to negotiate entry, assured the House of Commons in 1961 that he accepted de Gaulle's view of sovereignty.[3] A decade later Edward Heath was moved to reaffirm, in the White Paper on the terms of accession, that 'There is no question of any erosion of essential national sovereignty'.[4] What national sovereignty was essential? The Labour government that followed Heath in 1974, and Mrs Thatcher, who followed them in 1979, proved more jealous of Britain's sovereignty than Heath would probably have been. All member states behaved defensively during the economic troubles of the 1970s. They reacted in dispersed order to the oil shock of 1973–4; protection through non-tariff barriers fragmented the Community market; the Americans were less supportive of integration than they had been before. The member governments were generally reluctant to take decisions in the Council. But the Labour government was more insistent on sovereignty, more inclined to block Community action, than most of its partners. With the Labour Party swinging temporarily towards autarkic state socialism, it went so far as to campaign in the 1983 elections for British withdrawal from the Community, causing many social democrats to leave the party in order to create, with the Liberals, a pro-European Alliance. Mrs Thatcher was a strong proponent of free trade, and hence of the single market programme. But her attitude towards sovereignty was at least as intransigent as that of the Labour government had been. In her speech at Bruges in 1988, she asserted that 'some in the European Community seem to want . . . a European super-state exercising a new dominance from Brussels', which would 'suppress nationhood' and lead to an 'identikit European personality'.[5] Specific targets of this general anathema appear to have been monetary union and stronger powers for the European Parliament; and in place of such sharing of sovereignty, she proposed 'cooperation between independent sovereign states'. Unlike most political leaders in the Community, she saw German union as another argument against further integration, preferring to rely on more traditional inter-state relationships rather than on federal links as the framework for containing German power.

Most Members of the House of Commons backed her view of the sovereignty of the Westminster parliament, in the sense of unlimited legislative authority, thus denying any case for representative government at the Community level. Among other members of the Community, the Danes shared this insistence on the sovereignty of their institutions; and such was one of the motives for other Scandinavians and the Swiss remaining outside the Community.

Germans have often resisted moves towards monetary union, because they feared they would catch inflation from their neighbours if they relinquished the monetary sovereignty of the Federal Republic, with its autonomous Bundesbank. While there were rational grounds for such fears, this resistance was also an example of a more general inertia that works against the transfer of powers to the Community. It was, after all, the governments and bureaucracies of all the member states that appeared content with the practice of unanimous voting in the Council for two whole decades, during which its inefficiency became increasingly evident; nor is efficiency the word to describe the system of committees of member states' officials that restrict the executive competence of the Commission. Official inertia is backed by protectionist pressure from the less dynamic parts of the economy.

This combination of hostility and inertia that impedes the sharing of sovereignty, and stunted Community development between 1965 and 1985, lent credibility to the theorists who saw the Community as a 'regime', or 'system', not essentially different from other international organizations or groups. One such view was that, although integration does go 'beyond the nation-state', it does not go 'very far beyond'.[6] Another, playing down formal international institutions in favour of 'clusters of intergovernmental and transnational networks' associated with them, concluded that 'very little in the record [of the three first post-war decades] suggests that international organizations such as ... the European Community, will become increasingly autonomous and powerful in world politics'.[7] Evidently, these people underestimated the forces that favour further integration.

Forces favouring federal Union

The Community was founded because it was felt that 'cooperation between independent sovereign states' would not satisfy vital national interests. France, in order to establish permanent peace with Germany, wanted to contain the resurgent Germans within a strong framework that would satisfy them because it did not hold them down, but bound all the member states equally. The Germans sought, first, to recover equal status after their defeat in war, then a stable base in the West from which they could conduct an Ostpolitik without endangering their prosperity and peace. Such motives led France and Germany to found the Community in the 1950s, to relaunch it in 1969, and to promote the convening of the Intergovernmental Conferences on economic and monetary union and on political union in 1990.

Specific political motives such as these were generalized into a critique of the nation-state as inadequate to deal with the contemporary economic and security problems that transcend its borders. This has caused Italians, reacting against their experiences of fascism and of World War II, and stimulated by the thinking of Altiero Spinelli, to promote the idea of a federal Union, from the project for a European Political Community associated with the European Defence Community in the 1950s to the European Parliament's Draft Treaty in the 1980s. The Benelux countries, smaller and hence yet more conscious of interdependence, have often shared this approach; and surveys show that it is widely held by Community citizens.

Thus political motives for founding and developing the Community, largely absent in Britain with its different wartime experience and its long insular and imperial tradition, have been prevalent on the Continent, and have been powerful forces when the political conjuncture allowed; and the uniting of Germany in 1990 appeared to reinforce them, with most political leaders among both the Germans and their Continental partners seeing a more federal Community as the best framework for the more powerful German state. These motives have been reinforced by the desire of European countries to improve their status and influence in the wider world.

Already in 1950, the six founder members of the Community saw clearly how Europeans, weakened by their divisions that had led to two great fratricidal wars, had forfeited their capacity to defend their interests, let alone apply their full weight to shaping the course of world politics. To combine their strength to deal with external challenges was another motive for integration. While the British, less conscious of their reduced circumstances, held back, French diplomacy seized the opportunity to lead the Continent and thus reverse Britain's post-war superiority: a more traditional aim than that of Monnet, but the two combined were a powerful force for creating and defending the Community and its customs union.

Bargaining power in international trade negotiations, particularly in relation to the United States, was a motive for the customs union. Greater autonomy in relation to the dollar was a reason for the drive by Schmidt and Giscard to establish the EMS. The need to meet Japanese and American competition was the prime mover behind the single market programme. While Europeans have thus sought to redress the balance of power with respect to the United States and later Japan by developing the Community, the Americans have significantly helped them to do so. US support was a powerful force in favour of building the Community in its earlier days and, after a lapse, showed some signs that it might work again in the same direction in the 1990s.

The Community's preferential arrangements were a response to pressures from developing countries and from European neighbours for access to the EC market. The readiness to respond was motivated partly by French, then British desire to secure Community support for French Union and Commonwealth countries, partly by the European interest in stability around the Mediterranean, and partly in order to strengthen economic and political links with other West European and developing countries. Having established the customs union, the member states could no longer conduct separate trade policies and were obliged to develop relationships, and hence the Community, in these ways; and this experience enabled the Community to respond strongly to the emergence of pluralist democracies in Central Europe, thus adding to its capacity to conduct a common external policy. Behind its policy towards Central and Eastern Europe lay the motive of redressing the balance of power with the Soviet Union. Securing the autonomy of the former satellites was one way of doing this, in which common action by the Community was more powerful than the member states acting separately. The desire to counterbalance the Soviet Union motivated the project for a European Defence Community; and the need for an effective European security system, as well as to respond to events outside Europe such as the Iraqi invasion of Kuwait, may move EC member states towards security integration in the future, while efforts to help Russia and other former Soviet republics to succeed in reform may favour economic and political integration in order to match the size of the problem.

In short, the increasingly interdependent world presses on the member states to defend their interests through the Community, in particular in relation to the United States, Russia, and Japan, but also in the promotion of a safe and prosperous international order.

The political motives are underpinned by economic forces favouring integration. The more dynamic elements in the member states' economies have pressed for the wide market in which to develop the new technologies and compete with the Americans and Japanese.[8] They supported the creation of the common market, the acceleration of the customs union, the Community's collective research programmes, and the single market programme; and they likewise support the economic and monetary union, as a stable framework for industrial and financial development. Among Germany's partners there has been official support for the Exchange Rate Mechanism as an anchor against inflation through acceptance of the leading role of the Bundesbank; and now that most of them have got inflation down, they see Emu as a way of regaining control over monetary policy by ensuring that Germany shares it with the other participants.

The continued pressure for economic integration reflects the growth of interdependence that follows from technological development. The same root cause lies behind the rising demand for common action to protect the environment.

Thus substantial political, economic, and external forces, inherent in the growing interdependence among European countries and in the world, favour the building of a federal Union in Europe. There is also the question, posed by the neo-functionalists, of linkages between one step of integration and subsequent steps.

Linkages and neofunctionalism

We have seen how Monnet, determined to establish an authority to govern the coal and steel industries of France, Germany, and other countries, engendered a Community with a court that would subject the authority's actions to the rule of law and with an assembly for an element of democratic scrutiny and control. Given that pluralist democracies were setting up an executive that was independent of them in order to undertake common action more effectively than an international organization, the logic of applying to it some of the principles that underlay their own form of government could hardly be ignored.

The juridical implications of common action expanded with the creation of the common market with its four freedoms of movement for goods, services, capital, and people, together with the other provisions of the EEC. The Court's judgements on Cassis de Dijon, transport policy, and isoglucose have shown how it can apply the treaties so as to develop Community law and policy and to strengthen the institutions. Its ability to develop Community law by direct application of the treaties has, moreover, spurred the Council to perform its legislative duties, not only when the Court found that its failure to do so was illegal, as with the transport policy, but also, as in the case of legislation to control mergers, because the alternative was that the law would be shaped by the judges rather than by the Council.

The enactment of laws by the Council, by procedures that are more diplomatic than parliamentary, has provoked pressures for a stronger legislative role for the European Parliament. The original example was the Dutch insistence on parliamentary control of the European budget. More recently, there was the pressure from Italy and elsewhere that led to the co-operation procedure in the Single European Act, and from Germany in particular for the codecision agreed at Maastricht. The Parliament has also been able to use its own powers as leverage to enhance its role. It has gained some influence over policy through its budgetary powers, as with research, education, and aid for Hungary and Poland. Its power to increase non-compulsory expenditure and alter its pattern, thus potentially upsetting the Council's financial perspective for 1988–92, gave it the clout to secure some control over the Council's decisions on total agricultural spending, and to break the Agriculture Council's habit of taking decisions that required expenditure beyond what the budget allowed. The Parliament has also used its powers under the assent procedure of the Single Act, to influence policy towards the Community's associates; and it can do the same with respect to applications to join the Community. It has also used its various powers so as to influence the Commission; and Maastricht has substantially enhanced its potential.

Against the trend of the Court and Parliament, the Commission lost ground to the member governments following the early days after the foundation of the Communities. Coreper and its subordinate committees have kept the Commission's scope for executive action in check. But the need for effective action sometimes works the other way. The British government, among the most insistent on keeping the Commission under the Council's control, has supported greater power for the Commission to prevent excess agricultural expenditure, and an expanded role for it in securing member states' compliance with Community legislation. Independent action by the Commission in exploring with the trading partners solutions to the problems under negotiation, which the member governments were then obliged to accept for fear the negotiations would otherwise fail, contributed to the success of the Kennedy round and the Community's offer of generalized preferences to developing countries. Commission proposals provided the basis for the European Council's agreements on such crucial matters as the Single European Act and agri-budgetary reform; and its position was also strengthened at Maastricht.

The need for effectiveness, this time in legislating for the single market, has also led to the use of majority voting in the Council, as provided in the Single Act. Majority voting has also been applied in fields where it long lay dormant; and the Maastricht Treaty further extends it. While making a big contribution to legislative efficiency, this has also introduced a normal democratic principle into the Council's proceedings.

Thus the original creation of independent institutions with certain powers has led to their further development in response to the demands of effectiveness, democracy, and the rule of law, that is of principles on which the member states' polities are based, even if this has been countered, in relations between the Council and the Commission and Parliament, by the reluctance of member governments to relinquish power. In addition to these institutional linkages, working both for and against a federal Union, have been those derived from member states' efforts to secure their shares of advantage from the Community.

French insistence on the agricultural policy to counterbalance the gains to German industry from the common market was the first, classic example. The British demand for the Regional Development Fund was intended, in turn, to counterweigh the effect on Britain of the agricultural policy. But the long struggle, first by the Labour government then by Mrs Thatcher, to secure compensation through the budget had much greater impact on the Community's development, working against movement towards Union as decision-taking was frustrated by the conflict. The British insistence on effective Community controls over agricultural expenditure, embodied in the agri-budgetary reform, was more positive; and the doubling of structural funds, decided at the same time to benefit the weaker economies where there was fear about the competition from the stronger in the single market, followed by the further boost to cohesion at Maastricht, is another major example, leading towards a distributional policy such as is likely to be required in a Union or federation. From the countries with higher standards of protection for workers and for the environment, there has been a demand for Community safeguards against the 'social dumping' of competition from those with lower standards.

While linkages can come from the desire to redress a disadvantage, they can also result from determination to consolidate a gain. The French insisted that the Community have its own tax resources in order to safeguard their gains from the agricultural policy. Acceleration of the customs union was supported in order to make the common external tariff and the internal free trade irreversible. One motive for the single market programme was fear that the internal free trade would be negated by the proliferation of non-tariff barriers. The project for economic and monetary union arose partly because it was feared that free movement of capital would undermine the currency stability achieved through the Exchange Rate Mechanism unless the participants took the further step to a single currency.

More generally, one success can lead to others. Had the customs union not been seen as the context for prosperity in the 1960s, it is not likely that the single market programme would have been so strongly supported in the 1980s. The successful launching of that programme gave the Community the confidence needed to decide on the agri-budgetary reform, double the structural funds, and convene the Intergovernmental Conferences on economic and monetary union and political union. These successes helped to make the Community a pole of attraction for the countries of Central Europe.

There are, then, a number of ways in which linkages can favour steps towards union or impede them.

The original concept of the neofunctionalists laid emphasis on one particular form of linkage. They held that, because economic problems were interdependent, solution of one by joint action would lead to joint action to deal with others. From the starting-point of 'a real delegation of decision-making to a supranational agency', there would be 'a cumulative and expansive process whereby the supranational agency slowly extends its authority so as to progressively undermine the independence of the nation-state'; and as this happened, 'relevant interest groups would shift their attention and ultimately their loyalties from the nation-state'.[9] There were even hopes, raised by the Community's early success, that the process was inevitable.[10] But the neofunctionalists soon found that they had underestimated the power of national loyalties and the nation-state. Writing in 1970, after this had been demonstrated by de Gaulle, two of them maintained the emphasis on internal linkages, but accepted that these could move the Community either forward or back. There was a new focus on leadership, as distinct from automatic process, but this was not held likely to promote 'important new tasks or powers for the Community system'. The result would be a Community in equilibrium, conserving a balance between forces for and against further integration.[11]

In concentrating on linkages within the integration process, the neofunctionalists underrated the exogenous forces: first nationalism and the nation-state, embodied in particular by de Gaulle; then the contrary political, economic, and external forces and motives considered above. They also failed to give weight to constitutional values such as democracy and the rule of law. One of them defined political integration as 'a process, but without reference to an end point';[12] and this deflected attention from the constitutional principles that might underlie the Community's political order. It also appears to have impeded thinking about the functions that the Community might be called upon to perform in order to deal with the member states' political and economic problems. In particular the neofunctionalists gave little attention to the possibility that free movement of capital would lead on towards monetary union. Yet monetary union and institutional reform remained central to the prospects for the Community's future development.

Federalists

Unlike the neofunctionalists, the federalists have had a clear idea about the problems common to nation-states that would require common action to resolve, and about the form of institutions that would be needed to undertake it. The common problems are in the fields of trade, money, security, and now, evidently, the environment; the institutions are those of constitutional government to deal with the common affairs, leaving the member states to manage their own affairs with their own institutions. The problems have been identified through observation and analysis of how capable states are to deal with them independently; and it has been assumed that democracies would not wish to entrust important functions of government to institutions other than those of representative government, in a framework of the rule of law.[13]

Federalists have adopted two main approaches to the achievement of such a federal system. One, pioneered in post-war Europe by Altiero Spinelli, was that of a constituent assembly of people's representatives drawing up a federal constitution for ratification by the member states. With the direct election of the European Parliament in 1979, the people's representatives were in place; and Spinelli, as one of their number, persuaded them to design and approve the Draft Treaty on European Union. Without going so far as a federal state with integrated armed forces, this did propose to reform the Community's institutions to create a federal system for economic and monetary affairs; and although the immediate result was not a federal Union, but an impulse towards the more modest Single European Act, the Draft Treaty remained a benchmark against which federalists have measured subsequent proposals for Community reform.

The other approach, of steps towards federation, was developed by Jean Monnet. While he was often not explicit about a federal aim, he did insert it in his draft of the Schuman Declaration and in the statutes of his Action Committee for the United States of Europe, as well as expressing it on various other occasions. His close advisers, such as Etienne Hirsch, Pierre Uri, and Robert Triffin, were also federalists. Despite his pragmatic nature and his commitment to the art of the possible, it may be doubted whether he would have been able to initiate the creation of institutions with such scope for development in a federal direction had he not seen them as part of a process that would lead to federation.

Paul-Henri Spaak, the architect of the Rome Treaties, was also a federalist. So was Walter Hallstein, the President of the dynamic initial EEC Commission, and, in their different ways, Sicco Mansholt, Robert Marjolin, and Jean Rey, his colleagues in that Commission who shared much of the credit for its performance. The Community's successes in the 1970s owed much to statesmen who, if not at the time explicitly federalist, have since shown a commitment to at least most of the federalist programme: Willy Brandt, Valéry Giscard d'Estaing, Edward Heath, Roy Jenkins, and Helmut Schmidt. More recently Jacques Delors, who has initiated key steps towards Union, has been explicit about his federal aim, and in his advocacy of political union, the same may be said of Helmut Kohl.

Thus most of the steps towards Union have been promoted by people for whom a federal Union itself was an objective. The steps have also been supported by institutions that generally shared the aim: in particular the Commission and European Parliament, but also the parliaments of certain member states, including in various ways the Italian, Belgian, and Dutch parliaments and the German Bundestag. There has also been much support from European party groups, interest groups, and federalist movements.

These federalist statesmen and bodies have been central to the Community's foundation and development by steps towards a federal Union. But they would not have been likely to succeed had they not allied themselves with forces that had a particular interest in a given step rather than in the federal Union towards which it could lead. Industrial and financial interests supported the acceleration of the customs union, the single market programme, and the Emu project. Monnet harnessed the specific interests of France and West Germany to the ECSC project. The Commission had French and Dutch support for the establishment of the common agricultural policy, and that of the Dutch parliament for control of the budget by the European Parliament, of Spain for the cohesion policy, and of Britain for the agri-budgetary controls. The European Parliament's Draft Treaty owed its political impact to its favourable reception by President Mitterrand, who was at the time occupying the presidency of the European Council—although in this case his interest too may have been at least in part that of promoting the general idea of European Union.

The concept of steps towards federal Union, promoted by federalists and supported by more specific interests, may be seen as a neo-federal idea, more conscious than neofunctionalism of federalist motives and exogenous forces favouring movement towards Union, more explicit than classical federalists about the process that can lead up to acceptance of a federal constitution.

A neo-federal idea

This neo-federal idea[14] as it applies in Europe now may be summarized in seven propositions.

1. The process of movement towards a federal Union involves both a federal aim and steps towards it.
2. A federal Union and federation are rational solutions to problems that face European states at the end of the second millennium. A federal Union requires a single market, economic and monetary union, and a common external policy, with co-operation on security; federation requires control of armed forces. Both are governed by federal institutions, based on the rule of law, for which the independent Court of Justice is the ultimate juridical authority, and on representative government, which can be achieved through majority voting in the Community's Council, co-legislation by the Council and the European Parliament, and full executive competence for the Commission. Following the principle of subsidiarity, member states retain control over their domestic affairs.
3. Forces in favour are strong enough to make a federal Union a feasible political project for this century. They include federalist statesmen and, for each step, official and private interests specific to the problem with which it deals. Underlying these forces is the growth of interdependence, due mainly to technological development.
4. Forces against are enough to make such a Union uncertain.

They include nationalist opposition, the inertia of state bureaucracies and political systems, and protectionist interests.

5. The balance of forces for and against has been such as to allow steps towards a federal Union, with specific powers given to proto-federal institutions, but not the adoption of a federal constitution. Most steps are the subject of political conflict, and are taken as a result of federalist initiative combined with the support of more specific interests.

6. Steps make a federal Union more feasible in various ways. If successfully accomplished, they lend conviction to the idea that the Community institutions can be entrusted with new tasks. They increase, as they accumulate, the potency of internal linkages, for example as the capital liberalization in the single market context has led to the Emu project, and that has raised the demand for institutional reform. They increase the strength and prestige of federalists.

7. While a federal Union could be accomplished by a series of specific steps, the main ones remaining being the completion of Emu, full codecision of Parliament with Council, and a phased assimilation of the common foreign and security policy into the Community institutions, constitution arising from a formal constituent process would have the merit of being more clear and comprehensible to the citizens on whose support the Union's success must ultimately depend.

The idea expressed in these propositions is in some respects a synthesis of the federalist and the neofunctionalist approaches. It offers a way to supplement federalist theory, which has tended to focus on the design of a constitution by a constituent assembly without considering the process of steps which may make that feasible; and it fills gaps in neofunctionalism caused by neglect of some essential political and economic forces, including the federalist motive, and of constitutional questions. It is hoped, in these ways, to help understanding of the historic process of unification in Europe, and in particular to help understanding in Britain, where the case and prospects for a federal European Union have been underrated, owing partly to wartime experience and partly to a defensive mentality that followed the retreat from empire. Along with this reluctance to contemplate a federal Union has gone a disinclination to think rigorously about the development of the Community's institutions, with the term *sui generis* often employed to avoid examining them in the light of constitutional principles. The conclusion of this book is that principles of federal government are relevant to consideration of the development of the Community and of the European Union as established by the Maastricht Treaty; and that, given the balance of forces in favour over against the contrary forces, a federal Union is not unlikely to become a reality in the 1990s. It is also suggested that the neo-federal idea will be relevant, not only for the Community of twelve, but also for its extension to include most of Europe, and for eventual application in the wider world.

That is my judgement. I hope the book will have given readers the material on which they can form their own.

Postscript: The Maastrict Treaty

The Treaty on European Union that was agreed by the European Council at Maastricht in December 1991 and signed there in February 1992 was a considerable new step towards a federal Union as defined at the end of Chapter 1. The centrepiece was the decision to establish the economic and monetary union (Emu) which should go far to complete the economic competences that a federal Union requires. Along with this were included a number of other new competences and of reforms to the Community institutions, as well as the provision, under different institutional arrangements, for a 'common foreign and security policy' and for 'co-operation' on 'justice and home affairs'. The European Union, as defined by the Treaty, is the Community plus these two more intergovernmental wings. Taken together, they represent a qualitative shift in the Community's development which will affect its working in many ways.

It has not been possible in revisions to the preceding chapters to do full justice to the Maastricht Treaty. The text has been revised where the Treaty is germane to the argument; but it remains necessary to give here, at the risk of some repetition, a view of the Treaty as a whole.

The strongest pressure for Emu came from the French government, which saw it as a means of containing German monetary power and of anchoring the united Germany in a strengthened European Community. There was strong support from some other governments, from industrial interests, and from federalists, foremost among them President Delors, who secured the establishment of the Delors Committee in June 1988, leading to the decision in June 1989 to convene the Intergovernmental Conference on economic and monetary union. While Germans were reluctant to exchange the mark for an ecu that might well be less sound, the German government was a strong supporter of political union, as a way to ensure the stability of its western relationships following German unification. Chancellor Kohl became explicitly federalist, promoting the idea of the Community as a federal democracy with a common foreign and security policy. France, though less inclined to strengthen the European Parliament, also backed political union, as did most other member governments; and it was agreed in June 1990 to convene the parallel IGC on political union.

The British government had opposed the idea of amending the treaties through the IGCs. Mrs Thatcher had added her own brand of militancy to Britain's habitual resistance to moves in a federal direction. While John Major's attitude to the Community was friendlier, he adhered in the IGCs to the negotiating position that had been formed before she left office. But while the British government resisted many of the proposed changes, it did not wish to become isolated. So it accepted quite far-reaching reforms at Maastricht, with the proviso that it could stand aside from the social provisions and from the commitment to participate in the single currency. Thus the substantial Treaty on European Union emerged, due to come into force by 1993 when it has been ratified by all the member states.

Institutional reforms

The European Parliament has been given more power. The assent procedure, whereby the Council cannot enact a measure without the Parliament's approval, was extended. Introduced in the Single European Act with respect to accession and association agreements, Maastricht went on to apply it to all international agreements with an institutional framework or budgetary implications and to those involving subjects where the Parliament has a power of 'codecision' with the Council. The Parliament's assent will also be required to a uniform procedure for European elections, measures to effect the citizens' right to move and reside throughout the Community, amendment of the statutes of the European System of Central

Banks (ESCB) and the European Central Bank (ECB), major decisions regarding the structural funds; and, most significantly, the Parliament's approval is also required for the nomination of a new Commission.

The Maastricht Treaty also introduced a new procedure of 'codecision' which gives the Parliament the power to reject, by an absolute majority, a measure approved by the Council. But unlike the assent procedure, this gives the Parliament the right to propose amendments which, if not initially accepted by the Council, are to be considered in a conciliation committee, comprising the members of the Council or their representatives, and an equal number of members of the Parliament; and the Council cannot ignore the MEPs because, if agreement is not reached, the Parliament can reject the measure as a whole. This codecision is to apply in some of the Community's existing areas of competence: the single market; free movement of workers and the right of establishment; some environmental matters; framework programmes for research and technological development. It also applies to some new competences created at Maastricht: consumer protection, guidelines for trans-European infrastructure networks, and incentives for co-operation in public health, culture, education, vocational training, and youth.

Most of the other new competences introduced at Maastricht, apart from Emu, are subject to the co-operation procedure which was devised in the Single European Act for measures concerning the single market and a few other subjects (see p.38, above); and it applies to most aspects of the social policy agreement among eleven of the Maastricht signatories. It was also extended to competition policy and transport policy, which were among the original competences of the EEC. The subjects to which neither co-operation, codecision, nor assent applies are now few, although they include some of the most important: agriculture, tax, much of commercial policy, Emu—and, of course, the more intergovernmental common foreign and security policy and co-operation on justice and home affairs.

Assent and codecision, then, give the Parliament real power in some key fields of legislation, such as accession, association, single market, and free movement of citizens, as well as of workers and enterprises, together with others that concern the citizens closely, such as environmental programmes and consumer protection; and the Parliament's influence has been enlarged with the assignment of new fields to the co-operation procedure. The Parliament's power to influence the Commission, too, has been markedly increased by the Maastricht Treaty.

The Parliament's power to approve the Commission's appointment may be particularly significant. The next European elections are due in June 1994. The Commission that takes office on 1 January 1993 is to serve for two years only; and from 1 January 1995 onwards, each Commission is to serve for five years, starting its term half a year after the European elections. Thus each new Parliament will exercise its power to approve each new Commission. The Parliament's position is further strengthened by the requirement that the governments must first consult it before nominating a new President of the Commission. They can hardly ignore its advice, since it could then refuse to approve the Commission as a whole. The relationship begins to look more like that between parliament and government in a system of parliamentary democracy, particularly when the Parliament's right to dismiss the Commission, albeit by a two-thirds majority, is taken into account, in addition to its budgetary and legislative powers. The Maastricht Treaty has also given the Parliament further leverage over the Commission, with powers to scrutinize its conduct of Community expenditure and to set up temporary Committees of Enquiry to investigate maladministration or contraventions in implementing Community law.

The Council is to vote by the procedure of qualified majority on most of the new Community competences. Majority voting is, indeed, now the normal rule, with some vital exceptions, such as tax; major appointments to the Commission, the Court of Justice, and the Executive Board of the ECB, where the heads of state or government act by common agreement; and the new fields of foreign and security policy and of justice and home affairs.

When codecision was first discussed, the Commission was concerned lest it be frozen out of the process of conciliation between Parliament and Council. But it is to participate in that process and can take 'all the necessary initiatives' to reconcile the positions of the Parliament and the Council. The scope of the Commission's activity is widened along with that of Community competences. The Commission as well as the member states will moreover have the right to initiate policy proposals on any question relating to the common foreign and security policy and on much of the area of co-operation in justice and home affairs; the Treaty also provides that in these fields, the Commission is to be 'fully associated with the work'. An important change in the Commission's role should stem from its new relationship with the European Parliament, which may cause it inconvenience but should also strengthen its political base.

The scope of the Court of Justice, like that of the Commission, is widened along with that of Community competences, including the Emu. Unlike the Commission, however, the Court has been given no role in the new field of foreign and security policy and little in that of co-operation in justice and home affairs. The Court has, on the other hand, been given the power to fine member states that fail to comply with its judgements, which should help to strengthen the rule of law in the Community.

The Maastricht Treaty establishes a common citizenship. All nationals of member states are to be citizens of the Union, with the rights and duties conferred by the Treaty. The rights include that to move and reside throughout the Union; to vote and stand as a candidate in European and local elections though not in member states' national elections; to have diplomatic and consular protection from another member state where the citizen's own is not represented; and to petition the European Parliament. The Union is to respect the fundamental rights and freedoms as guaranteed by the European Convention; and for protection against maladministration by Community bodies, the citizen may complain to an Ombudsman appointed by the European Parliament.

The effort to bring the Community closer to the citizen also resulted in the establishment of a Committee of the Regions, to contain representatives of regional and local bodies. Like the Economic and Social Committee, its opinion is to be sought on proposed measures within its field of interest and it will have the right to volunteer its opinion when it sees fit. More generally, the Maastricht Treaty introduced the principle of subsidiarity, providing that the Community should act only where the objectives cannot be sufficiently achieved by the member states and can be better achieved by the Community; nor should the Community 'go beyond what is necessary to achieve the objectives of this Treaty'. Thus the Treaty sought to allay fears of excessive centralization.

Economic and monetary union

Probably the most important words in the Maastricht Treaty were in its provision for 'the irrevocable fixing of exchange rates leading to the introduction of a single currency, the ecu'. This is to take place when the participating states enter stage 3 of Emu, which is to be by 1 January 1999 at the latest and could be soon after the end of 1996, if the Council decides that a majority of the member states are ready by then. But readiness is to be judged by strict criteria; Germany insisted on the principles of sound money and price stability.

In order to be regarded as ready to participate, member states should keep their rates of inflation, measured by the consumer price index, not more than 1.5 per cent above that of the average of the three least inflationary members during the year before the Commission makes its examination prior to the decision. Long-term interest rates are not to be more than 2 per cent above the average for those three countries in that year. Exchange rates are to be kept within the normal fluctuation margins of the Exchange Rate Mechanism for two years, without devaluation against any other member state's currency. The government's deficit is not to exceed 3 per cent of GDP. When the Commission reports on the member states' readiness according to these criteria, as well as on whether their legislation, in particular regarding the independence of their central banks, responds to Emu's requirements, the Council is to decide by a qualified majority, not later than the end of 1996, which member states are ready. If they comprise a majority, the Council is to fix a date for the start of stage 3, when the participating countries' rates of exchange with the ecu are to be fixed irrevocably. Those countries that are not deemed ready are to have a derogation until they fulfil the conditions; and Britain may have an exemption unless it decides to join.

If a majority are indeed judged ready, the ecu will become a major factor in the European economy, and consequently in the international system; and the member states with a derogation or exemption may be expected to strive to participate. If a majority are not ready, the commitment in the Maastricht Treaty to start stage 3 by 1 January 1999 at the latest could be less significant. It could, at the limit, apply to only three member states, probably Germany and the two others with the lowest inflation rates. While such an extreme outcome is unlikely, the importance of the move to stage 3 will depend on whether other large member states, particularly France or Britain, join Germany in it; if not, it will be a new deutschmark zone under another name. France does, however, treat the Emu project as a major national interest and is likely to make every effort to be ready for it. If France is to participate as well as Germany, the importance of Emu will be assured; and Britain will not be likely to take the risk of financial exclusion by making use of its right to exemption. Thus while it remains possible that Emu will be stillborn, its successful development is more probable; and if the financial markets believe in it, their behaviour could accelerate its introduction, to a date earlier than foreseen in the Treaty.

The ESCB, comprising the ECB and the member states' central banks, is to manage the new monetary system. It is to be responsible for monetary policy, with the exclusive right to authorize the issue of banknotes; it is to hold and manage official reserves and conduct foreign exchange operations, and to promote the smooth operation of payments systems. Its primary aim is to be price stability; without prejudice to that, it is, however, to support the Community's general economic policies. As a guarantee against political interference that could undermine price stability, the members of the Governing Council and the Executive Board, which are to be the governing bodies of both the ECB and the ESCB, will not be allowed to take instructions from any other bodies. The Governing Council is to comprise the governors of the member states' central banks, themselves by then independent of governments, and the members of the Executive Board, which is to have a President, Vice-President and four other members, appointed for eight-year terms by common accord among the heads of state or government, on a recommendation of the Council after consulting the European Parliament and the Governing Council.

While independent of political pressures, the ECB is to be accountable to the Community institutions. It must make an annual report to the Commission, Council, and Parliament, which may have a debate on it. The main responsibility for the relationship between the ecu and the international monetary system lies with the Council. The Council is to decide the arrangements for international monetary negotiations, with which the Commission is to be 'fully associated', and the Council is to be responsible for the strategic decisions on exchange rate policy: it is to decide by unanimity, on a proposal from the Commission, on formal agreements regarding any system linking the ecu with other currencies; and by qualified majority on changes in the central rates or on general orientations for floating.

The Council is also to formulate guidelines for the Community's general economic policy, as well as for those of the member states; and the Council is to make recommendations to member states that breach them, which it may decide by a qualified majority to publish, thus bringing pressure to bear through public opinion and the financial markets.

The Emu is to have strict rules about government deficits. There is to be no printing of money to cover them, or bailing out of governments with unmanageable debts: that is to say, member states' governments or public bodies are to receive no form of official credits or privileged access to EC or member states' institutions, neither is the Community nor another member state to undertake responsibility for their commitments. Nor are governments to run deficits exceeding 3 per cent of GDP, or to have debt which is over 60 per cent of GDP and is not being reduced so as to approach that level at a satisfactory pace. Sanctions against an offending government may be decided by the Council, by a qualified majority excluding the vote of the government in question; the Council may publish its recommendations to that government, so influencing its borrowing power in the markets, and may require specific information to be published before the government issues bonds or securities; the Council can ask the European Investment Bank to reconsider its lending policy to that member state; and it may require a non-interest-bearing deposit, or impose fines. In short, laxity in public finance is to be severely discouraged.

The transitional period up to stage 3 is to be spent preparing for its rigours. Before stage 2 begins in January 1994, all member states are to free payments and movements of capital. Those that need to converge on the standards of price stability and sound public finance of the better performers are to adopt multi-annual convergence programmes; and all are to cease printing money to cover deficits, covering them instead by borrowing from the markets. During stage 2, member governments must 'endeavour' to avoid excessive deficits (whereas in stage 3 they 'shall' avoid them). If they fail to do so, the Council may make its recommendations public, but will not, until stage 3, be able to impose the other sanctions. The European Monetary Institute (EMI) is to be established at the start of stage 2, as a forerunner of the ECB. Its Council will include the governors of the member states' central banks, one of whom will be its Vice-President, together with a President appointed by common accord among the heads of state or government. It is to give advice, opinions and recommendations to the member states, seek to co-ordinate their economic policies and secure co-operation among their central banks; and it is to monitor the European Monetary System, take over the European Monetary Co-operation Fund, and develop the use of the ecu. In general, it is to prepare for stage 3.

Common foreign and security policy

The Maastricht Treaty provided that the Union and the member states are to define and implement a common foreign and security policy (CFSP), covering all the areas of foreign and security policy. As already under the European Political Co-operation, the member governments are to inform and consult each other, and the Council can define common positions only by unanimity. But the new arrangements should be more effective.

Although the Council is to decide unanimously that a matter is to be the subject of joint action, binding the member states, it may at the same time decide how far majority voting is to be used to implement the action. Examples of matters for joint action in the first instance include the Conference on Security and Co-operation in Europe; disarmament, arms control, and non-proliferation; and economic aspects of security. It is notable that the CFSP is to comprise all questions relating to the security of the Union, including the eventual framing of a common defence policy, which 'might' in time lead to a common defence. This is not to prejudice member states' existing orientations, such as their Nato obligations or the specific character of certain policies, such as Irish neutrality. But the beginning of co-operation among member states in this field could prove a turning-point.

The defence activities of the Union are to be carried out through the Western European Union (WEU), which the Treaty calls an 'integral part' of the Union's development. The nine member states of the Union that are the existing members of WEU declared that the others were invited to join them; Greece will probably do so, Denmark maybe, Ireland probably not. The nine agreed, in a declaration annexed to the Treaty, on the need for a genuine European identity and greater responsibility in defence matters, 'to strengthen the European pillar of the Atlantic Alliance'. They also agreed to co-operate in planning, logistics, and making military units 'answerable' to WEU, and perhaps in creating a European armaments agency and a European Security and Defence Academy. The Council is to report to the European Council in 1996 on any need to revise the Union Treaty, in view of the expiry of the WEU treaty in 1998.

The CFSP wing of the Union is not subject to the normal Community institutional arrangements. The Court of Justice, in particular, has no role in relation to it. The European

Parliament, on the other hand, is to be informed and consulted; may put questions or recommendations; and is to hold an annual debate. The Commission's role has considerable potential. It is to have, alongside the member governments, the right to propose policies, sometimes called 'co-initiative', and is, as we saw, to be 'fully associated' with the work. It is also to be responsible, together with the Council, for ensuring the consistency of the Union's external relations as a whole, including economic, development, and security policies. The economic and development policies are part of Community competence; and the Community has shown, in relation to Central Europe for example, that it can be quite effective. The Commission will certainly seek to ensure that the strength of the Community is not sapped by the weaker institutional structure of the CFSP.

Co-operation on 'justice and home affairs'

The Maastricht Treaty provided for a second wing, alongside the Community, for co-operation on 'justice and home affairs'. This was wanted by Germany in particular, with its exposure to problems of asylum and immigration. Britain wished to keep such co-operation separate from the Community and without majority voting.

Asylum, immigration, and treatment of nationals of third countries were among the subjects covered by this part of the Treaty. It also provided for collaboration in combating drug addiction and fraud, and for judicial, customs, and police co-operation—the latter against terrorism, drug trafficking, and other serious forms of international crime. The Council is, with unanimous voting, to adopt joint positions, promote co-operation, and decide on joint actions; and it can draw up conventions for ratification by the member states. Measures to implement such conventions can be adopted by a majority of two-thirds of the governments in the Council, and the Court of Justice may be given jurisdiction to interpret them and to rule on any disputes. Otherwise the Court is to have no role in this field. The Parliament is to be informed and consulted, and can put questions or recommendations, and debate. The Commission is to have the right of co-initiative and, again, to be 'fully associated' with the work. Some subjects may, however, be transferred by unanimous agreement to Community competence, and hence to its institutional procedures, without the need for further treaty amendment.

Other new Community competences

The new Treaty has strengthened some of the competences already broached in the Single European Act. Research and technological development is one. Environment is another; and with ecological considerations in view, the Union's aim is to be 'sustainable' economic progress. The cohesion policy is also to be enhanced. Spain led the other lower-income countries, as at the time of the Single European Act which provided for the single market programme, in demanding this as a condition for accepting Emu and the principle of the single currency. A new Cohesion Fund is to be set up to help finance projects in the fields of environment and cross-frontier transport infrastructures in member states with GNP per head less than 90 per cent of the Community average; the structural funds are to be reformed; and a protocol indicated the intention to increase the finance for cohesion and to correct the degressive elements in the Community's system of own resources.

The other eleven member states wished to strengthen the provisions for social policy. But the British government held out against this, so that while the Single European Act still applies in this field to all twelve members, the other eleven bound themselves at Maastricht, through a protocol, to use the Community institutions, without British participation, to take decisions by qualified majority on a number of matters such as working conditions and consultation of workers, though some subjects, such as social security, are to be subject to unanimity.

The new Treaty also breaks new ground with a number of competences, relating to fields in which the Community may have been active on the basis of other treaty articles, but in which specific articles now strengthen the juridical basis. These new competences are: development co-operation with less-developed countries; trans-European networks of infrastructure for transport, telecommunications, or energy; education, vocational training, and youth; culture; public health; consumer protection; and industry, where differences of philosophy regarding industrial policy led to the retention of unanimous voting in the Council, whereas qualified majority is to be the rule for the other new Community competences.

How big a step towards a federal Union?

The Emu will, barring accidents, give the Community the main economic power that it has lacked hitherto: that over currency, alongside its existing powers over trade. The timetable for establishing the single currency and the ECB, moreover, gives the Maastricht Treaty its backbone, just as the single market programme did for the Single Act and the customs union timetable for the original EEC, lending conviction to the many other measures included in the Treaty. Among these measures, the increase in the European Parliament's legislative powers and in its authority over the Commission are particularly significant, even though the Parliament still falls far short of equality with the Council; and the common foreign and security policy with its defence element has much potential for development, although it can also be argued that its intergovernmental character might cause a reversal of the movement towards a federal Union.

The institutional arrangements for the CFSP are indeed likely to be less effective than those of the Community; and the division between the responsibility of this less effective institutional structure for the CFSP and that of the Community for external economic relations is a further source of weakness. It was widely agreed that defence integration could not immediately be made a responsibility of the Community institutions without exposing them to greater strains than they might be able to bear. There was, however, support from most governments in the IGC for the development of majority voting in the making of policy in those fields where security questions are not likely to prove divisive; but this was prevented by British opposition. Is the CFSP likely to move in the future

towards the Community institutions or may the intergovern-
mentalism of the CFSP, on the contrary, begin to influence the
formation of the Community's external economic policy?

The major achievements of the external economic policy, for
which the Community institutions have been responsible, are a
standing argument against any tendency to intergovern-
mentalism in the Community. The Commission, with its strong
position in the common commercial policy, its right of co-
initiative for the CFSP, and its responsibility for consistency in
the Union's external relations as a whole, is well placed to resist
it. Since most member states favoured the development of
majority voting for the CFSP, there will be pressure for it to
move towards the Community procedures, rather than the
other way about. This was, indeed, a major reason why they
insisted that another Conference be held in 1996 on further
treaty revision in order, among other things, to ensure 'the
effectiveness of the mechanisms and the institutions of the
Community' and to consider the future of the defence
component. But for the opposition of the British government,
the Treaty would have stated that the aim would be to
strengthen 'the federal character of the Union'. The commitment of other member states to this would also have been
underlined by the affirmation, in the opening words of the
Treaty, that it was to mark 'a new stage in the process leading
gradually to a Union with a federal goal'; but this too was
replaced, on British insistence, by the original EEC Treaty's
vague term of 'an ever closer union'. The desire of the majority
that the Community be central to the Union was, however,
expressed by the provision that the Union 'shall be founded on
the European Communities, supplemented by the policies and
forms of cooperation established by this Treaty'.

British governments may continue to resist movement in a
federal direction. Germany, its federal aspirations rebuffed at
Maastricht, may lose interest in the Community. France may,
reacting against a more independent, powerful Germany, react
against the Community too. Economic divergence may dim the
prospects for Emu. The federalist tide, having risen into the
early 1990s, may fall again. If these things happen, the
Conference in 1996 will not strengthen the Community or the

Union. But the economic interests that support the Emu and the French commitment to it are strong, as is the German commitment to political union. The British may become less averse to federalism. It will be increasingly evident that enlargement requires stronger institutions if the Community is not to be paralysed. There will be external pressures that work towards closer integration in defence and foreign policy. Underlying these influences, interdependence in the economy, security, and ecology will continue to intensify.

Thus the Conference in 1996 may be more federalist than the IGCs of 1991. The Maastricht Treaty that was their outcome produced a Union that will become federal if three main conditions are fulfilled: the assured completion of Emu; the reform of the procedure of codecision to give the Parliament full equality with the Council and its extension to cover the main fields of Community activity; and movement of the CFSP by stages into the Community institutions, so that the Community will not be weakened by the more intergovernmental CFSP but will strengthen the Union's external policy as a whole.

Before Maastricht, I wrote that a federal Union was 'not unlikely to become a reality in the 1990s' (p. 222, above). After Maastricht, this judgement still stands: the conditions may well be fulfilled sufficiently by the end of this decade to justify calling the Union federal.

Notes

Chapter 1: Creating the Community

1. Statement by Robert Schuman, French foreign minister, 9 May 1950.
2. See Walter Lipgens (ed.), *Documents on the History of European Integration*: vol. 1, *Continental Plans for European Union 1939–1945*; vol. 2, *Plans for European Union in Great Britain and in Exile 1939–1945* (Berlin and New York, 1985, 1986).
3. Alan S. Milward, *The Reconstruction of Western Europe 1945–51* (London, 1984), pp. 310–11.
4. John Pinder, 'Federal Union 1939–41', in Lipgens (ed.), *Documents*, vol. 2, pp. 26–155; Richard Mayne and John Pinder, with John Roberts, *Federal Union: The Pioneers* (London, 1990).
5. Jean Monnet, *Les États-Unis d'Europe ont commencé: Discours et allocutions 1952–1954* (Paris, 1955), pp. 51–60; Altiero Spinelli, *Diario europeo: 1948–1969*, ed. Edmondo Paolini (Bologna, 1989), p. 142.
6. Jean Monnet, *Memoirs*, trans. by Richard Mayne (London, 1978), p. 343.
7. Luigi Vittorio Majocchi and Francesco Rossolillo, *Il Parlamento europeo* (Naples, 1979), pp. 163–216, with introduction by Mario Albertini.
8. The principal neofunctionalist works were Ernst B. Haas, *The Uniting of Europe: Political, Social and Economical Forces 1950–1957* (London, 1958); Leon N. Lindberg, *The Political Dynamics of European Economic Integration* (Stanford, California, 1963); Leon N. Lindberg and Stuart A. Scheingold, *Europe's Would-be Polity: Patterns of Change in the European Community* (Englewood Cliffs, New Jersey, 1970).
9. Press Conference, 15 May 1962.

Chapter 2: Institutions or Constitution

1. Press Conference, 9 Sept. 1965.
2. See Altiero Spinelli, *The Eurocrats: Conflict and Crisis in the European Community*, trans. by C. Grove Haines (Baltimore,

Maryland, 1966); David Coombes, *Politics and Bureaucracy in the European Community: A Portrait of the Commission of the E.E.C.* (London, 1970).

3. Commission of the EC, *Mémorandum sur la réforme de l'agriculture dans la Communauté Économique Européenne: Agriculture 1980*, COM (68) 1000 (Brussels, 21 Dec. 1968).

4. See Donald J. Puchala, 'Worm Cans and Worth Taxes: Fiscal Harmonization and the European Policy Process', in Helen Wallace, William Wallace, and Carole Webb (eds.), *Policy Making in the European Community* (Chichester, 1983; 1st edn. London, 1977).

5. T. C. Hartley, *The Foundations of European Community Law* (Oxford, 1988), p. 47.

6. Monnet, *Les États-Unis d'Europe*, p. 57; the French member of parliament was André Philip, see Etienne Hirsch, *Ainsi va la vie* (Lausanne, 1988), p. 107.

7. Monnet, *Memoirs*, pp. 512–13.

8. Sir Michael Butler, *Europe: More than a Continent* (London, 1986), p. 158.

9. See Ch. 8, below, and Michael Shackleton, *Financing the European Community* (London, 1990), ch. 2.

10. B. M. Key, 'The Exercise by the European Parliament of its Power of Discharge', in R. Hrbek, J. Jamar, and W. Wessels (eds.), *The European Parliament on the Eve of the Second Direct Election: Balance Sheet and Prospects* (Bruges, 1984), p. 788.

11. Butler, *Europe*, p. 22.

12. Altiero Spinelli, *Towards the European Union*, Sixth Jean Monnet Lecture (European University Institute, Florence, 1984).

13. *Interim Report on the Intergovernmental Conference in the context of Parliament's strategy for European Union*, A3–47/90, approved by European Parliament, 14 Mar. 1990.

14. These concepts are summarized in Vernon Bogdanor (ed.), *The Blackwell Encyclopaedia of Political Institutions* (Oxford, 1987), pp. 146–8, 532–4, 547–8.

15. Richard Corbett and Juliet Lodge, 'Progress and Prospects', in Juliet Lodge (ed.), *European Union: The European Community in Search of a Future* (London, 1986).

Chapter 3: From Six to Twelve

1. Mayne, Pinder, and Roberts, *Federal Union*, pp. 26–8.

2. Michael Charlton, *The Price of Victory* (London, 1983), pp. 99, 102, 104, 106.

3 See Miriam Camps, *Britain and the European Community 1955–1963* (London, 1964), ch. 5.

4. Charlton, *The Price of Victory*, p. 304.

5. Camps, *Britain and the European Community*, p. 360; Charlton, *The Price of Victory*, p. 246.

6. Eric Roll, *Crowded Hours* (London, 1985), p. 115.

7. Marcus H. Miller, 'Estimates of the Static Balance-of-Payments and Welfare Costs Compared', in John Pinder (ed.), *The Economics of Europe: What the Common Market Means for Britain* (London, 1971), p. 147. For an account of the politics and diplomacy of British entry, see Uwe Kitzinger, *Diplomacy and Persuasion: How Britain Joined the Common Market* (London, 1973).

8. *The United Kingdom and the European Communities*, Cmnd 4715 (London, July 1971), p. 16.

9. Ibid., p. 25.

10. Ibid., p. 8.

11. See Michael Hodges and William Wallace (eds.), *Economic Divergence in the European Community* (London, 1981).

12. See Helen Wallace with Adam Ridley, *Europe: The Challenge of Diversity* (London, 1985).

Chapter 4: From Customs Union to Single Market

1. Comité Intergouvernemental créé par la Conférence de Messine, *Rapport des Chefs de Délégation aux Ministres des Affaires Étrangères*, the Spaak Report (Brussels, 21 Apr. 1956), pp. 9–10. The economic arguments were later developed in Bela Balassa, *The Theory of Economic Integration* (London, 1961); Jacques Pelkmans, *Market Integration in the European Community* (The Hague, 1984); Paolo Cecchini with Michael Catinat and Alexis Jacquemin, *The European Challenge 1992: The Benefits of a Single Market* (Aldershot, 1988).

2. This 'acceleration' is analysed in Lindberg, *Political Dynamics*, ch. 9.

3. For example, Commission of the EC, *The Competitiveness of the European Community Industry*, Document III/387/82 (Brussels, Mar. 1982); M. Albert and Professor J. Ball, *Towards European Economic Recovery in the 1980s* (European Parliament, 31 Aug. 1983); Jacques Pelkmans, *Completing the Internal Market for Industrial Products* (Commission of the EC, Brussels, 1986).

4. Wisse Dekker, *Europe–1990* (Eindhoven, 1985); *Completing the*

Internal Market, White Paper from the Commission to the European Council, June 1985.

5. *Completing the Internal Market.* The programme is analysed in Roland Bieber, Renaud Dehousse, John Pinder, and Joseph H. H. Weiler (eds.), *1992: One European Market? A Critical Analysis of the Commission's Internal Market Strategy* (Baden-Baden, 1988); Jacques Pelkmans and Alan Winters, *Europe's Domestic Market* (London, 1988); Cecchini, *European Challenge.*

6. Cecchini, *European Challenge*, pp. 10–11.

7. Ibid., p. 27.

8. Ibid., p. 16; Pelkmans and Winters, *Europe's Domestic Market*, pp. 32–4.

9. Richard H. Lauwaars, 'The "Model Directive" on Technical Harmonization', in Bieber, Dehousse, Pinder, and Weiler (eds.), *1992*, pp. 152–5. In the same book see also Christian Joerges, 'The New Approach to Technical Harmonization and the Interests of Consumers: Reflections on the Requirements and Difficulties of a Europeanization Product Safety Policy', and Pieter VerLoren van Themaat, 'The Contributions to the Establishment of the Internal Market by the Case-Law of the Court of Justice of the European Communities'.

10. See Lauwaars, 'Model Directive'.

11. Cecchini, *European Challenge*; the reports on which this summary book was based are explained and listed in it on pp. 115–27.

12. John Pinder, 'Positive Integration and Negative Integration: Some Problems of Economic Union in the EEC', *The World Today*, Jan. 1968.

Chapter 5: Agricultural Policy

1. Miriam Camps, *European Unification in the Sixties: From the Veto to the Crisis* (New York, 1966), pp. 15 ff.

2. Ibid., pp. 40 ff.

3. Commission of the EC, *Mémorandum sur la réforme de l'agriculture.* This episode is explained in Edmund Neville-Rolfe, *The Politics of Agriculture in the European Community* (London, 1984), which gives a detailed account of the development of the common agricultural policy up to 1983.

4. Glenda Goldstone Rosenthal, *The Men Behind the Decisions: Cases in European Policy-Making* (Lexington, Massachusetts, 1975), ch. 6.

5. D. Biehl (chairman) and members of a study group of the Institut

für Europäische Politik, *Common Agricultural Policy, European Integration and International Division of Labour* (Bonn, 1987), pp. 8, 10, 20.

6. Commission of the EC, *Making a Success of the Single Act*, COM (87) 100, and *Report by the Commission to the Council and the Parliament on the Financing of the Community Budget*, COM (87) 101 (Brussels, 1987).

Chapter 6: Industrial and Social Policy

1. See John Pinder (ed.), *National Industrial Strategies and the World Economy* (Totowa, New Jersey, 1982). See also the chapters by Christopher Wilkinson and Jean Waelbroeck in Alexis Jacquemin (ed.), *European Industry: Public Policy and Corporate Strategy* (Oxford, 1984).

2. The complexities of the steel industry in that region are discussed in Milward, *Reconstruction*, ch. 12.

3. See Pinder (ed.), *National Industrial Strategies*, chs. 3 and 5.

4. Dennis Swann, *Competition and Industrial Policy in the European Community* (London, 1983), p. 92.

5. Ibid., p. 95.

6. See Emmanuel de Robien, 'The Role of European Industry in European Standardization: The Case of Information Technology', in Rita Beuter and Jacques Pelkmans (eds.), *Cementing the Internal Market* (Maastricht, 1986); and Margaret Sharp, 'The Community and New Technologies', in Juliet Lodge (ed.), *The European Community and the Challenge of the Future* (London, 1989), pp. 207 ff.

7. Sharp, 'Community', p. 203.

8. Nigel Haigh and Konrad von Moltke, 'The European Community: An Environmental Force', *EPA Journal*, Washington DC, July/Aug. 1990, p. 60. On EC environmental policy, see also Nigel Haigh, *EEC Environmental Policy and Britain* (London, 1984; revised edn., Harlow, 1989).

Chapter 7: Monetary System and Monetary Union

1. Tommaso Padoa-Schioppa, *Financial and Monetary Integration in Europe: 1990, 1992 and Beyond* (Group of Thirty, New York and London, 1990), p. 18.

2. Spaak Report (see n.1 to Ch.4), p.74. For the part played by Triffin and Uri, see Pierre Uri, 'Réflexion sur l'approche

fonctionnaliste de Jean Monnet et suggestions pour l'avenir', in Giandomenico Majone, Emile Noël, and Peter Van den Bossche (eds.), *Jean Monnet et l'Europe d'aujourd'hui* (Baden-Baden, 1989), p. 76.

3. Robert Triffin, 'Note sur ma collaboration avec Jean Monnet', in *Témoignages à la mémoire de Jean Monnet* (Fondation Jean Monnet pour l'Europe and Centre de Recherches Européennes, Lausanne, 1989), p. 531.

4. For Triffin's proposals during that period on monetary reform, see his *Europe and the Money Muddle: From Bilateralism to Near-Convertibility, 1947–1956* (New Haven, Connecticut, 1957), pp. 287–94; and his *Gold and the Dollar Crisis: The Future of Convertibility* (New Haven, 1961), pp. 131–44.

5. *Action Committee for the United States of Europe: Statements and Declarations 1955–67* (London, 1969), pp. 46, 60–2; and Triffin, 'Note', p. 531.

6. Robert Marjolin, *Le Travail d'une vie: Mémoires 1911–1986* (Paris, 1986), p. 312; Commission of the EEC, *Action Programme of the Community for the Second Stage* (Brussels, 1962). The development of monetary integration up to the mid-1970s is recounted in Loukas Tsoukalis, *The Politics and Economics of European Monetary Integration* (London, 1977).

7. See Triffin, *Gold and the Dollar Crisis*; Robert Mundell, 'A Theory of Optimum Currency Areas', *American Economic Review*, Sept. 1961; R. I. McKinnon, 'Optimum Currency Areas', *American Economic Review*, Sept. 1963.

8. Commission of the EEC, *Eighth General Report* (Brussels, 1965).

9. Tsoukalis, *Politics and Economics*, p. 72.

10. Monnet, *Memoirs*, pp. 194–5.

11. Tsoukalis, *Politics and Economics*, pp. 88–9.

12. Herman Wortmann and Florent Bonn, 'Theorie und Praxis der Währungsunion in Europa', in R. Regul and H. Wolff (eds.), *Das Bankwesen im grösseren Europa* (Baden-Baden, 1963), cited in Tsoukalis, *Politics and Economics*, p. 36; Max Corden, 'The Adjustment Problem', in L. B. Krause and W. S. Salant (eds.), *European Monetary Unification and its Meaning for the United States* (Washington DC, 1973); Giovanni Magnifico, *European Monetary Unification* (London, 1973); Peter Oppenheimer, 'The Problem of Monetary Union', in D. Evans (ed.), *Britain in the EEC* (London, 1973). Compare also with the literature on divergence, for example Hodges and Wallace (eds.), *Economic Divergence*.

13. Giovanni Magnifico and John Williamson, *European Monetary Integration*, Federal Trust Study Group Report (London, 1972).

14. Commission of the EC, *Report on European Union*, Supplement to Bulletin, 5-1975 (Brussels, 1975).

15. Commission of the EC, *Economic and Monetary Union: The Economic Rationale and Design of the System* (Brussels, 20 Mar. 1990), para. IV. 1. 3; speech by John Major, Chancellor of the Exchequer, 20 June 1990.

16. Roy Jenkins, *European Diary: 1977–1981* (London, 1989), p. 22. For a complete account of the establishment of the EMS, see Peter Ludlow, *The Making of the European Monetary System* (London, 1982).

17. Jenkins, *European Diary*, pp. 22–3.

18. Roy Jenkins, *Europe's Present Challenge and Future Opportunity*, First Jean Monnet Lecture (European University Institute, Florence, 1977), cited in Ludlow, *Making of the EMS*, pp. 47–9.

19. Jenkins, *European Diary*, pp. 197, 223–4.

20. Helmut Schmidt, Preface to Jean Monnet, *Errinerungen eines Europäers* (Munich, 1978); Jenkins, *European Diary*, p. 286.

21. Ludlow, *Making of the EMS*, p. 76; Jenkins, *European Diary*, p. 137.

22. *The Times*, 11 July 1978, cited in Ludlow, *Making of the EMS*, pp. 112–13.

23. Ludlow, *Making of the EMS*, p. 220.

24. Jenkins, *European Diary*, p. 353.

25. Commission of the EC, 'Benefits and Costs of Economic and Monetary Union', annex to Commission, *Economic and Monetary Union*; Michael J. Artis and Mark P. Taylor, 'Exchange Rates, Interest Rates, Capital Controls and the European Monetary System: Assessing the Track Record', in Francesco Giavazzi, Stefano Micossi, and Marcus Miller (eds.), *The European Monetary System* (Cambridge, 1988), pp. 188, 202; and Emil-Maria Claassen and Eric Perée, 'Discussion' following Artis and Taylor, ibid., p. 209.

26. J. Godeaux, 'The Working of the EMS: A Personal Assessment', in Committee for the Study of Economic and Monetary Union, *Report on Economic and Monetary Union in the European Community*, the Delors report (Luxembourg, 1989), p. 192.

27. Case 203/80, Casati (1981) ECR 2595, cited in VerLoren van Themaat, 'Contributions', pp. 112, 121.

28. Cecchini, *European Challenge*, pp. 37–42, 84, 95.

29. Padoa-Schioppa, *Financial and Monetary Integration*, p. 19.

30. See n. 26 above.

31. Padoa-Schioppa, *Financial and Monetary Integration*, p. 22.

32. Commission, *Economic and Monetary Union*, para. II. 2.

33. Karl Otto Pöhl, 'The Further Development of the European Monetary System', in Delors report (see n. 26 above), pp. 129–55.

34. Maurice F. Doyle, 'Regional Policy and European Economic Integration', and J. Delors, 'Regional Implications of Economic and Monetary Integration', in Delors report, pp. 61–79, 81–9.

35. Commission, 'Benefits and Costs'.

Chapter 8: European Budget and Public Finance Union

1. David Coombes with Ilka Wiebecke, *The Power of the Purse in the European Communities* (London, 1972), p. 10.

2. Monnet, *Les États-Unis d'Europe*, pp. 57–8.

3. Commission of the EC, *Report of the Study Group on the Role of Public Finance in European Integration*, the MacDougall report (Brussels, 1977), vol. 2, p. 483; Dieter Biehl, 'A Federalist Budgetary Strategy for European Union', *Policy Studies*, Oct. 1985, p. 67.

4. Camps, *European Unification*, pp. 38 ff.

5. See Coombes, *Power of the Purse*, and Helen Wallace, *Budgetary Politics: The Finances of the European Communities* (London, 1980).

6. Commission of the EC, *Rapport du groupe ad hoc pour l'examen du problème de l'accroissement des compétences du parlement européen*, the Vedel report (Brussels, 1972).

7. Loc. cit., n. 10 to Ch. 2.

8. The MacDougall report (see n. 3 above) included two annexes in vol. 2 on the subject of fiscal federalism: Wallace E. Oates, 'Fiscal Federalism in Theory and Practice: Applications to the European Community'; Francesco Forte, 'Principles for the Assignment of Public Economic Functions in a Setting of Multilayer Government'.

9. MacDougall report, vol. 1, p. 16; Oates, 'Fiscal Federalism', p. 296.

10. MacDougall report, vol. 1, p. 20.

11. Ibid., p. 17.

12. An economic analysis of the British budget question is given in Geoffrey Denton, *The British Budget Problem and the Future of the EEC Budget* (London, 1982). Accounts from participants include Butler, *Europe*, ch. 7; Jenkins, *European Diary*, *passim*.

13. Marcus Miller, 'Estimates', pp. 120, 147; John Pinder, 'What Membership Means for Britain', in Pinder (ed.), *Economics of Europe*, p. 13.

14. *The United Kingdom and the European Communities*, Cmnd 4715, p. 25.

15. J. Ørstrøm Møller, 'Budgetary Imbalances', *Journal of European Integration*, 1985, Nos. 2–3, p. 128.

16. Delors, 'Regional Implications', p. 88; MacDougall report, vol. 1, pp. 32–3.

17. Commission of the EC, *Making a Success of the Single Act: A New Frontier for Europe*, COM (87) 100 (Brussels, 1987); Commission, *Report to the Council and Parliament on the Financing of the Community Budget*, COM (87) 101 (Brussels, 1987); Michael Shackleton, *Financing the European Community* (London, 1990), gives a full account of this decision and of subsequent events relating to the EC budget.

18. Shackleton, *Financing*, pp. 30–1.

19. The future of the budget is considered in ibid., pp. 57 ff.

20. Ibid., p. 61.

21. Doyle, 'Regional Policy'.

22. Delors, 'Regional Implications'.

23. Delors report (see n. 26 to Ch. 7), p. 22.

24. Commission of the EC, *Efficiency, Stability and Equity: A Strategy for the Evolution of the Economic System of the European Community*, the Padoa-Schioppa report (Brussels, 1987), pp. 137–41.

25. Biehl, 'A Federalist Budgetary Strategy', p. 71.

26. Commission of the EC, Communication from the Commission to the Council, *A Community Strategy to Limit Carbon Dioxide Emissions and to Improve Energy Efficiency*, SEC (91) 1744 final (Brussels: October 1991).

27. Albert and Ball, *Towards European Economic Recovery*, ch. 5, para. 31.

28. Commission of the EC, *Economic and Monetary Union*, para. IV. 2. 2.

29. Shackleton, *Financing*, p. 30.

30. Biehl, 'A Federalist Budgetary Strategy', p. 66.

Chapter 9: From Common Tariff to Great Civilian Power

1. See John Pinder, 'Integrating Divergent Economies: The Extra-national Method', in Hodges and Wallace (eds.), *Economic Divergence*, pp. 194–5.

2. Camps, *Britain and the European Community*, pp. 24, 32.
3. Spaak report (see n. 1 to Ch. 4), pp. 21–2, 30–1.
4. Cited in Murray Forsyth, *Unions of States: The Theory and Practice of Confederation* (Leicester, 1981), p. 162.
5. Balassa, *Theory of Economic Integration*, ch. 2. The original work on this subject was Jacob Viner, *The Customs Union Issue* (New York, 1950).
6. Michael Davenport, 'The Economic Impact of the EEC', in Andrea Boltho (ed.), *The European Economy: Growth and Crisis* (London, 1982), p. 227.
7. *Action Committee for the United States of Europe*, pp. 62–5.
8. Coombes, *Politics and Bureaucracy*, ch. 8.
9. Bela Balassa, *Trade Liberalization among Industrial Countries: Objectives and Alternatives* (New York, 1967), p. 122.
10. Lawrence B. Krause, *European Economic Integration and the United States* (Washington DC, 1968), pp. 224–5.
11. François Duchêne, 'Europe's Role in World Peace', in Richard Mayne (ed.), *Europe Tomorrow: Sixteen Europeans Look Ahead* (London, 1972), p. 43.
12. Gunnar Myrdal, *An International Economy: Problems and Prospects* (London, 1956), ch. 4.
13. Padoa-Schioppa, *Financial and Monetary Integration*, p. 28.
14. Camps, *Britain and the European Community*, p. 65.
15. Rosenthal, *The Men Behind The Decisions*, ch. 3.
16. For a view from the EC Commission, see Eberhard Rhein, 'Die Europäische Gemeinschaft und das Mittelmeer', *Europa-Archiv*, 22/1986, pp. 641–8.
17. Victoria Curzon, *The Essentials of Economic Integration: Lessons of EFTA Experience* (London, 1974), p. 303.
18. *Memoirs*, p. 343.
19. 'Report of the Ministers of Foreign Affairs of the Member States on the Problems of Political Unification', the Davignon report, EC *Bulletin*, 11/1970 (Luxembourg, 1970).
20. Wilhelm Späth, 'Die Arbeit des EPZ-Sekretariats: Eine Bilanz', *Europa-Archiv*, 6/1990, pp. 213–20.
21. Alfred Pijpers, Elfriede Regelsberger, and Wolfgang Wessels, 'A Common Foreign Policy for Western Europe?', in Pijpers *et al.* with Geoffrey Edwards (eds.), *European Political Cooperation in the 1980s* (Dordrecht, 1988), pp. 271–2.
22. *European Union*, Report by Mr Leo Tindemans to the European Council, EC *Bulletin*, Supplement 1/1976.

23. Helmut Schmidt, 'Deutsch-französische Zusammenarbeit in der Sicherheitspolitik', *Europa-Archiv*, 11/1987.
24. Monnet, *Les États-Unis d'Europe*, pp. 127–8.

Chapter 10: The Building of a Union

1. For an explanation of the concepts of allocation, stabilization, and distribution as they apply to the Community, see Padoa-Schioppa report (n. 24 to Ch. 8), pp. 22–3.
2. Press Conference, 15 May 1962.
3. Camps, *Britain and the European Community*, p. 360.
4. *The United Kingdom and the European Communities*, Cmnd 4715, p. 8.
5. Speech delivered in Bruges on 20 Sept. 1988.
6. Donald Puchala, 'Of Blind Men, Elephants and International Integration', *Journal of Common Market Studies*, Mar. 1972, p. 168.
7. Robert O. Keohane and Joseph S. Nye, *Power and Interdependence: World Politics in Transition* (Boston, 1977), p. 240.
8. See Dekker, *Europe-1990* and Cecchini, *European Challenge*.
9. Lindberg and Scheingold, *Europe's Would-be Polity*, p. 7.
10. Lindberg, *Political Dynamics*, p. 10.
11. Lindberg and Scheingold, *Europe's Would-be Polity*, pp. 118, 282, 285, 296.
12. Lindberg, *Political Dynamics*, p. 6.
13. Basic works of modern federalist literature are: the Marquis of Lothian, *Pacifism is not Enough (Nor Patriotism Either)* (London, 1935, reprinted in John Pinder and Andrea Bosco (eds.), *Pacifism is not Enough: Collected Lectures and Speeches of Lord Lothian (Philip Kerr)*, (London, 1990); Lionel Robbins, *The Economic Causes of War* (London, 1939). See also Richard Mayne and John Pinder with John Roberts, *Federal Union: The Pioneers* (London, 1990).
14. John Pinder, 'European Community and Nation-State: A Case for a Neo-Federalism?', *International Affairs*, Jan. 1986.

Select Bibliography

The sources are listed here in six groups, corresponding to chapters in this book or to groups of chapters with related subjects: general and institutional (Chapters 1, 2, 10); enlargement and external relations (3, 9); market integration and industrial policy (4, 6); agriculture (5); money (7); budget (8).

General and institutional

Action Committee for the United States of Europe: Statements and Declarations 1955–67, Chatham House and PEP Joint European Series No. 9 (London, 1969).

Bieber, Roland, Jacqué, Jean-Paul, and Weiler, Joseph H. H. (eds.), *An Ever Closer Union: A Critical Analysis of the Draft Treaty Establishing the European Union*, The European Perspectives Series (Commission of the EC, Luxembourg, 1985).

Bulmer, Simon, and Wessels, Wolfgang, *The European Council: Decision-Making in European Politics* (London, 1987).

Butler, Sir Michael, *Europe: More than a Continent* (London, 1986).

Camps, Miriam, *European Unification in the Sixties: From the Veto to the Crisis* (New York, 1966).

Charlton, Michael, *The Price of Victory* (London, 1983).

Commission of the EC, *Efficiency, Stability and Equity: A Strategy for the Evolution of the Economic System of the European Community*, the Padoa-Schioppa report (Brussels, 1987).

Coombes, David, *Politics and Bureaucracy in the European Community: A Portrait of the Commission of the E.E.C.* (London, 1970).

—— *The Future of the European Parliament* (London, 1979).

Haas, Ernst B., *The Uniting of Europe: Political, Social and Economical Forces 1950–1957* (London, 1958).

Harrop, Jeffrey, *The Political Economy of Integration in the European Community* (Aldershot and Brookfield, Vermont, 1989).

Hartley, T. C., *The Foundations of European Community Law* (Oxford, 1988).

Lindberg, Leon N., *The Political Dynamics of European Economic Integration* (Stanford, California, 1963).

—— and Scheingold, Stuart A., *Europe's Would-be Polity: Patterns of Change in the European Community* (Englewood Cliffs, New Jersey, 1970).

Lodge, Juliet (ed.), *European Union: The European Community in Search of a Future* (London, 1986).

—— (ed.), *The European Community and the Challenge of the Future* (London, 1989).

Marquand, David, *Parliament for Europe* (London, 1979).

Mayne, Richard, and Pinder, John, with Roberts, John, *Federal Union: The Pioneers* (London, 1990).

Monnet, Jean, *Memoirs*, trans. by Richard Mayne (London, 1978).

Padoa-Schioppa report, *see* Commission of the EC, *above*.

Pinder, John, 'Positive Integration and Negative Integration: Some Problems of Economic Union in the EEC', *The World Today*, Jan. 1968.

—— 'European Community and Nation-State: A Case for a Neo-Federalism?', *International Affairs*, Jan. 1986.

Pryce, Roy (ed.), *The Dynamics of European Union* (Beckenham and New York, 1987).

Swann, Dennis, *The Economics of the Common Market*, 6th edn. (Harmondsworth, 1988).

Tugendhat, Christopher, *Making Sense of Europe* (Harmondsworth, 1986).

Wallace, Helen, Wallace, William, and Webb, Carole (eds.), *Policy Making in the European Community*, 2nd edn. (Chichester, 1983).

Enlargement, external relations

Camps, Miriam, *Britain and the European Community 1955–1963* (London, 1964).

Hine, R. C., *The Political Economy of European Trade: An Introduction to the Trade Policies of the EEC* (Brighton, 1985).

HMSO, White Paper, *The United Kingdom and the European Communities*, Cmnd 4715 (London, 1971).

Kitzinger, Uwe, *Diplomacy and Persuasion: How Britain Joined the Common Market* (London, 1973).

Lodge, Juliet, Tsakaloyannis, Panos, Ginsberg, Roy H., Daniels, Gordon, and Hewitt, Adrian, 'Part III, External Perspectives', in Lodge (ed.), *European Community* (1989).

Nicholson, Francis, and East, Roger, *From the Six to the Twelve: The Enlargement of the European Communities* (Harlow, 1987).

Pijpers, Alfred, Regelsberger, Elfriede, and Wessels, Wolfgang, with Edwards, Geoffrey (eds.), *European Political Cooperation in the 1980s* (Dordrecht, 1988).

Pinder, John (ed.), *The Economics of Europe: What the Common Market Means for Britain* (London, 1971).

Pomfret, Richard, *Mediterranean Policy of the European Community* (London, 1986).

Tsoukalis, Loukas, *The European Community and its Mediterranean Enlargement* (London, 1981).

—— (ed.), *Europe, America and the World Economy* (Oxford, 1986).

Wallace, Helen, and Wessels, Wolfgang, *Towards a New Partnership: The EC and EFTA in the Wider Western Europe*, Occasional Paper No. 28 (Geneva, EFTA, 1989).

Market integration, industrial policy

Bieber, Roland, Dehousse, Renaud, Pinder, John, and Weiler, Joseph H. H. (eds.), *1992: One European Market? A Critical Analysis of the Commission's Internal Market Strategy* (Baden-Baden, 1988).

Cecchini, Paolo, with Catinat, Michael, and Jacquemin, Alexis, *The European Challenge 1992: The Benefits of a Single Market* (Aldershot, 1988).

Commission of the EC, *Completing the Internal Market*, White Paper from the Commission to the Council (Luxembourg, 1985).

Jacquemin, Alexis (ed.), *European Industry: Public Policy and Corporate Strategy* (Oxford, 1984).

Pearce, Joan, and Sutton, John, with Batchelor, Roy, *Protection and Industrial Policy in Europe* (London, 1985).

Pelkmans, Jacques, *Market Integration in the European Community* (The Hague, 1984).

—— *Completing the Internal Market for Industrial Products* (Commission of the EC, Brussels, 1986).

—— and Winters, Alan, *Europe's Domestic Market* (London, 1988).

Pinder, John (ed.), *National Industrial Strategies and the World Economy* (Totowa, New Jersey, 1982).

Sharp, Margaret, and Shearman, Claire, *European Technological Collaboration* (London, 1987).

Swann, Dennis, *Competition and Industrial Policy in the European Community* (London, 1983).

Agriculture

Biehl, Dieter, *et al.*, *Common Agricultural Policy, European Integration and International Division of Labour* (Bonn, 1987).

Commission of the EC, *Mémorandum sur la réforme de l'agriculture dans la Communauté Économique Européenne: Agriculture 1980*, COM (68) 1000 (Brussels, 21 Dec. 1968).

Duchêne, François, Szczepanik, Edward, and Legg, Wilfred, *New Limits on Agriculture* (Beckenham, 1985).

Franklin, Michael, *Rich Man's Farming: The Crisis in Agriculture* (London, 1988).

Josling, Tim, 'Agricultural Policies and World Trade: The US and the European Community at Bay', in Tsoukalis (ed.), *Europe, America* (1986).

Marsh, John S., 'The Common Agricultural Policy', in Lodge (ed.), *European Community* (1989).

Neville-Rolfe, Edmund, *The Politics of Agriculture in the European Community* (London, 1984).

Tracy, Michael, *Government and Agriculture in Western Europe 1880–1988* (London and New York, 1989).

—— 'Agricultural Policy and European Integration', in John Davis and Peter Mathias (eds.), *The Nature of Industrialisation*, vol. 5 (Oxford, 1990).

Money

Committee for the Study of Economic and Monetary Union, *Report on Economic and Monetary Union in the European Community*, the Delors report (Luxembourg, 1989).

Delors report, *see preceding entry.*

Giavazzi, Francesco, Micossi, Stefano, and Miller, Marcus (eds.), *The European Monetary System* (Cambridge, 1988).

Ludlow, Peter, *The Making of the European Monetary System* (London, 1982).

Magnifico, Giovanni, *European Monetary Unification* (London, 1973).

Padoa-Schioppa, Tommaso, *Financial and Monetary Integration in Europe: 1990, 1992 and Beyond* (Group of Thirty, New York and London, 1990).

Werner report, *Report to the Council and the Commission on the Realisation by Stages of Economic and Monetary Union in the Community*, Supplement to Bulletin 11-1970 of the EC (Luxembourg, 1970).

Budget

Biehl, Dieter, 'A Federalist Budgetary Strategy for European Union', *Policy Studies*, Oct. 1985.

Commission of the EC, *Report of the Study Group on the Role of Public Finance in European Integration*, the MacDougall report (Brussels, 1977).

—— *Making a Success of the Single Act: A New Frontier for Europe*, COM (87) 100 (Brussels, 1987).

—— *Report to the Council and Parliament on the Financing of the Community Budget*, COM (87) 101 (Brussels, 1987).

Coombes, David, with Wiebecke, Ilke, *The Power of the Purse in the European Communities* (London, 1972).

Denton, Geoffrey, *The British Budget Problem and the Future of the EEC Budget* (London, 1982).

MacDougall report, *see* Commission of the EC, *above*.

Shackleton, Michael, *Financing the European Community* (London, 1990).

Wallace, Helen, *Budgetary Politics: The Finances of the European Communities* (London, 1980).

Index

OXFORD

MORE OXFORD PAPERBACKS

This book is just one of nearly 1000 Oxford Paperbacks currently in print. If you would like details of other Oxford Paperbacks, including titles in the World's Classics, Oxford Reference, Oxford Books, OPUS, Past Masters, Oxford Authors, and Oxford Shakespeare series, please write to:

UK and Europe: Oxford Paperbacks Publicity Manager, Arts and Reference Publicity Department, Oxford University Press, Walton Street, Oxford OX2 6DP.

Customers in UK and Europe will find Oxford Paperbacks available in all good bookshops. But in case of difficulty please send orders to the Cash-with-Order Department, Oxford University Press Distribution Services, Saxon Way West, Corby, Northants NN18 9ES. Tel: 0536 741519; Fax: 0536 746337. Please send a cheque for the total cost of the books, plus £1.75 postage and packing for orders under £20; £2.75 for orders over £20. Customers outside the UK should add 10% of the cost of the books for postage and packing.

USA: Oxford Paperbacks Marketing Manager, Oxford University Press, Inc., 200 Madison Avenue, New York, N.Y. 10016.

Canada: Trade Department, Oxford University Press, 70 Wynford Drive, Don Mills, Ontario M3C 1J9.

Australia: Trade Marketing Manager, Oxford University Press, G.P.O. Box 2784Y, Melbourne 3001, Victoria.

South Africa: Oxford University Press, P.O. Box 1141, Cape Town 8000.

POLITICS IN OXFORD PAPERBACKS

Oxford Paperbacks offers incisive and provocative studies of the political ideologies and institutions that have shaped the modern world since 1945.

GOD SAVE ULSTER!

The Religion and Politics of Paisleyism

Steve Bruce

Ian Paisley is the only modern Western leader to have founded his own Church and political party, and his enduring popularity and success mirror the complicated issues which continue to plague Northern Ireland. This book is the first serious analysis of his religious and political careers and a unique insight into Unionist politics and religion in Northern Ireland today.

Since it was founded in 1951, the Free Presbyterian Church of Ulster has grown steadily; it now comprises some 14,000 members in fifty congregations in Ulster and ten branches overseas. The Democratic Unionist Party, formed in 1971, now speaks for about half of the Unionist voters in Northern Ireland, and the personal standing of the man who leads both these movements was confirmed in 1979 when Ian R. K. Paisley received more votes than any other member of the European Parliament. While not neglecting Paisley's 'charismatic' qualities, Steve Bruce argues that the key to his success has been his ability to embody and represent traditional evangelical Protestantism and traditional Ulster Unionism.

'original and profound . . . I cannot praise this book too highly.'
Bernard Crick, *New Society*

Also in Oxford Paperbacks:

Freedom Under Thatcher   Keith Ewing and Conor Gearty
Strong Leadership   Graham Little
The Thatcher Effect   Dennis Kavanagh and Anthony Seldon

HISTORY IN OXFORD PAPERBACKS

Oxford Paperbacks' superb history list offers books on a wide range of topics from ancient to modern times, whether general period studies or assessments of particular events, movements, or personalities.

THE STRUGGLE FOR
THE MASTERY OF EUROPE 1848–1918

A. J. P. Taylor

The fall of Metternich in the revolutions of 1848 heralded an era of unprecedented nationalism in Europe, culminating in the collapse of the Hapsburg, Romanov, and Hohenzollern dynasties at the end of the First World War. In the intervening seventy years the boundaries of Europe changed dramatically from those established at Vienna in 1815. Cavour championed the cause of *Risorgimento* in Italy; Bismarck's three wars brought about the unification of Germany; Serbia and Bulgaria gained their independence courtesy of the decline of Turkey—'the sick man of Europe'; while the great powers scrambled for places in the sun in Africa. However, with America's entry into the war and President Wilson's adherence to idealistic internationalist principles, Europe ceased to be the centre of the world, although its problems, still primarily revolving around nationalist aspirations, were to smash the Treaty of Versailles and plunge the world into war once more.

A. J. P. Taylor has drawn the material for his account of this turbulent period from the many volumes of diplomatic documents which have been published in the five major European languages. By using vivid language and forceful characterization, he has produced a book that is as much a work of literature as a contribution to scientific history.

'One of the glories of twentieth-century writing.' *Observer*

Also in Oxford Paperbacks:

Portrait of an Age: Victorian England   G. M. Young
Germany 1866–1945   Gorden A. Craig
The Russian Revolution 1917–1932   Sheila Fitzpatrick
France 1848–1945   Theodore Zeldin

PHILOSOPHY IN OXFORD PAPERBACKS

Ranging from authoritative introductions in the Past Masters and OPUS series to in-depth studies of classical and modern thought, the Oxford Paperbacks' philosophy list is one of the most provocative and challenging available.

THE GREAT PHILOSOPHERS
Bryan Magee

Beginning with the death of Socrates in 399, and following the story through the centuries to recent figures such as Bertrand Russell and Wittgenstein, Bryan Magee and fifteen contemporary writers and philosophers provide an accessible and exciting introduction to Western philosophy and its greatest thinkers.

Bryan Magee in conversation with:

A. J. Ayer
Michael Ayers
Miles Burnyeat
Frederick Copleston
Hubert Dreyfus
Anthony Kenny
Sidney Morgenbesser
Martha Nussbaum

John Passmore
Anthony Quinton
John Searle
Peter Singer
J. P. Stern
Geoffrey Warnock
Bernard Williams

'Magee is to be congratulated . . . anyone who sees the programmes or reads the book will be left in no danger of believing philosophical thinking is unpractical and uninteresting.' Ronald Hayman, *Times Educational Supplement*

'one of the liveliest, fast-paced introductions to philosophy, ancient and modern that one could wish for' *Universe*

Also by Bryan Magee in Oxford Paperbacks:

Men of Ideas
Aspects of Wagner 2/e

PAST MASTERS

General Editor: Keith Thomas

The *Past Masters* series offers students and general readers alike concise introductions to the lives and works of the world's greatest literary figures, composers, philosophers, religious leaders, scientists, and social and political thinkers.

'Put end to end, this series will constitute a noble encyclopaedia of the history of ideas.' Mary Warnock

HOBBES

Richard Tuck

Thomas Hobbes (1588–1679) was the first great English political philosopher, and his book *Leviathan* was one of the first truly modern works of philosophy. He has long had the reputation of being a pessimistic atheist, who saw human nature as inevitably evil, and who proposed a totalitarian state to subdue human failings. In this new study, Richard Tuck shows that while Hobbes may indeed have been an atheist, he was far from pessimistic about human nature, nor did he advocate totalitarianism. By locating him against the context of his age, Dr Tuck reveals Hobbs to have been passionately concerned with the refutation of scepticism in both science and ethics, and to have developed a theory of knowledge which rivalled that of Descartes in its importance for the formation of modern philosophy.

Also available in Past Masters:

Spinoza   Roger Scruton
Bach   Denis Arnold
Machiavelli   Quentin Skinner
Darwin   Jonathan Howard

RELIGION AND THEOLOGY
IN OXFORD PAPERBACKS

Oxford Paperbacks offers incisive studies of the philosophies and ceremonies of the world's major religions, including Christianity, Judaism, Islam, Buddhism, and Hinduism.

A HISTORY OF HERESY

David Christie-Murray

'Heresy, a cynic might say, is the opinion held by a minority of men which the majority declares unacceptable and is strong enough to punish.'

What is heresy? Who were the great heretics and what did they believe? Why might those originally condemned as heretics come to be regarded as martyrs and cherished as saints?

Heretics, those who dissent from orthodox Christian belief, have existed at all times since the Christian Church was founded and the first Christians became themselves heretics within Judaism. From earliest times too, politics, orthodoxy, and heresy have been inextricably entwined—to be a heretic was often to be a traitor and punishable by death at the stake—and heresy deserves to be placed against the background of political and social developments which shaped it.

This book is a vivid combination of narrative and comment which succeeds in both re-creating historical events and elucidating the most important—and most disputed—doctrines and philosophies.

Also in Oxford Paperbacks:

Christianity in the West 1400–1700   John Bossy
John Henry Newman: A Biography   Ian Ker
Islam: The Straight Path   John L. Esposito

LAW FROM OXFORD PAPERBACKS

Oxford Paperbacks's law list ranges from introductions to the English legal system to reference books and in-depth studies of contemporary legal issues.

INTRODUCTION TO ENGLISH LAW
Tenth Edition

William Geldart
Edited by D. C. M. Yardley

'Geldart' has over the years established itself as a standard account of English law, expounding the body of modern law as set in its historical context. Regularly updated since its first publication, it remains indispensable to student and layman alike as a concise, reliable guide.

Since publication of the ninth edition in 1984 there have been important court decisions and a great deal of relevant new legislation. D. C. M. Yardley, Chairman of the Commission for Local Administration in England, has taken account of all these developments and the result has been a considerable rewriting of several parts of the book. These include the sections dealing with the contractual liability of minors, the abolition of the concept of illegitimacy, the liability of a trade union in tort for inducing a person to break his/her contract of employment, the new public order offences, and the intent necessary for a conviction of murder.

Other law titles:

Freedom Under Thatcher: Civil Liberties in Modern Britain
Keith Ewing and Conor Gearty
Doing the Business   Dick Hobbs
Judges   David Pannick
Law and Modern Society   P. S. Atiyah

SCIENCE IN OXFORD PAPERBACKS

Oxford Paperbacks' expanding science and mathematics list offers a range of books across the scientific spectrum by men and women at the forefront of their fields, including Richard Dawkins, Martin Gardner, James Lovelock, Raymond Smullyan, and Nobel Prize winners Peter Medawar and Gerald Edelman.

THE SELFISH GENE

Second Edition

Richard Dawkins

Our genes made us. We animals exist for their preservation and are nothing more than their throwaway survival machines. The world of the selfish gene is one of savage competition, ruthless exploitation, and deceit. But what of the acts of apparent altruism found in nature—the bees who commit suicide when they sting to protect the hive, or the birds who risk their lives to warn the flock of an approaching hawk? Do they contravene the fundamental law of gene selfishness? By no means: Dawkins shows that the selfish gene is also the subtle gene. And he holds out the hope that our species—alone on earth—has the power to rebel against the designs of the selfish gene. This book is a call to arms. It is both manual and manifesto, and it grips like a thriller.

The Selfish Gene, Richard Dawkins's brilliant first book and still his most famous, is an international bestseller in thirteen languages. For this greatly expanded edition, endnotes have been added, giving fascinating reflections on the original text, and there are two major new chapters.

'learned, witty, and very well written . . . exhilaratingly good.' Sir Peter Medawar, *Spectator*

'Who should read this book? Everyone interested in the universe and their place in it.' Jeffrey R. Baylis, *Animal Behaviour*

'the sort of popular science writing that makes the reader feel like a genius' *New York Times*

Also in Oxford Paperbacks:

The Extended Phenotype   Richard Dawkins
The Ages of Gaia   James Lovelock
The Unheeded Cry   Bernard E. Rollin

MEDICINE IN OXFORD PAPERBACKS

Oxford Paperbacks offers an increasing list of medical studies and reference books of interest to the specialist and general reader alike, including The Facts series, authoritative and practical guides to a wide range of common diseases and conditions.

CONCISE MEDICAL DICTIONARY
Third Edition

Written without the use of unnecessary technical jargon, this illustrated medical dictionary will be welcomed as a home reference, as well as an indispensible aid for all those working in the medical profession.

Nearly 10,000 important terms and concepts are explained, including all the major medical and surgical specialities, such as gynaecology and obstetrics, paediatrics, dermatology, neurology, cardiology, and tropical medicine. This third edition contains much new material on pre-natal diagnosis, infertility treatment, nuclear medicine, community health, and immunology. Terms relating to advances in molecular biology and genetic engineering have been added, and recently developed drugs in clinical use are included. A feature of the dictionary is its unusually full coverage of the fields of community health, psychology, and psychiatry.

Each entry contains a straightforward definition, followed by a more detailed description, while an extensive crossreference system provides the reader with a comprehensive view of a particular subject.

Also in Oxford Paperbacks:

Drugs and Medicine   Roderick Cawson and Roy Spector
Travellers' Health: How to Stay Healthy Abroad 2/e
Richard Dawood
I'm a Health Freak Too!
Aidan Macfarlane and Ann McPherson
Problem Drinking   Nick Heather and Ian Robertson

RECREATIONS IN MATHEMATICS

Recreations in Mathematics covers all aspects of this diverse, ancient, and popular subject. There are books on puzzles and games, original studies of particular topics, translations, and reprints of classical works. Offering new versions of old problems and old versions of problems thought to be new, the series will interest lovers of mathematics—students and teachers, amateurs and professionals, young and old.

THE PUZZLING WORLD OF POLYHEDRAL DISSECTIONS
Stewart T. Coffin

This fascinating and fully illustrated book examines the history, geometry, and practical construction of three-dimensional puzzles. Containing solid puzzles, such as burrs, Tangrams, polyominoes, and those using rhombic dodecahedron and truncated octahedron, this collection includes a variety of unsolved and previously unpublished problems.

MATHEMATICAL BYWAYS IN AYLING, BEELING, AND CEILING
Hugh ApSimon

Set in the fictional villages of Ayling, Beeling, and Ceiling, and requiring little formal mathematical experience, this entertaining collection of problems develop a wide range of problem-solving techniques, which can then be used to tackle the more complex extensions to each puzzle.

Also available:

The Mathematics of Games   John D. Beasley
The Ins and Outs of Peg Solitaire   John D. Beasley